Person-Centred Practice:
The BAPCA Reader

edited by
Tony Merry

PCCS BOOKS
Ross-on-Wye

First published in 2000
Reprinted in 2004

PCCS BOOKS Ltd
Llangarron
Ross-on-Wye
Herefordshire
HR9 6PT
UK
Tel +44 (0)1989 77 07 07

Person-Centred Practice: The BAPCA Reader

ISBN 1 898059 16 0

Cover design by Denis Postle.
Printed by Bath Press, Bath, UK

Contents

Acknowledgement

Particular thanks go to Pete Sanders, BAPCA member and publisher of the journal, for preparing this book for publication. Once again, he and Maggie Taylor-Sanders have turned an idea into a reality. They are rather good at that.

Tony Merry

Introduction

The idea for a British Association for the Person-Centred Approach (BAPCA) was born during the summer of 1987, in a car on the way to Heathrow Airport. The official inaugural meeting of BAPCA was held in 1989 after a number of preliminary meetings at the Holbrook site of what was then the Polytechnic of East London.

The first edition of the journal *Person-Centred Practice* appeared in the Spring of 1993, even though the Association was perilously close to insolvency with only about 100 members. Since then, under the guidance of Irene Fairhurst, then Paul Marchant and, at the time of writing, Steve Vincent as Chair of the Association, things gradually improved as BAPCA became more widely known until there are, at the end of the millennium, nearly 700 members.

One of the general aims of BAPCA is to communicate ideas central to the PCA more widely, both within the PCA 'community' and outside of it. Over the past seven years, from the rather humble photocopied beginnings, the journal has grown up into an increasingly effective means of contributing to that aim. As Editor, I wanted to encourage people, some perhaps not used to writing for 'academic' journals, to share with others what they were thinking and doing. Many practitioners felt isolated from other like-minded people, and the main application of the PCA — counselling and psychotherapy — can be a lonely and private business.

Members of BAPCA were, at first, slow to respond, and there were times when I wondered if a journal was viable. But gradually people began to gain in confidence and some really excellent contributions began to land on my doorstep. Now, seven years on, *Person-Centred Practice* is professionally produced by PCCS Books and I am fortunate that the publisher lives and works separated from me only by a field of sheep in a village just outside Ross-on-Wye. The articles comprising this volume have been chosen to represent the broad range of material published in the journal since its inception. They come from students and experienced practitioners — in some cases internationally known. They are a testament to the energy and creativity of the Person-Centred Approach and they provide a resource and valuable record for BAPCA members and others interested in this most humanistic approach to working, and being, with people.

Unfortunately, there is not room for everything. Some people may be disappointed to find their contribution missing, but we tried to find as much space as possible for as many articles as we could. Sharp-eyed readers may spot some slight variations in print-size in places — evidence that we crammed as much on to each page as technology would allow.

Please read and enjoy the material contained in this book. If your article is not here, or not yet written, there may be space for it in the next volume.

Tony Merry
Editor
January 2000

Themes from Selected Editorials

Tony Merry

The Sufficiency of the 'Core Conditions' and Creative or Expressive Art Methods *(Vol.2. No. 1. 1994)*

This editorial revisits the current debate in the person-centred world about maintaining philosophical allegiance to Rogers whilst developing new ways of working with clients and client groups. To some the issue is a complex one involving reaching newer, more contemporary understandings of the spirit of Rogers' 'message'. To others the issue is how to introduce more creative forms of expression, not whether to.

I do not wish, as editor, to take advantage of my position in having easy access to the pages of this Journal by arguing for a particular position. Neither do I wish to see this Journal lining up on one side rather than the other. However, it does seem legitimate to try and summarise the stage the debate seems to have reached so far, and to highlight the problems that exist in all positions as I see them.

The 'traditional line' taken,for example, by Jerold Bozarth and Barbara Brodley from the USA, David Mearns and Brian Thorne in *Person Centred Counselling in Action,* and Irene Fairhurst in an earlier edition of this Journal, and others from the UK and elsewhere, see the PCA as resting on the Rogers 1957 position of 'necessary and sufficient'. Bozarth has recently modified his position, arguing that the core conditions are not necessarily necessary, but always sufficient (Bozarth, 1993). One of the implications of the traditional position is that person-centred therapy proceeds on the assumption that the therapist's job is to attend *to the client's process as his or her sole activity.* To introduce anything at all from the therapist's 'frame of reference' in the form of exercises, games, suggestions or direction is, by definition, in contravention of the basic philosophical assumption that each person's actualising tendency will become mobilised in personal and, in its specific form, unpredictable ways, within a person-centred psychological environment.

In support of this position, some have turned to an examination of what Rogers actually did, and they point out that he listened, understood and communicated his understanding non-judgementally and congruently, and very little else. Brodley and Brody (1990), for example, found that over 90 per cent of all of Rogers' responses in therapeutic situations were verbal 'empathic following' responses. My own work (Merry, 1994) has confirmed this. I found 88 per cent of all Rogers' responses to be statements which responded empathically to the client's present expression of self. These figures won't surprise anyone familiar with Rogers' work.

Of those who take the 'non-traditional' position, one group believes that it is legitimate to supplement, or even replace, verbal interaction with other forms of expression. A second group, exemplified by Gendlin and his work with 'focussing', believe that therapist-initiated ideas for action are still person-centred, provided those ideas are not formulated as instructions, but leave the decision on whether to use them or not to the client. (To be accurate, Gendlin refers to his work as 'experiential therapy', and this distinguishes it from 'traditional' person-centred therapy.)

The tension is around the word 'sufficient'. Someone who claims that the core conditions are not sufficient must doubt the effectiveness of person-centred therapy, at least in some circumstances with some clients. (However, it is rare for which clients or what circumstances to be specified.) Logically, I cannot see how any other position could be taken. The more extreme position is that the core conditions are never sufficient, typified by Egan (e.g. Egan, 1990) and others. Egan's work is sometimes described as an integration of person-centred and cognitive-behavioural approaches; he describes stages of the counselling process, and suggests necessary counsellor skills to facilitate progress through each of the stages.

It would be too simplistic to leave the matter there, it is complicated by those who take something of a middle ground. To them, it is not inconsistent with person-centred principles explicitly to include in the therapeutic process the use of means of communication other than the purely verbal. Their reasoning is that human beings are themselves not.purely verbal in their expression, and to ignore other aspects of communication is to 'hive off' part of a person, a process which diminishes creativity. They argue, in essence, that the core conditions remain central, as does the belief in the actualising tendency; it is only the means of communication that are different. What is less often made explicit, however, is the accompanying belief that different forms of expression are more efficient, or more readily access emotional material that purely verbal communication would exclude. Nevertheless, the argument is not that the core conditions themselves are not sufficient. Brian Thorne, described above as a 'traditionalist', wrote an enthusiastic foreword for Liesi Silverstone's book on Person-Centred Art Therapy (Silverstone, 1993), but Thorne has never argued that the core conditions are not sufficient.

Hardline traditionalists view any incorporation of non-verbal means of communication (or other therapist-directed interventions) with suspicion, unless they are introduced (without prompting) by the client. But the 'non-traditionalists' argue that if you advertise yourself as a 'Person-Centred Art Therapist', for example, then clients will come to you with the expectation that they will be involved in a process that explicitly includes 'creative' means of expression. The therapist will communicate the core conditions through non-verbal as well as verbal means, and will still rely on the actualising tendency to motivate change and development. Natalie Rogers' Person-Centred Expressive Therapy also seems to take this position.

The real problem comes when those who argue that the core conditions are not sufficient, then go on to put the deficiency right by introducing techniques derived from other approaches, *but still call themselves person-centred.* This, it seems to me, is an untenable position. For example, there are those who claim they 'integrate' person-centred therapy with gestalt therapy. But how far has this 'integration' gone? It is not an 'integration' simply to use gestalt techniques with the person-centred approach. It is not an integration sometimes to be 'pure' person centred, and sometimes to use gestalt techniques. An integration implies that the product of integrating two things is not either of those things but is something new which contains elements of each thing. This might lead to the conclusion that there can be no such thing as Person-Centred Gestalt, or Person-Centred Psychodrama. To call it Person-Centred Gestalt, for example, is not identifying the new thing that has emerged from the integration of the PCA and Gestalt. You cannot 'do' Gestalt in a 'person-centred way' any more than you can 'do' the PCA in a Gestalt way. This, of course, represents the difference between 'eclectic' and 'integrated' approaches. There are arguments for and against both sides (e.g. Dryden and Norcross, 1990).

The discussion within the person-centred community reflects this wider discussion about integrated, eclectic or 'pure'. The research, as in most research relating to psychotherapy, is not at present able to settle the matter. Those against both 'integrationism' and 'eclecticism' include representatives of the psychoanalytical school (Szasz, 1974), and the behaviourist school (Eysenck, 1970), so the discussion is by no means limited to the PCA.

Economic factors also play a part. The present climate insists on cost-effectiveness and quick results; many counselling agencies limit the number of allowable sessions, sometimes to as few as six. This is not the most helpful environment for person-centred therapy. Six sessions hardly gives time to form much of a relationship, and so relationship-based therapies are at a disadvantage. The pressure is on to stimulate rapid change, and, inevitably, therapists become more directive in their approach, and less person-centred. This means that person centred therapists have fewer chances to do what Rogers urged them to do — to treat the PCA as a hypothesis to be tested against experience, not as a series of facts to be implemented.

What does seem to be clear is that the PCA cannot ignore modern trends and economic and cultural pressures. We need to engage in the debate, not to defend a corner but to learn from each other.

References

Bozarth, J. (1993) *Not necessarily necessary, but always sufficient* in Brazier, D (Ed) *Beyond Carl Rogers*. London: Constable.

Brodley, B. & Brody, A. (1990) Understanding client-centred therapy through interviews conducted by Carl Rogers. Paper presented for the panel: Fifty Years of Client-Centred Therapy: Recent Research, at American Psychological Association annual meeting, Boston, Ma.

Dryden, W. & Norcross, J. (Eds) (1990) Eclecticism and Integration in Counselling and Psychotherapy, Gale Centre.

Egan, G. (1990) *The Skilled Helper*, Brooks/Cole.

Eysenck, H.J. (1970) *A mish-mash of theories*. International Journal of Psychiatry (9) pp.140–6

Merry, T. (1994) An analysis of ten demonstration interviews by Carl Rogers: implications for the training of client-centred counsellors. Paper prepared for the 3rd International Conference on Client-Centred and Experiential Psychotherapy, Austria.

Silverstone, L. (1993) *Art Therapy — The Person Centred Way.* Autonomy Books.

Szasz, T.S. (1974) The Ethics of Psycho-Analysis: The Theory and Method of Autonomous Psychotherapy. London: Routledge and Kegan Paul.

You Wouldn't Ask a Roofer to Fix Your Washing Machine *(Vol 2. No.2. 1994)*

In client-centred counselling, and, indeed, in all other applications of the Person-Centred Approach, there is a suspicion of 'skills', 'techniques' and 'methods' — and for justifiable reasons. A review of some of the most well-known counsellor training books, *The Skilled Helper* (Egan, 4th edition 1990), and *Practical Counselling and Helping Skills* (Nelson-Jones, 2nd edition 1988), for example, can lead the unwary reader to believe that counselling (and other forms of helping) is simply a matter of learning the correct response to every situation one is likely to encounter. Without being too unkind to Egan, his breaking up of the counselling process into three stages, each with three substages and each with its own set of counsellor skills and techniques, is not attractive to person-centred counsellors who view the counselling process as less predictable than Egan seems to imply.

There is now a growing literature that concerns itself with counselling in special, closely defined contexts. The Sage *Counselling in Practice* series, edited by Windy Dryden is a good example, covering sexual abuse counselling, counselling for depression and anxiety, careers counselling, alcohol counselling and post-traumatic stress disorder counselling. There seems to be almost no human experience that has not developed its concomitant helping strategy, each claiming that the special circumstances involved call for specialised knowledge and skills on the part of the helper.

It appears to be a matter of common sense that some knowledge of a wide variety of human situations is an essential prerequisite of the effective helper. The literature claims to have identified patterns of experience expected from people who have fallen victim to the kinds of troubles identified above, along with a range of psychological strategies that need to be adopted by the counsellor. Cycles of emotional response have been noted, stages of experiencing identified, and an array of intervention techniques developed. It gets to the point where nobody who is not familiar with Murray-Parkes or Kubler-Ross should presume to counsel the recently bereaved or terminally ill, and nobody who has not been trained in the progression of HIV infection to full-blown AIDS should offer help to someone diagnosed as HIV positive.

This diversification into specialised areas reflects the more general cultural expectation that there exists an expert to put right whatever has gone wrong, and that the choice of the right expert for the right problem is crucial. A dentist fixes your teeth, and a mechanic fixes your car. (Mechanics are good examples. Some will only fix Fords, others will only fix Volkswagens.) You wouldn't ask a roofer to mend your washing machine, and you wouldn't expect a landscape gardener to treat your abdominal pains. The logic of this argument now extends to the counselling situation. Trainee counsellors have come to expect courses to offer sessions on 'dealing with sexual abuse', 'counselling the recently bereaved', 'dealing with stress', 'psychosexual therapy', 'alcohol and drug addiction counselling', 'eating disorders', and so on.

It is certainly no intention of this article to belittle the valuable work done by experts in each of these, and other, fields. A knowledge at some level of special issues like HIV infection, or recovering from sexual abuse and so on, should be part of every counsellor's repertoire. However, counsellors, especially beginning counsellors, often feel lost or uncertain when faced with a client with a particular presenting problem. They know a specialised field of knowledge exists in this area, but, usually, they are very vague about it themselves. Advice, instruction and guidelines are not in short supply, but they bring with them the implicit warning, 'Don't go into areas you don't understand'.

In the person-centred approach, there are not, as far as I know, any books that deal explicitly with specific problems. There is no 'Person-Centred Approach to Sexual Abuse Counselling', no 'Person-Centred Approach to Bereavement Counselling', for example. Apart from the very general 'beginning', 'middle' and 'ending', described in, for example, Mearns and Thorne (1988) there are no 'stages' in client-centred counselling. There is no advice in any of Carl Rogers' books on how to establish a counselling contract, what to do if . . . , or how to deal with particular groups of people, or when to mobilise particular skills in response to specific situations during the counselling hour.

The growing idea that counselling is no longer the 'generic' activity it was once thought to be is given substance by the existence of counsellors who have adopted a professional specialisation in a clearly defined field of human experience. Past categories like 'children', 'adolescents', 'adults' are now considered too vague and general. Sub-grouping into closer defined categories is now common place: 'assertiveness', 'school phobic children', 'counselling anger', 'sons and mothers counselling', 'dealing with difficult people', 'hyperactive children', 'redundancy counselling', for example, now regularly appear in advertisements for counsellor training programmes and workshops.

What are person-centred practitioners to make of all this when, generally speaking, we do not subdivide human experiences into these kinds of categories? Neither have we developed approaches to different experiences that call upon us to exercise specifically designed skills, techniques or methods. What we know, in the person-centred approach, as core qualities (or 'a way of being'), in other approaches have become demoted into 'core *skills*'. For example, one Training Institute in the UK, for its 'Diploma in Humanistic Counselling', announces Year One as 'Person-Centred Counselling and Practice', and Year Two as 'Advanced Counselling'. Is the implication here that Year Two provides something more 'advanced' than person-centred counselling?

Person-centred counselling will gain more credibility if we can become better at describing what we do and how what we do is appropriate to the clients we get. Does a person-centred counsellor *do* anything differently when faced with a bereaved client, or a client with HIV or a client who was sexually abused as a child? If not, are 'core qualities' all it takes? Is the same kind of relationship, based on the same core qualities, sufficient for all clients, no matter what their immediate concerns or personal history?

I think we should not be afraid to answer, 'Yes', to this last question, whilst acknowledging that limitations of the effectiveness of person-centred therapy are as likely to reside within us as individual practitioners, as with any shortcomings of the theory itself. As far as the PCA is concerned, there is a real and present danger in categorising human suffering into subgroups of the type described above.

Social scientists tend (in this area) to be interested in generalities. That is, they are interested in describing typical or expected patterns of behaviour, emotional reactions and so forth. I have no doubt that understanding general human experience in this way is useful, but its usefulness can turn destructive if we expect each person we see to conform to the pattern predicted for them. How many times have you heard the idea, for example, that because a person was sexually abused as a child, that person *must* be experiencing anger (however that anger is denied or covered up), and that the person *must* discover and express that anger if he or she is to 'recover'?

Person-centred psychotherapy proceeds from a basic attitude on behalf of the therapist of 'not knowing'. This does not mean being ignorant or unaware. Therapists are interested to discover what is new and unexpected from this person, as well as what is familiar. Being empathic means to enter the world of another person from a starting point of genuinely wanting to discover both what it contains, and what it means. Its content may be more predictable (or familiar) than its meaning. Each person's inner world will contain a unique set of conditions of worth, and each person's locus of evaluation will reside on a different point of an internal-external axis. There will be an interaction between conditions of worth and the locus of evaluation. This interaction will inspire an inner dialogue with which, as practitioners, we must be prepared to engage with sensitivity and respect for the unique nuances that will, if we are open-minded, become revealed. The situation is further complicated by the tendency for people to distort or deny into awareness those experiences that challenge their self-concept including its internalised conditions of worth.

Knowing how, in general, people respond to a bereavement, or to being diagnosed as HIV positive, or to having experienced abusive relationships, will help us in some measure. But our task is to accompany our clients in their experiencing and we cannot know in advance what that experiencing might contain, or what meaning it has for this person. The strength of the PCA is that it is open-minded and open-hearted. We can discover what is the same in us, and what is different. If we only look for what is the same because we want people to fit our pre-existing theories, we will miss what is different — in short, we will prevent ourselves from encountering others. Not only is this bad phenomenology, it is bad therapy.

Responding to a Serious Misrepresentation of Person-Centred Therapy *(Vol 3. No.2. 1995)*

In July of this year I received a copy of an article published in *Nursing Times* written by Philip Burnard, Director of Nursing Studies at University of Wales College of Medicine, titled *Implications of client-centred counselling for nursing practice.* Person-centred people are quite used to Rogers' work being misrepresented by those who purport to know something about counselling and psychotherapy, but who have never closely studied what Rogers really said. They have a view about it, often based on oversimplification, misunderstandings and distortion. Normally, this doesn't worry me overmuch. The same could be said about Freud's work, for example, and I know that many Freudians are often irritated by the distortions they hear being promulgated about psychodynamic therapy (sometimes from person-centred practitioners!). The *Nursing Times* article is, however, a different kettle of fish. *Nursing Times* is read by nurses (of course), hospital administrators, and other medical and paramedical staff. Maybe a quarter of a million of them. The Burnard article remains the most serious case of misrepresentation of Rogers' work I have ever seen. It is naive, simplistic and factually incorrect. It breaks the first rule of good scholarship: check your sources (then check them again). Burnard is an influential member of the 'caring professions' — he holds a responsible position and writes copiously. Nurses, and others in the medical profession, don't have the time or the resources to check the accuracy of what they read in their journal. Quite rightly I imagine they assume that someone of Burnard's standing knows what he is talking about, and that *Nursing Times* is sufficiently responsible and respected to rely on.

I wrote to *Nursing Times* pointing out to them that they had carried an article that misleads rather than informs. Apparently, a number of other people did as well, and the *Nursing Times* letters-page subsequently contained a number of contributions, together with a reply from Burnard. I haven't seen this issue of *Nursing Times,* so I don't know what was said (perhaps someone could send me a copy or a photocopy). *Nursing Times* thanked me for the points I made, and called my response 'elegant'. However, they did not wish to publish it on the grounds that they didn't think it moved the debate forward. They are entitled to their opinion, of course, but while I respect it, I disagree. Whilst there is no point in reproducing Burnard's article here (it's main arguments can be gleaned from the contents of my reply, which 1 reproduce below), there are several things Dr. Burnard might keep in mind should he ever decide to write about client-centred counselling again.

1. Some people have tried to link Rogers with Rousseau, but, in a letter to me in 1984, Rogers said he found Rousseau too 'sentimental' for his liking.
2. It was a potato, not a bean, that Rogers used as an example to show how an organism will attempt to grow even in adverse environmental conditions.
3. Rogers did not argue that people are 'free to be good', or that people are 'somehow programmed to be good'. To invent these two statements, and to imply that they form part of client-centred theory, or attribute them to someone

given the American Psychological Association's special award for his *scientific* contribution to psychology, is a reckless disregard for good scholarship.

4. A belief in the 'inherent goodness' of people is not a necessary or sufficient condition for the successful practice of client-centred counselling.

5. Client-centred counselling can hardly be a 'form of tyranny' when the counsellor's fundamental intentions are empathically to understand you, your thoughts, feelings and experiences, and actively to communicate and check-out that understanding. What sort of tyranny is that? I've not heard the word 'tyranny' used before in connection with Rogers, a man nominated for the Nobel Peace Prize. Burnard's prescription for avoiding becoming tyrannical is to give advice, make suggestions and give information.

6. There is no evidence that 'counsellors who offer the greatest range and flexibility of approaches are likely to be of most value overall'. Burnard completely ignores the widely discussed problems of 'eclecticism'.

By the way, Burnard, in at least one other publication *(What is Counselling?,* Gale Centre, 1992) has talked about what he calls 'evangelists' in the 'client-centred movement'. He implies that people believe in the effectiveness of client-centred counselling through some sort of blind faith. Personally, I find this deeply insulting. My assessment of the effectiveness of client-centred counselling, which is not uncritical, is based on twenty-five years of close study, practice and research. I don't believe we have all the answers, or even most of them, or even know many of the right questions. What I do know is that my original training as a scientist impressed on me the need for a hard-headed evaluation of the evidence, and that an opinion that does not incorporate a sound familiarity with it is hardly worth the air used in expressing it.

A Reply to Philip Burnard — Nursing Times, Volume 91, No. 26

If client-centred counselling bore any real resemblance to the parody of it produced by Philip Burnard *(Nursing Times,* Vol. 91, No. 26), I for one, and I suspect all others, would give it up immediately. There are just so many mistakes, misrepresentations and distortions in his piece that space does not allow for a full discussion of all of them, but I feel that some at least must be put right or many nurses and others, perhaps contemplating some training in counselling, will be sadly influenced by Burnard into making misinformed decisions.

Firstly, let's remind ourselves that nursing and counselling are not the same thing. Obvious enough, but a point Burnard completely overlooks. Of course, nurses and all other health professionals are often asked for advice or information during their work. To withhold it would, in most cases, be a dereliction of duty. But counselling is not a process in which advice-giving has a very high priority, and most clients who come for counselling do not expect it.

Leaving aside Burnard's eccentric assertion that 'Existentialism underwent a transition, becoming client-centred counselling in the process', it is a distortion of Rogers' position to imply that he believed people to be basically 'good'. Rogers' theory rests partly on the concept of 'actualisation' — the tendency in all forms of organic life (including people) to progress towards the maximisation of potential. In ideal environmental conditions (which includes relationships with others for example) actualisation can occur unimpeded, and in the case of people will result in development towards the 'fully functioning person' who Rogers described as constructive, social and open to experience without the need to deny or distort that experiencing. This is vastly different from saying that people are 'basically good', which is a value judgement dependent on the time and culture in which that judgement is made (and by whom, of course). But environmental conditions are never ideal, and a person develops 'conditions of worth' created most usually by the negative evaluations of others becoming incorporated into the self-concept. The actualising process can, in this way, become distorted and that person's behaviour and feelings will reflect the degree of distortion present. It is simply not true that 'growth' was never clearly defined (which is what Burnard claims) and I suggest that interested people read Rogers' very clear and detailed descriptions for themselves (see, for example *On Becoming a Person*, Constable, 1961).

Client-centred counsellors do not 'maintain a low profile', and client-centred counselling cannot be summed up by the phrase 'pick yourself up by your bootstraps'. Burnard's article completely ignores one of Rogers' central and most enduring ideas concerning the relationship between client and counsellor. It is within a relationship with a person able and willing empathically to understand you and to communicate and check out that understanding, who can remain real and present with you (Rogers called this 'being congruent or authentic') and who is not in the business of making value judgements about you, that change and personal growth are more likely to occur. Almost no form of counselling disputes that the quality of the relationship between client and counsellor is of critical importance in determining the success or otherwise of the counselling process. A counselling relationship characterised by what Rogers called these 'core conditions' of empathic understanding, authenticity and non-judgementalism provides the psychological safety for clients to embark on a journey of self-discovery. The vital role of the counsellor is to provide understanding companionship on that journey, not to give advice on its direction. This is the very opposite from Burnard's statement that clients are 'forced into the unenviable position of being totally alone in their decision making'. I once heard client-centred counselling described as 'people doing it for themselves, but not by themselves'.

Burnard offers an extraordinarily simplistic example to illustrate his point of view, but one that serves only to reveal his near total misunderstanding of the client-centred counselling process. No client-centred counsellor would 'advise a client to accept their highly negative or aggressive feelings', especially if there were grounds for believing that the client was contemplating murder. Apart from the fact that this example contradicts Burnard's previous assertion that Rogers' 'commandment to practitioners' was that they should 'eschew offering advice', a counsellor in the situation Burnard describes would be morally and legally obliged to act to protect any potential victim. In any case, client-centred counselling is not a process of advising clients to accept negative feelings, which implies a somewhat static view of the personality.

Where in Rogers' writing has Burnard found Rogers saying or implying that 'all problems are seen as individual and not one is believed to have been previously experienced by another'? Whilst it is true that each of us is likely to experience the same situation differently, Rogers never believed that experiences did not significantly overlap very often. In fact, one of Rogers' favourite remarks can be summed up by the phrase, 'If it's personal, it's universal', meaning that, paradoxically, the more deeply we speak of our own experience, the more recognisable it is to others. We have all had different experiences of death and illness for example, but we all know something about the pain, fear and grief that can accompany those experiences.

Perhaps the most disturbing of Burnard's comments concern his view that client-centred counselling is 'simple', and that it is 'relatively easy to train nurses in client-centred counselling'. Rogers did not train 'thousands of ex-services personnel after the Second World War . . . in a short space of time' in client-centred counselling. What he and his colleagues did was to help people appreciate the creative results of listening to others in trouble with higher levels of empathic understanding, respect and authenticity, and if you wanted to help them this was a good place to start. He did something similar with schoolteachers and medical personnel. This is not the same, by a very long chalk, as training in client-centred counselling, which is neither simple nor easy. The client-centred training course with which I am involved lasts for three years and includes five or six hundred hours of learning and training as well as a requirement for 150 hours of supervised practice. It is a travesty of client-centred theory, philosophy and practice to describe it, as Burnard does, as an 'agreeable and acceptable form of communications training', or as 'a relatively easy path of communication'.

Just as astonishing is Burnard's claim that 'there is almost no empirical evidence that any sort of counselling — client-centred or not — actually works'. It is hard to believe that Burnard has not read any of the hundreds of studies now completed on the effectiveness of counselling and psychotherapy. Whilst it is true that many research studies suffer from methodological problems, the evidence is now overwhelming that people who get counselling when they need it are better off than about 80 per cent of people who don't get counselling when they need it. If Burnard really believes that there is almost no evidence that counselling is effective, why is he so involved with it, and why does he write so much about it?

As far as nurses in clinical and community practice are concerned, of course they should give their clients information about personal and emotional issues when it is needed or requested. Whoever said they shouldn't? Where nurses have incorporated client-centred theory into their work (whether they have had formal training or not) they will continue to give information as well as understanding and respect for their clients as people; that's their job and most are extremely good at it. My experience is that nurses and all other medical personnel are well aware of the differences between nursing and counselling. When they have trained as counsellors in addition to their nurse training and experience, nurses know that offering a counselling 'contract' to a client involves a relationship in which understanding, exploration genuineness and non-judgementalism take precedence over the more familiar activities of advising and informing.

Nurses also know that all strongly held positions they take in relation to their work should be constantly reviewed, challenged and revised if necessary. This includes their work as counsellors if counselling is what they also do. Rogers offered his ideas, supported by rigorous research and enquiry, as a set of hypotheses to be continually tested, not as statements of 'fact'. If Burnard is right and the client-centred approach is a popular one, it is not because there is anything easy about it. More likely it is popular because nurses and their 'trainers' know that the work of Rogers and his colleagues has endured for more than fifty years and has been the subject of more research and evaluation studies than any other approach to counselling. They know, too, that it is based not on the erroneous belief that 'people are basically good', but that everyone, no matter how hurt or damaged, can still grow, change and develop constructively when they experience a relationship in which they are deeply understood as fallible human beings without the threat of being judged.

On Congruence . . . *(Vol.4. No.1. 1996)*

For some time now I have been getting involved in a number of discussions about what Rogers meant by his term 'congruence'. Of the three core conditions, this is the one that seems to lead to most confusion. The confusion arises, as often as not, in terms of muddling congruence with 'self-disclosure'. Some practitioners seem to think that self-disclosure and congruence are the same thing, in other words that you are not being congruent if you do not communicate your feelings to your client. I've also heard the expression 'use of congruence', but this is, in fact, very misleading. Since congruence is a state of being or an attitude existing within the therapist, it is inaccurate to refer to it as if it were something that could, from time to time, be 'used'. Used for what? Happiness is also a state of being, and it doesn't make sense to say we 'use' our happiness in order to achieve something. We are happy, and our happiness enables us to experience life in ways that are different from experiences of life when we are unhappy. When we are (relatively) congruent (at least in this present relationship in this present time), we are free to admit into our awareness more of our experience, both of our 'self' and of the relationship more accurately, than when we are (relatively) incongruent. Talk of 'using congruence' (rather than 'being congruent') leads on to the erroneous conclusion that congruence is a skill, technique or method. It isn't, any more than happiness is a skill, technique or method. There may be skill involved in communicating (if that is what we choose to do) our current experiencing to our client, but that's not the same thing.

Congruence (in counselling and psychotherapy) is one of the core conditions of effective therapy and was defined in several different ways by Rogers. For example, the Rogers (1959) definition includes, '. . . when self-experiences are accurately symbolized (in awareness), and are included in the self-concept in this accurately symbolized form, then the state is one of congruence of self and experience . . . terms which are synonymous . . . [are] integrated, whole, genuine' (p. 206). As Brodley (1995, unpublished) points out, this definition is couched in terms of Rogers' distinction between self and experience, not in terms of therapist's behaviour. This emphasis is consistent with Rogers (1957) definition where, in discussing the six necessary and sufficient conditions for therapeutic personality change, Rogers defined congruence in the following terms:

> . . . the therapist should be, within the confines of this relationship, a congruent, genuine, integrated person. It means that within the relationship he is freely and deeply himself, with his actual experience accurately represented by his awareness of himself . . . It should be clear that this includes being himself even in ways which are not regarded as ideal for psychotherapy. His experience may be, 'I am afraid of this client', or, 'My attention is so focussed on my own problems that I can scarcely listen to him'. If the therapist is not denying these feelings to awareness, but is able freely to be them (as well as being other feelings), then the condition (congruence) we have stated is met (p. 97).

In counselling and psychotherapy, congruence is a condition in the sense that it must be a:

> state or condition within the therapist. This state permits the therapist to succeed in his intentions to experience unconditional positive regard and empathic understanding. It does so by permitting the therapist to experience an unconflicted and undistracted dedication to acceptant empathy. The therapist's integrated authentic appearance facilitates the client's clear perception of the therapist's attitudes of unconditional positive regard and empathic understanding (Brodley, 1995 pp. 3–4).

In ideal terms, the core conditions (all subjective states or attitudes existing within the therapist) need to be fully present together, but in practice it is rarely possible for a therapist to be so consistent:

> The theory predicts that to the extent the therapist experiences these three therapeutic attitudes while with the client and if the client perceives the unconditional positive regard and the empathic understanding, to that extent the client will experience therapeutic change. The therapeutic attitudes are experienced only to some degree, not absolutely, in any relationship (Brodley, 1995 p. 4).

Because the therapeutic attitudes are seen as existing together rather than separately, it is not usually helpful to ascribe more importance to one or other of them, but Rogers did believe that therapist congruence sometimes takes priority (Rogers, 1959 p. 215). In other words, at those times when therapists are unable to experience empathic understanding, or are unable to be unconditionally accepting, then therapists should be aware of those experiences, attend to them and allow them accurately into awareness. Most certainly, therapists should not attempt to deny such experiences or distort them in awareness, because to do so would result in therapists becoming unintegrated and thus incongruent in the relationship.

The question often arises about the degree to which it is necessary for therapists directly to communicate their feelings and thoughts to their clients in pursuance of congruence. In his 1957 paper, Rogers did not refer to any necessity directly (or otherwise) to communicate congruence. He did, however, (pp. 97–8) make the following comment: 'It would take us too far afield to consider the puzzling matter as to the degree to which the therapist overtly communicates this reality [referring to a therapist who is afraid of a client, or unable to listen to the client] in himself to the client. Certainly the aim is not for the therapist to express or talk out his own feelings, but primarily that he should not be deceiving the client as to himself.' Later (Rogers, 1959), the wording of the 'Necessary and Sufficient Conditions' changed slightly: 'The therapist is congruent (or genuine or real) in the relationship, his picture of himself and *the way he communicates matches his immediate experiencing*' (my italics). However, Rogers, in this instance, is still referring to the way a therapist communicates, not what a therapist communicates, and there is still no component of the condition that a therapist *should* communicate thoughts and feelings that arise from within the therapist's frame of reference.

In a 1980 article (Rogers and Sanford, 1980 p. 1381), the question of the communication of therapist's thoughts and feelings was taken up again in the section on 'Genuineness or Congruence'. Here, Rogers and Sanford went into some detail:

> Being real involves being thoroughly acquainted with the flow of experiencing going on within, a complex and continuing flow. It means being willing to express the attitudes that come persistently to the fore, especially perhaps the negative attitudes, inasmuch as the positive ones can rather easily be inferred from behaviour and tone. If the therapist is bored with the client, it is only real to express this feeling . . .

Rogers and Sanford gave a number of examples of therapists experiencing and expressing negative feelings, including boredom and anger, but:

> Note that in each instance the therapist is voicing a feeling within herself, not a fact or judgement about the client. To say, 'I feel bored at the moment', does not pass any judgement on the client as a boring person. It merely puts into the relationship the basic data of the therapist's own feelings. As this boredom and sense of remoteness are shared, the therapist's feelings change; certainly she is not bored when trying to communicate self in this way. The therapist who expressed anger could then more clearly hear the client, and the client caught a glimpse of his own behaviour, which seemed to have been hidden from him. The therapist is, in fact, quite sensitively eager to hear the client's response. Empathic responses begin again to be experienced. To be real is to reduce barriers. The client is now likely to find himself speaking more congruently because the therapist has dared to be real. It is a genuine

person-to-person relationship between two imperfect human beings.

Rogers and Sanford realised that this concept could create difficulties and was open to misinterpretation:

> It certainly does not mean that the therapist burdens the client with all her problems or feelings. It does not mean that the therapist blurts out impulsively any attitude that comes to mind. It does mean, however, that the therapist does not deny to herself the feelings being experienced and that the therapist is willing to express and to be any persistent feelings that exist in the relationship . . . When the therapist is feeling neither empathic nor caring, she must discover what the flow of experiencing is and must be willing to express that flow, whether it seems embarrassing, too revealing, or whatever.

Key phrases here are, 'the therapist does not deny to herself the feelings being experienced', and the therapist is willing to express and to be any persistent feelings that exist'. In other words, the critical issues are the therapist's ability to remain open to her experiencing without the need to distort or deny that experiencing, and the existence of persistent feelings, i.e. those that have remained for some time and are interfering with the therapist's experiencing of empathic understanding and unconditional positive regard.

An obvious implication here is that self-disclosure, i.e. giving open expression to the 'flow of experiencing' can have the effect of returning the therapist to experiencing empathic understanding and unconditional positive regard when those experiences have, for some reason, been interrupted. But it is not incongruent to choose not to give expression to the flow of experiencing. There may be many factors that determine whether or not a therapist chooses to self-disclose. The therapist may decide that these experiences are best left undisclosed, perhaps to be explored elsewhere, but the therapist is not being incongruent if she takes this decision because she is still allowing those experiences into her awareness, and is not denying them. It may be that the internal act of taking the decision not to self-disclose at this time is all that is needed to enable the therapist to return to experiencing empathic understanding and unconditional positive regard.

References

Brodley, B. (1995) Congruence and its relation to communication in client-centered therapy and the person-centered approach. *Unpublished.*

Rogers, C. R. (1957) The necessary and sufficient conditions for therapeutic personality change. *Journal of Consulting Psychology,* 21,(2), *pp. 95–* 103.

Rogers, C. R. (1959) A theory of therapy personality and interpersonal relationships as developed in the client-centred framework. In Koch, S. (Ed), *Psychology: A Study of Science, Vol 3. Formulations of the Person and the Social Context.* New York: McGraw-Hill. pp. 184–256.

Rogers, C. R. and Sanford, R. (1980) Client-centered psychotherapy. In Kaplan, H,

Sadock, B. and Freeman, A. (Eds), *Comprehensive Textbook of Psychiatry, Vol. 3.*
Baltimore, MD: Williams and Wilkins.

Can the Core Principles of Person-Centred Counselling be Described? *(Vol.6. No.2. 1998)*

Recently I have been struck by the diversity of thought and opinion within the person-centred tradition, and I found myself somewhat nonplussed on reading *Person-Centred Counselling: An Experiential Approach*, by David L. Rennie (Sage, 1998). Much of the language of this book is recognisably person-centred, but, by the author's own admission, his approach 'was developed with one foot — but only one — in the person-centred and experiential mainstream' (p. v). I review this book in detail elsewhere in this issue, but what reading it did do for me was to interest me in retracing some of the historical developments of person-centred ideas. In doing this I was (again) impressed by the consistency of the set of core principles that can be found within the PCA at all stages of its development, though emphasis shifts slightly at various times, and basic ideas are developed and refined. As far as I can see them, the core principles that emerge are:

1. The belief that the actualising tendency is the sole motivator of human growth, change and development. It is the estrangement between actualisation and self-actualisation that accounts for all psychological disturbance. The actualising tendency is a universal characteristic of humankind and, whilst its specific manifestations are different in different cultures, it is a tendency towards the fulfilment of human potential.
2. Each individual has the right to their own psychological determination.
3. The individual functions as an organised whole, responds to its perceptual field and develops a sense of 'self' that is vulnerable to the imposition by others of conditions of worth.
4. The principle of 'non-directivity', explicitly present in early formulations of the PCA, remains as central today as it was in the early years. Non-directivity implies an enduring trust in the inherent wisdom of every organism to develop a 'way of being' that is creative, social and constructive. One way of developing this 'way of being' is in a psychological climate that conforms (however idiosyncratically) to the six necessary and sufficient conditions postulated by Rogers initially in 1957.
5. Related to the principle of non-directivity, the role of change-agent (e.g. counsellor, therapist, teacher, parent, etc.) as perceived in the PCA is non-intrusive and non-technological. It is concerned with the discovery of what is already present, rather than with 'change', *per se*.

References

Rennie, D.L. (1998) *Person-Centred Counselling: An Experiential Approach.* London: Sage.

Client-Centred Therapy: Origins and Influences

Tony Merry

All therapeutic systems contain elements and repercussions of their antecedents, some more obviously so than others. Client-centred psychotherapy arose at a time when the dominating influences in the main were the various Freudian schools — it was not until much later that 'Humanistic Psychology' emerged as a significant trend in psychology. When it did, the principles of the PCA had already been established.

In a book chapter published in 1980 (Rogers and Sanford, 1980) Rogers himself takes credit for originating client-centred psychotherapy: 'Client-centered psycho-therapy was conceived of primarily by Rogers and came into being in the period from 1938 through 1950; it was further elaborated at the Counselling Center at the University of Chicago' (p.1374). However, Rogers did acknowledge some of the influences that significantly shaped his thinking.[1] They include John Dewey, William H. Kilpatrick, Kurt Lewin and Lao Tse, and most relevant to the present discussion, Otto Rank.

Otto Rank and 'Will Therapy' (or 'Relationship Therapy')

Rank was, for a long time, one of Freud's closest associates; a position he was to sacrifice eventually with the publication of *The Trauma of Birth* in 1924 (see Rank, 1994). Here, 'birth replaced castration as the original trauma, and the breast took precedence over the penis as the first libido object. In addition, Rank identified the origin of fear with the birth process' (Raskin, 1948).

Raskin (1948) credits Rank with responsibility for the initiation in psychotherapy of seven significant ideas, summarised below:
1. The individual seeking help has creative powers of his own, a will. When the individual is threatened, when a strange will is forced on him, this positive will

---

First Published in *Person-Centred Practice*, Volume 6, Number 2, 1998.

1. A number of people have tried to claim that Rogers was significantly influenced by Rousseau, largely because of Rogers' ideas about education and/or because they believe (wrongly) that Rogers thought people to be basically 'good'. However, in a private communication (1983) Rogers describes Rousseau as 'too sentimentally optimistic'. Rogers also remarks, 'I try to be careful not to speak about the goodness of human nature, because I don't know who is judging that quality. I do feel that human nature is constructive in that it has a tendency to work toward the fulfilment of its own potential.'

becomes counter-will.

2. Because of the dangers involved in living and the fear of dying, everybody experiences a basic ambivalence. There is a conflict between will-to-health and will-to-illness, between self-determination and acceptance of fate, etc. This ambivalence is characteristic not just of neurotics, but is an integral part of life.

3. The distinguishing characteristic of the neurotic is that he is 'ego-bound', both his destructive and productive tendencies are directed towards the self.

4. The aim of therapy is the acceptance by the individual of himself as unique and self-reliant, with all his ambivalencies, and the freeing of the positive will through the elimination of the temporary blocking which consists of the concentration of creative energies on the ego.

5. In order to achieve this goal, the patient rather than the therapist must become the central figure in the therapeutic process. The patient is his own therapist, he has within him forces of self-creation as well as of self-destruction, and the former can be brought into play if the therapist will play the role, not of authority, but of ego-helper or ego-assistant, not of positive will but of counter-will to strengthen the patient's positive will, etc.

6. The goals of therapy are achieved by the patient not through an explanation of the past, which he would resist if interpreted to him, and which, even if accepted by him, would serve to lessen his responsibility for his present adjustment, but rather through the experiencing of the present in the therapeutic situation.

7. The ending of therapy, the separation of patient from therapist, is a symbol of all separations in life, starting with the separation of foetus from womb in birth, and if the patient can be made to understand the will-conflict present here, the conflict over growth towards independence and self-reliance, and if he can exercise the separation as something which he wills himself, despite the pain of it, then it can symbolise the birth of a new individual.

In 1945, during the formative years of client-centred therapy, Rank wrote:
> For real psychotherapy is not concerned primarily with adaptation to any kind of reality, but with the adjustment of the patient to himself, that is, with his acceptance of his own individuality or that part of his personality which he has formerly denied (Rank, 1945).

Self-acceptance (or positive self-regard) is a key concept within client-centred psychotherapy, and it is clear from the above quote and from Raskin's list that Rank's 'Will Therapy' (or 'Relationship Therapy') and Rogers' 'Client-Centred Therapy' share many common characteristics — at least philosophically. However, Raskin believes that the differences between the two are significant, especially in terms of therapist behaviour and intention during the therapy process,
> . . . we find, despite all the venom heaped by Rank on the techniques of education and interpretation, and despite all the emphasis placed on the autotherapeutic abilities of the patient, that 'I [Rank] unmask all the reactions of the patient even if they apparently refer to the

analyst, as projections of his own inner conflict and bring them back to his own ego', that 'interpretation on the part of the analyst is worthless as long as it does not lead to understanding of this denial mechanism itself and its relation to the yielding of the will under emotion', and that 'here is the place [the therapeutic hour] to show him how he tries to destroy the connections with this experience just as he does with the past' (Rank, 1945) (Raskin, 1948).

So, Rank does not reject interpretation as a therapeutic technique as long as it leads to understanding of denial mechanisms, etc. Here is a clear difference between Rank, who maintained allegiance to some, at least, of the techniques of psychoanalysis, and Rogers, who never adopted them.

Otto Rank and Carl Rogers met once, in June 1938, when Rank accepted an invitation from Rogers to address a 3-day seminar in Rochester, New York. At this time, Rogers was working for the Society for the Prevention of Cruelty to Children, his first professional position after graduating from Columbia University. According to his biographer:

If Rogers favored any one deep, therapeutic approach when he came to Rochester, it was interpretive therapy, the major goal of which is to help the child or parent achieve insight into his own behavior and motives, past and present (Kirschenbaum, 1979, p. 86).

Exactly what occurred at this seminar, apart from the formal talk given by Rank, is now impossible to determine. Rank, according to Kramer (1995 p. 77), mentioned the seminar only twice in correspondence with a friend, Jessie Taft (of whom, more later). However, there can be little doubt that the seminar itself, and Rogers' contact with students of Rank's on the staff of the Rochester clinic, did have a significant impact on Rogers' thinking. In an interview with his biographer, Howerd Kirschenbaum, Rogers remarked:

I became infected with Rankian ideas and began to realise the possibilities of the individual being self-directing . . . I was clearly fascinated by Rankian ideas but didn't quite adopt his emphases for myself until I left Rochester. But the core idea did develop. I came to believe in the individual's capacity. I value the dignity and rights of the individual sufficiently that I do not want to impose my way upon him. These two aspects of the core idea haven't changed since that time (Kirschenbaum, 1979 p. 95).

Nowhere in Rogers' writing is there a direct quotation from Rank, but Kramer (1995) remarks (echoing Raskin, 1948),

Yet Rogers was evidently so moved by the seminar with Rank in 1936, and later by the lucid writings of Jessie Taft and Frederick Allen, two leading American students of Rank, that his view of the helping profession changed radically (Kramer, 1995 p. 78).

In his essay, *Empathic: An Un-appreciated Way of Being* (in Rogers, 1980, pp. 137–138), Rogers commented:

> A little later a social worker,[2] who had a background of Rankian training, helped me to learn that the most effective approach was to listen for the feelings, the emotions, whose patterns could be discerned through the client's word. I believe she was the one who suggested that the best response was to 'reflect' these feelings back to the client - "reflect" becoming in time a word that made me cringe. But at that time, it improved my work as a therapist, and I was grateful.

Kramer (1995, p. 78) speculates, 'What might Rank have "taught" Rogers?' Invited to deliver a lecture in 1938 at the University of Minnesota before Psi Chi, the psychology honour society, Rank summarised his post-Freudian learnings with unusual clarity:

> From my own experience, I learned that the therapeutic process is basically an emotional experience — which takes place independently of the theoretical concepts of the analyst, a statement that is borne out by the fact that the therapeutic results have been attained and achieved by various methods of psychotherapy, based on different theories. Furthermore, the emphasis on the emotional experience — instead of on the intellectual enlightenment of the patient — brings two essential principles of my dynamic therapy into focus. Firstly, the emphasis is shifted from the past to the present, in which all emotional experience takes place; secondly, the therapeutic process allows the patient a much more active role than being merely an object on whom the therapist operates . . .
>
> *All living psychology is relationship psychology* . . . What we learned from the analysis and understanding of this therapeutic relationship seems to have a bearing on other forms and types of relationships . . . Simply speaking, this is the definition of relationship: *one individual is helping the other to develop and grow*, without infringing too much on the other's personality (Rank, in Kramer, 1995).

The birth of client-centred psychotherapy
Rogers nominated December 11, 1940 as 'the day on which client-centred therapy was born' (Kirschenbaum, 1979, p. 112), the day he delivered a paper before Psi Chi (coincidentally at the University of Minnesota where Rank had spoken in 1938). This paper, *Newer Concepts in Psychotherapy* publicly credited the thinking of Otto Rank and went on:

> the aim of this newer therapy is not to solve one particular problem, but to assist the individual to grow . . . This newer therapy places

---

2. According to Raskin (in Lynn and Garske, 1985) this social worker was Elizabeth Davis who had been trained at the University of Pennsylvania School of Social Work.

greater stress upon the emotional elements, the feeling aspects of the situation, than upon the intellectual aspects . . . In the third place, this newer therapy places greater stress upon the immediate situation than upon the individual's past . . . Finally this approach lays stress upon the therapeutic relationship itself as a growth experience (Kirschenbaum, 1979, p 113).

Kramer[3] (1995, p. 80) concluded:

Somehow the ideas of Otto Rank had germinated in the mind of Carl Rogers, whether directly as a result of the 1936 seminar or indirectly through Rank's students . . . Echoing Rank's old-world philosophy of life . . . Rogers came to define the fully functioning person as one who deliberately and creatively says 'Yes' to the 'Must'. By doing so, the person affirms the loan of life, a loan that is fated to be repaid in full at the end — 'returned', so to speak, to the Cosmos, to 'the ALL' (Rank, 1936/1978, p. 155) Such a person, concluded Rogers, in words that are almost identical to Rank's, 'voluntarily chooses and wills that which is absolutely determined'.

Taft and 'The Pennsylvania School'

The name, Jessie Taft, occurs several times in exploring early influences on the development of client-centred therapy. Taft was Rank's student, patient and translator, and for a short time his associate at the Pennsylvania School of Social Work. According to Thorne (1992, p. 9), 'She [Taft] and her colleague, Frederick Allen, became a major influence in Rogers' professional life and it was their version of Rank's ideas and practice which gradually permeated Rogers' own thinking and clinical behaviour'.

Apart from her work in translating Rank, Taft is best known for her book, *The Dynamics of Therapy in a Controlled Relationship* (Taft, 1933).[4] This book contains Taft's unique theoretical contribution to the development of theory and practice in psychotherapy — the emphasis she placed on time as a significant factor of the therapeutic endeavour:

If there is no therapeutic understanding and use of one interview, many interviews equally barren cannot help. In the single interview, if that is all I allow myself to count upon, if I am willing to take that

---

3. In a personal communication (1996), Robert Kramer added: 'Needless to say, there were many influences on Rank as well. For example, my article did not highlight enough the fruitful contribution of Sandor Ferenczi, who was Rank's closest friend and colleague during the early Twenties. There has been a remarkable revival of interest in Ferenczi in the last ten years, and he is now recognized even by the analysts for his pioneering stress on empathic understanding and mutuality. If Carl had encountered Ferenczi rather than Rank, the results would probably have been the same.'

4. Republished in 1962 by Dover Publications (USA), and by Constable in London. Reprinted in 1973.

> one hour in and for itself, there is no time to hide behind material, no time to explore the past or the future. I myself am the remedy at this moment if there is any and I can no longer escape my responsibility, not for the client, but for myself and my role in the situation. Here is just one hour to be lived through as it goes, one hour of present immediate relationship, however limited, with another human being who has brought himself to the point of asking for help (p.11).

Taft and her Rankian colleague, Frederick Allen are, however, important to this present discussion because they both have provided more-or-less verbatim transcripts of therapy sessions. This enables a more direct comparison with Rogers on a practical level as well as a theoretical one. Raskin (1948), in reviewing Taft's transcripts of her work with two children (Helen P and John) made four observations:

1. There is only incidental attempt on the part of the therapist to bring out content material.
2. There are leading questions as to past feelings and warnings as to future feelings.
3. The therapist sometimes takes the lead in bringing out attitudes on the time element and on other aspects of the dynamics of the therapeutic situation.
4. The main resource of the therapist here is her general attitude of understanding and respect for the child. In the absence of any specific techniques the therapist appears to respond on an intuitive emotional basis.

It is interesting to note that in 1933, seven years before client-centred therapy was born, i.e. during the years when Rogers was formulating his theory, one of his working colleagues was already conducting therapy in a way that was remarkably similar to the approach that Rogers eventually called client-centred therapy. Rank's influence, both direct and indirect, is there for all to see.

Raskin (1948) has a word of warning, however:

> It may be recalled that in evaluating Rank's contribution, it was stated that while his renunciation of the past for the present and of the therapeutic content for dynamics was complete, his abandonment of the Freudian techniques of therapist-direction and interpretation was not, at least where the dynamics of will in the therapeutic situation were concerned.

Frederick Allen

The same comment can be made in regard to Frederick Allen, but with more certainty, since we have a much clearer record of his therapeutic technique.

In reviewing Allen's work with 'a fearful child' [Solomon], Raskin again makes four observations:

1. The therapist may be accepting Solomon as an individual who can help himself get well, but he is not accepting the boy's capacity to arrive at that insight himself, he is not accepting the expressed feeling that he does not know how to

get well and needs the therapist to help him.

2. The therapist plays the role of interpreter of the dynamics of the child's will-conflict, and of the relationship of the child to the therapist and to the therapeutic situation in general.

3. Solomon resists all these attempts at interpretation, and in being forced to express his counter-will against the therapist's will, is given no opportunity to assert the positive will which would make for growth.

4. Any progress made by Solomon is dependent upon the therapist's interpretation and is not apparent from the boy's statements and actions themselves.

The extent to which Rogers was influenced by Rankian ideas in the way he practised therapy does not seem as great as Rank's philosophical influence. Rogers and Sanford (1980) have summed up the various influences on the development of client-centred therapy, and do not identify any one theory or set of ideas as having any more importance than any other. In fact, Rogers avoided being associated with any particular school of thought, and saw this as a positive advantage, although he did identify some of Rank's influence specifically:

> Rank's emphasis on therapy being for the client, rather than being a channel for the high-blown theories of the therapist, appears to have left its mark. Also important was Rank's stress on the necessity for the individual clients to express their personal will, to take command of their own lives, and constantly to create their own reality.
>
> One important factor in the development of a client-centered approach is that Rogers never had just one mentor. He was, instead, influenced by many significant figures of widely differing views. Consequently, he was tied to no dogma nor to any previously held theory. It is fair to say that the client-centered view, although fed by various streams of thought, developed primarily out of the continuing examination by Rogers and his colleagues of their changing, broadening experience with their clients. It was the client in process who constituted the basic data of learning for the evolution of client-centered thought (Rogers and Sanford, 1980, p. 1375).

Client-centred therapy did not, then, develop as the result of a departure from an already existing system, in the way that Rank's therapy did. Rogers was never a member of the psychoanalytic community of his day, even though his early work was recognisably influenced by it. There were significant influences on Rogers' thinking, but they tended to reinforce and affirm his direction, rather than change it. His work did not even grow from an accumulated body of knowledge subsumed under the heading of Humanistic Psychology, as client-centred therapy was already well established before Humanistic Psychology became an acknowledged 'third force' in psychology. Whilst Rogers was certainly impressed by some of the theorists and practitioners with whom he came into contact, his approach did not evolve out of an earlier well-established one.

What remains is the thought that Rogers' work was truly original. His source of data was the people with whom he worked — his clients. Rogers' ability as an observer of human behaviour coupled with his determination to learn from his observations led him to a formulation that was, in the 1940s, quite revolutionary. Since then, much of what Rogers and his colleagues said and wrote has filtered into the 'mainstream'. Unfortunately, some it has become distorted and, ironically, misunderstood. It is time for a reappraisal of the revolutionary nature of the person-centred approach.

References

Kirschenbaum, H. (1979) *On Becoming Carl Rogers*. New York: Delacorte.

Kirschenbaum, H. and Henderson, V. (Eds). (1989) *The Carl Rogers Reader*. Boston: Houghton Mifflin.

Kramer, R. (1995) The birth of client-centered therapy: Carl Rogers, Otto Rank and 'the beyond'. *Journal of Humanistic Psychology*, 35, (4).

Lynn, S. J. and Garske, J. P. (1985) *Contemporary Psychotherapies.*Columbus, Ohio: Charles Merill.

Rank, O. (1945) *Will Therapy, and Truth and Reality*. New York: Knopf.

Rank, O. (1978) *Will Therapy: An analysis of the therapeutic process in terms of relationship* (J. Taft, trans.) New York: Norton. (Original work published 1936.)

Rank, O. (1994) *The Trauma of Birth*. New York: Dover. (Original work published in 1924.)

Raskin, N. (1948) The Development of Nondirective Therapy, *Journal of Consulting Psychology*, 12, pp. 92–110.

Rogers, C. R. (1980*) A Way of Being*. Boston: Houghton Mifflin.

Rogers, C. R. and Sanford, R. C. (1980) Client-Centred Psychotherapy. In Kaplan, G. H., Sadock, B., & Freeman, A. (Eds). *Comprehensive Textbook of Psychiatry,* Vol. 3. Baltimore: Williams and Wilkins.

Taft, J. (1933) *The Dynamics of Therapy in a Controlled Relationship*. New York: MacMillan. (Reprinted 1973)

Thorne, B.(1992) *Carl Rogers*. London: Sage.

Rigid, or Pure?

Irene Fairhurst

Since the death of Carl Rogers, six years ago, the debate about 'pure form' and 'person-centred eclecticism' has become more heated and, in my view, more vital than ever. It is easy to understand the need for security felt by client-centred therapists and counsellors who lost the personal reference point Carl provided. He displayed an unpossessive generosity, and no feelings of threat or jealousy when faced with such terms as 'Person-Centred Gestalt', or 'Person-Centred psychodrama'. On the other hand, there is a fear amongst some that 'eclecticism' might undermine the scientific discipline of the PCA, and that recognition of the validity and value of this approach will be threatened.

One of the problems is a lack of understanding of what the term 'person-centred' means. A central hypothesis and conviction of the PCA is that individuals have the potential for finding their own meaning, solutions, autonomy and personal responsibility. Carl Rogers referred to this potential as the organism's actualising tendency. An acceptance of the actualising tendency is central to person-centred personality theory, and provides a contrast to other theories which look to external constructs, reinforcements or cognitive learning. It offers an optimistic alternative to Freud's death instinct, and notions of the 'savage beast'.

In other words, Rogers believed that the organism is capable of promoting its own health and wholeness if the right psychological climate is provided. He did not see clients as sick and in need of treatment from someone who knows what is best for them.

> The organism has one basic tendency and striving — to actualise, maintain, and enhance the experiencing organism (Rogers, 1951).

In therapy, the theory continues that this growth-promoting psychological climate is more likely to occur when the therapist or counsellor possesses and communicates empathy, congruence and unconditional positive regard. It is my experience that it is here that many practitioners jump on the person-centred bandwagon. The reasoning goes:

> 'If I understand my clients and let them know I understand them from time to time, I am being empathic (I can do that by nodding and repeating back the last three words of any sentence when they pause long enough). If I let them know my opinions, particularly if I disagree and confront and challenge them, I am being real. If I am warm and supportive, give them lots of hugs and assure them

First published in *Person-Centred Practice*, Volume 1, Number 1, 1993.

of my love and acceptance whatever they are telling me, and provide a nice atmosphere with flowers and armchairs, I am being warm and non-judgemental — ergo I am person-centred and can now get on with the *real work* with empty chairs, cushion-thumping, interpreting, explaining, stage-managing and suggesting.'

The fundamental precept of the PCA theory — the actualising tendency of the organism — is either unheard of or conveniently forgotten. Do I *really* believe that my poor, confused clients, who are after all coming to me for help, could possibly know what is best for them, even more than I do? Rogers (1951) wrote :

> If the counsellor feels, in the middle of an interview, that this client may not have the capacity for reorganising himself, and shifts to the hypothesis that the counsellor must bear a considerable responsibility for this reorganisation, he confuses the client and defeats himself. He has shut himself off from proving or disproving either hypothesis. This confused eclecticism, which has been prevalent in psychotherapy, has blocked scientific progress in the field. Actually, it is only by acting *consistently* upon a well selected hypothesis that its elements of truth and untruth can become known.

So, we have practitioners, both eclectic and integrative, who believe themselves, understandably but, in my view, mistakenly, to be person-centred, and those who do know the theory, but have very individualistic interpretations of it. This brings me to the core of this paper — rigid, or pure?

In Rogers' (1951) words:

> There has been a tendency to regard the non-directive or client-centered approach as something static — a method, a technique, a rather rigid system. Nothing could be further from the truth. A group of professional workers in this field are working with dynamic concepts which they are constantly revising in the light of continuing clinical experience and in the light of research findings. The picture is one of fluid changes in a general approach to problems of human relationships, rather than a situation in which some relatively rigid technique is more or less mechanically applied.
>
> In this flux of changing thinking there are some central hypotheses which give unity to the search for further knowledge. Perhaps one of the reasons for the high stimulus value which client-centered therapy seems to have had is the fact that these hypotheses are testable, are capable of proof or disproof, and hence offer a hope of progress, rather than the stagnation of dogma. There appears to be more than a likelihood that psychotherapy is, by the efforts of various workers, being brought out of the realm of the mystical, the intuitive, the personal, the undefinable, into the full light of objective scrutiny. This inevitably means that change rather than rigidity

becomes the characteristic of such a field. To those at work in client-centered therapy, this characteristic of development, of reformulation, of change, appears to be one of its most outstanding qualities.

As someone who calls herself a 'pure' client-centred therapist, the words 'rigid' and 'dogma', when applied to the PCA are a contradiction in terms to me. When I began as a client-centred therapist some fifteen years ago, I would sometimes feel stuck with a client and wonder, for a fraction of a second, whether my knowledge of other techniques, such as Transactional Analysis, Gestalt or Bioenergetics, might help the client. With my supervisor's support, I realised that it was not the theory that was weak, but my experience and confidence in it. Often clients, if allowed freedom to experience their stuckness, would find *their own way out*.

As Rogers (1951) said,

> So it is with the counsellor. As he finds new and more subtle ways of implementing his client-centered hypothesis, new meanings are poured into it by experience, and its depth is seen to be greater than was first supposed.

I am continually excited and stimulated by the new thinking and research in this work which prevents me from becoming rigid and dogmatic, whilst trusting completely in the basic hypothesis. In the introduction to *Client-Centered Therapy* (Rogers, 1951), Leonard Carmichael writes,

> This volume is not a rigid presentation of a closed system. The author and his collaborators have captured the gift of making the reader feel, as he turns its pages, that he is already participating in the constructive and forward-looking thinking which characterises the basic point of view of this book.

However, I should like to finish this section with a later quote from Rogers (in Kutash and Wolf, 1986) :

> **One more characteristic**
>
> I described above the characteristics of a growth-promoting relationship that have been investigated and supported by research. But recently my view has broadened into a new area that cannot as yet be studied empirically.
>
> When I am at my best, as a group facilitator or a therapist, I discover another characteristic. I find that when I am closest to my inner, intuitive self, when I am somehow in touch with the unknown in me, when perhaps I am in a slightly altered state of consciousness in the relationship, then whatever I do seems to be full of healing. Then simply my *presence* is releasing and helpful. There is nothing I can do to force this experience, but when I can relax and be close to the transcendental core of me, then I may behave in strange and impulsive ways in the relationship, ways which I cannot justify

rationally, which have nothing to do with my thought processes. But these strange behaviours turn out to be right, in some *odd* way. At those moments it seems that my inner spirit has reached out and touched the inner spirit of the other. Our relationship transcends itself and becomes a part of something larger. Profound growth and healing and energy are present.

Does this sound like a rigid dogma? Whether you agree with this later thinking or not, and there are eminent client-centred theoreticians who do not (and I hope they will soon be putting their opinions in papers), the point is that Rogers was himself open to new thinking and development and identified himself, in the same paper, with the 'New Science :

The person-centered approach, then, is primarily a way of being that finds its expression in attitudes and behaviours that create a growth-promoting climate. It is a basic philosophy rather than simply a technique or a method. When this philosophy is lived, it helps the person expand the development of his or her own capacities. When it is lived, it also stimulates constructive change in others. It empowers the individual, and when this personal power is sensed, experience shows that it tends to be used for personal and social transformation.

When this person-centered way of being is lived in psychotherapy, it leads to a process of self-exploration and self-discovery in the client and eventually to constructive changes in personality and behaviour. As the therapist lives these conditions in the relationship, he or she becomes a companion to the client in this journey toward the core of self.

I do not intend to imply that other schools of thought, including eclecticism, are not effective, or that client-centred therapy is always the best approach for every client. I am saying that it is the only approach within which I can work happily, and the one I can be most effective in, because it comes closest to my own fundamental philosophy of humankind.

Implications for training

As a facilitator in a learning programme in client-centred psychotherapy, I become concerned when what I practice and believe in is misunderstood and misrepresented. Philosophical consistency in training in the PCA is a matter of great importance and passion for me. For over ten years I have been involved in learning/training programmes in client-centred therapy and the PCA, both in the UK and elsewhere. I have become aware of the importance for participants to be clear about the philosophical position of those who are included as facilitators of their learning. One of the factors which prompted me to write this paper was a debate about the inclusion of staff who are knowledgeable in the theory of the PCA, but are not 'rigid' in their commitment to it.

I have discussed this with participants on two learning programmes. These programmes run over three years, and are consistent with student-centred learning objectives. It was said that it would be confusing to have facilitators who did not operate from a person-centred position at the beginning of the programme. This seems to support Rogers (1951), who, in writing about therapist training, said :

> In so far as possible, the atmosphere of the course would be the atmosphere of client-centered therapy, and that we would endeavour to facilitate learning that was self-motivated . . . A Client-centered climate demands of the teacher a sensitivity to the values, feelings and ideas of students; it also demands a nondefensiveness on the part of the teacher so that students can deal with deeper feelings aroused by new learnings. It was assumed that, as a student's emotionalised viewpoint is understood by an accepting teacher, it becomes possible for the student to learn the teacher's viewpoint and independently establish his own altered viewpoint.

The participants in the groups referred to above, felt that at the beginning of a programme it would be difficult to challenge teaching methods which did not comply with the stated aim of the Institute — to practise a person-centred approach to learning. It would also be confusing, again at the beginning of a programme, to be presented with theories that were inconsistent with person-centred philosophy.

It was also thought that it would not be helpful to be exposed to facilitators who genuinely believe themselves to be person-centred, but who do not adhere to the basic philosophy of the actualising tendency. However, I have been with a group of participants towards the end of a programme who were sufficiently confident and knowledgeable to be challenging in such a situation.

The Institute of which I am part does not run an eclectic course which offers comparisons with other philosophies (there are many other courses which offer this valuable facility). However, Institute staff are willing and qualified to respond to *specific requests from participants* for comparisons of this kind. It is, perhaps, because the Institute includes facilitators both from a core staff, and from visitors from the USA and Europe, often invited at the request of participants themselves, that this debate has arisen.

I will finish where Carl Rogers began *Client-Centered Therapy:*

> We mark with light in the memory the few interviews we have had, in the dreary years of routine and of sin, with souls that made our souls wiser; that spoke what we thought; that told us what we knew; that gave us leave to be what we truly were (Emerson, Divinity School Address, 1838).

References

Rogers, C.R. (1951) *Client-Centred Therapy*. London: Constable.

Kutash, I. and Wolf, A. (1986)(Eds) *Psychotherapist's Casebook*. San Fransisco: Jossey Bass.

Carl Rogers and Experiential Therapies: A Dissonance?

Garry Prouty

Introduction

In recent months, there has been a growing impetus for the formation of a person-centered/experiential organization of an international nature. My initial response to this was relaxed, because it seemed to involve the same historical-theoretical framework I had previously been familiar with via Rogers and Gendlin. Several months later, I realized that a *new* person-centered/experiential organizational theme was being presented. Its proponents offer a view that is inclusive of different experiential approaches (Greenberg, et al. 1998). Since there are about two dozen experiential methods (Mahrer and Fairweather, 1993), it seems appropriate to examine the proposed theoretical–organizational fusion for its consistency with client-centered principles. However, this position *in no way* attempts to challenge the empirical efficacy of experiential therapies. Nor is it an exhaustive elucidation or comparison of theories. Rather, it is an attempt at an introductory exploration of theoretical dissonance between Rogers and experiential therapies — a necessary understanding for organizational development.

A major paradigm shift, from Rogers' (1959) view that relationship is primary in psychological healing to an emphasis on experiential factors, is perhaps a historical shift that is not appropriate. My major concern is the possible absorption and eventual vague dissolution of client-centered therapy into an experiential zeitgeist. In balance, it should be noted that I have written evolutions in both Rogers' client-centered theory and Gendlin's experiential theory, but they are clearly *differentiated* from each other (Prouty, 1994).

Is Rogers experiential?

Although Rogers (1961) explicitly acknowledges the influence of Gendlin's experiential theory on his own work, he did not subscribe to experiencing as an independent variable in psychotherapy research. He viewed it as a dependent variable. Experiencing was a *result* of therapy, not the *cause* of therapy (Prouty, 1994). This is illustrated in his 'Process Conception of Therapy' (Rogers, 1961). He clearly states that the 'attitudes' are the basic condition for experiential change. This is also illustrated in the Wisconsin project on schizophrenia (Rogers, Gendlin, et al. 1967). There, experiencing is again formulated as a function of the 'attitudes'.

First Published in *Person-Centred Practice,* Volume 7, Number 1, 1999.

If Rogers had intended Gendlin's experiencing to be the cause of therapy, it is not illustrated there, in their closest collaboration. In addition, while Rogers characterizes 'openness to experience' as one of the characteristics of the 'fully functioning person' (Rogers, 1989), he clearly rooted this in the safe and accepting relationship (Rogers, 1957).

Argument for the differentiation of Gendlin's experiential approach from Rogers' views are presented by Brodley (1990), who describes Rogers as trusting in the *whole person,* while in experiential therapy trust is placed in the *experiencing process.* She also suggests that 'listening' is different between the two approaches. Listening, in the experiential approach of Gendlin, is directed towards the felt sense (Hendricks, 1986). My views, and those of Brodley, point at what I would call 'phenomenological reductionism'. I interpret this to mean the reduction of *person* to a *process.*

The non-directive attitude

Although not formalized, a non-directive approach to psychotherapy is one of the distinctive features of client-centered therapy. It can be more fully understood if, first, its cultural roots are clarified. Rogers, in his early religious training, was raised and educated in a Protestant tradition. Simply put, Martin Luther's revolutionary doctrine was to shift the power of moral interpretation from the church to the conscience of the individual. Moral conscience became a form of self-empowerment. Rogers' (1977) distinct and revolutionary doctrine in mental health was to shift the power of understanding self-experience from the therapist to the client. The client was self-empowered about the meanings of his experience. Rogers' non-directive stance can be seen culturally as a form of Protestant individualism. As a theology student, he had studied Luther.

In terms of psychotherapy, Rogers (1942) described non-directivity in several forms. First, the client is described as taking responsibility for directing the interview. Second, the counselor responds in such a way as to indicate a recognition of the client's preceding message; the counselor responds to the client's immediate feeling and attitude. The counselor indicates that decisions are up to the client and accepting the client's actual decisions.

Rogers then abstracts non-directivity to a set of values to be held by the therapist. The client has the right to select individual goals; the client has the right to be psychologically independent and to maintain psychological integrity; the client has the right to choose the right reality adaptation. In more modern language, the client's autonomy is maximized, the therapeutic relationship is more democratized, and the client's individualization is more centered. It seems obvious that in order to implement this the therapist needs a genuine and congruent attitude. Raskin (1951) described the preceding construction as a 'non-directive attitude'.

I would say that Rogers formulated an approach that deeply values psychological freedom for the client to define and create himself. I further think that Rogers' formal description of the necessary and sufficient conditions of therapy (unconditional positive regard, empathy and congruence) does not *exclude* the 'non-directive attitude'. In the first place, Rogers never disconnected himself from the 'non-directive attitude': it has become subsumed and integrated within the practice of client-centered therapy. Second, the 'non-directive attitude' expresses unconditional positive regard in that a deep acceptance of the client is involved. Third, the 'non-directive attitude' is embodied in the disciplined following of client process, i.e. empathic understanding. Finally, the integration of the non-directive attitude, unconditional positive regard and empathy are achieved through the congruence of the therapist.

I think an issue of historical magnitude occurred when Rogers failed to formalize the 'non-directive attitude' along with the other necessary conditions of therapy. *The result is to create a theoretical situation where, as long as the necessary and sufficient conditions are present, any technique can be combined with them.* At practice levels this theoretical shifting is illustrated by the 'evocative reflections' suggested by Rice (1974) and by 'focused reflections' (Hendricks, 1986). Both of these authors direct technique towards the experiencing process.

The Process–Experiential Approach
The Process–Experiential Approach is examined because of its theoretical and organizational leadership in unifying or integrating client-centered therapy with experiential methods.

The Rice (1983) distinction between relationship and therapeutic task has 'allowed' the development of the Process–Experiential Approach, which blends the 'attitudes' with experiential processing encompassing multiple methods (Greenberg, et al. 1993). 'Direct the process, not the content' is a slogan which perhaps encapsulates this view. This illustrates the consequences of 'splitting' non-directivity from the attitudinal conditions of therapy and the philosophic and theoretical commitment to experiencing as a 'cause', not a 'result', of therapy.

The most basic description of process–experiential therapy is that it is a combination of the client-centered attitudes with various *process directive* experiential methods or techniques. Perhaps this view is most clearly presented in the following quotation (Greenberg, et al. 1993):

> Our approach involves a combination and a balance between client-centered empathic responding and the process directiveness of experiential and Gestalt therapies. In this approach, the therapist is highly empathically attuned to the client's moment-by-moment feelings and experience of being. He or she is also directive in process, guiding the client toward engaging in particular types of resolution-enhancing, affective information-processing strategies at different times. Our therapist thus facilitates the client's process, both by responding empathically to the client's experience and by providing directions or suggestions as to the actions or mental operations the client might engage in at the moment to enhance processing. The goal is to stimulate new awareness, experiencing and meaning construction, not to provide insight or modify cognition (p. 15).

The second 'pillar' of the Process–Experiential Approach is that process provides the basis for a diagnosis. *How* the client processes provides a 'marker' as to which experiential technique is appropriate: it is a *process diagnosis*. Different process problems result in differential application of technique. This view is expressed in the following quotation (Greenberg, et al. 1993):

> Based on the recognition of different emerging client states, the therapist intervenes in different ways at different times in order to facilitate particular types of constructive information processing. This intervention is guided by a type of 'process diagnosis' of the client's current state and by ideas of what would be most helpful at any particular moment in facilitating the client's cognitive/affective processing.
>
> Process diagnosis thus involves an identification of a 'marker' of emotional processing problems. When a 'marker' of a particular process emerges, the therapist facilitates particular types of processing activity designed to help resolve the currently experienced processing problem. An example of this would be if the client experiences conflict, the two-chair Gestalt technique would be applied. If the client experiences an unclear felt-sense, then focusing would be utilized. The therapist is the process expert (p. 17).

Since directivity is an acknowledged part of the Process–Experiential Approach, it is important to clarify fully and fairly the meaning of 'directive' in this therapy. Perhaps this is best conveyed by the following quotation (Greenberg, et al. 1993):

> However, the client is seen as an expert on what he or she is experiencing, and as an active agent in the change process. Throughout the therapy, even when being process directive, the therapist adopts an inquiring 'not knowing' attitude. This position entails a stance of curiosity and suggestion rather than one of a knowing authority. Therapists' actions and attitudes express a desire to know more about the client's experience, and suggestions are made to help explicate the implicit, rather than to convey that therapists are more knowing and searching for hidden material. This 'less knowing' position, adopted by process-experiential therapists, stands in contrast to the adoption of a more knowing position in an interpretive approach in which the therapist operates as an expert on the client's experience, on the basis of theoretical truths or professional knowledge. In being process directive the therapist engages with the clients, not to make meaning for them, nor to identify patterns, not to ferret out the hidden, nor to suggest better ways of seeing themselves or the world. Rather the therapist guides or stimulates the client to engage in certain information processing activities believed to enhance schematic information that will aid the client in reorganizing experience and in making new meaning in

areas that are troublesome to him or her. It is self-generated reorganization in areas of desired change that best helps people to see themselves, or their world in a new way (p. 16).

The directive attitude

The issue of the 'directive attitude' is difficult to articulate as it is subtly woven through the therapeutic approaches of Gendlin, Rice and Greenberg. Each of these theoreticians propose so to direct the client towards their experiencing. This attitude is expressed in such language as *guide, suggest, stimulate, explicate, enhance*. It is an attitude of theoretically and selectively listening with *technical intent*, and it is also the problem alluded to earlier — the problem of *phenomenological reductionism*.

In my understanding of the therapeutic experience, accurate empathy releases the client into the next organismically formed experience, i.e. a pattern of 'non-directive experiencing' where the flow of experiencing *naturally* follows the organism. Experiencing as a natural consequence, as compared with experiencing resulting from therapist intent, differentiates Rogers from experiential views. Why is this important?

Technical intent

The issue of therapist intent is important only when counterpoised with the issue of client intent. It seems reasonable to describe one of the differences between Rogers and the experiential therapies as one of therapist intent. It is the purpose of experiential therapies to 'guide' the client towards experiencing. This is not the intent of Rogers' view of client-centered therapy, which facilitates client intent through a 'surrender' to *client self-direction.*

The term 'technical intent' alludes to an attitude of paying attention to the *how* of experiential process. The therapist is 'empathically attuned' to the 'how' of experiencing. This sounds like a *selective listening* for process with the intent of therapeutic experiencing. It does not convey the existential attitude of hearing the client's grasp of their 'reality', which is a fuller expression of accurate empathy. The problem is that empathy is *used* for a therapist's technical concern for the 'how' of the process, as the basis for a diagnostic intervention — hardly a genuine 'I–thou' response.

However assuredly benign or helpful the therapist's motive might be, there are complex and difficult clinical situations surrounding the issue of directiveness. First, there is the issue of conscious client resistance. There are situations in therapy where 'experiencing' is threatening to the client, i.e. is a manifestation of client fear. To 'experience' may be actually be disintegrative of self. This can be the case when integrating homosexual feelings, psychotic experiences or certain aspects of multiple personality. These can be described as examples of 'fragile process' (Warner, 1991). These are feelings where *only* the client's sense provides a safe pathway. Many times I have seen 'experiences' too threatening for 'directive' experiencing. Only a slow surrender to the 'natural' experiencing and integration seems safe — certainly not therapist-intended interventions that are ahead of the client process. This is often true of psychotic and psychotic-like experiencing.

Phenomenological reductionism

A client recalled an experience that illustrates the problem of 'phenomenological reductionism'. She remembered needing the empathic presence and response of her therapist. Instead, she was 'guided' to her experiencing. She reported a visceral sense of not being related to. She felt her 'self' was ignored, and she experienced therapist intent rather than empathy. This example frames the problem of 'phenomenological reductionism', which can be described as empathy *to* experiencing rather than empathy *for* the self. The self is reduced to its experiencing. The *process* of experiencing rather than the existential *whole being* of self is empathically related to by the therapist.

An example is drawn from my experience as a therapist. I worked with a client who was schizophrenic and very homicidal. Her experiencing was one of homicidal feeling. The client reports that what was most helpful was my ability to discern between her self and her experiencing. Her existential self was not her experiencing process. Repeatedly, she expressed the feeling 'that's not me'. The distinction between self and experience had empathic and long-term therapeutic consequences.

Summary and conclusions

This article is an attempt to introduce a discussion about the dissonance between the client-centered theory of Carl Rogers and the experiential approach. The basis for such an effort is concern about an inaccurate absorbing of client-centered theory and therapy into an experiential zeitgeist and organizational unity. The first issue of concern was that there exist about two-dozen experiential methods and more clarity is needed. The major exploration concerned the Process–Experiential Approach because of its empirical and organizational leadership. It is clear that empirical validity was not questioned: rather, issues of theory and practice were explored.

The first issue explored was whether Rogers' client-centered therapy could be viewed as 'experiential'. This was considered a key issue because there are some scholars who do view Rogers as experiential. Experiencing is present in Rogers' work, but it is a function of the attitudes — a result. It was pointed out that experiencing is an outcome variable with Rogers. It is treated in that way in the Wisconsin project, as well as in his 'process conception of therapy'. Additionally, the 'openness to experience' characteristic of the 'fully functioning person' is a function of the attitudes. For Rogers, experiencing is a result, not the cause, of therapy.

The next important issue to be discussed was the theoretical construction of the 'attitudes' by Rogers. Although he never rejected his non-directive views, he did not formally include them in his theory of therapy. The result of this omission has been an interpretation that, as long as the conditions are present, any method can be used — which, of course, allows for directive techniques. This results in subtle movements towards directivity, in the work of both Gendlin (focusing), and Rice (evocative reflections), as well as, more explicitly, by Greenberg et al. (process directive).

Because of its role in the proposed organizational fusion between client-centered and experiential therapies, the tenets of the Process–Experiential Approach are examined. It presents itself as a fusion of 'traditional' client-centered therapy and directive experiential techniques based on diagnostic 'markers'. A descriptive slogan for this view is 'Direct the process, not the content'. This is based on the Gestalt theory of attention for the 'how' of experiential processing.

On the level of practice, several issues are raised. First is the issue of therapist intent. Self-directed intent of the client is compared with therapist direct intent. Therapist intent directed towards the 'how' of experiencing is described as technical intent, which is not the full empathic presence of the therapist. Listening with 'empathic attunement' to the 'how of experiencing' is described as selective listening, which can easily omit empathy for the existential self of the client — a very critical issue.

Finally, the issue of 'phenomenological reduction' is explored. Phenomenological reduction is defined as empathy towards experiential process in contrast to empathy for the whole being. We can describe this issue in terms of the I–it relation as contrasted to the I–thou relation. The philosopher Levinas (1989) suggests that, when we speak of the *psychological states* (experiential processing) of human beings, we are speaking in the mode of objectification: I–it not the existential I–thou mode — *person to person.*

The ultimate resolution of these fundamental issues is of course up to the individual practitioner. The issue is whether we follow the self actualizing, non-directive intent of Rogers' empathic view, or subscribe to an empathically reduced view of therapy.

References

Brodley, B. (1990) Client-centered and experiential: two different therapies. In C. Lietaer, J. Rombauts and R. Van Balen, (Eds.), *Client-Centered and Experiential Psychotherapy in the Nineties.* Leuven, Belgium: Leuven University Press, pp. 87–107.

Greenberg, L., Rice, L. and Elliot, R. (1993) *Facilitating Emotional Change.* New York: Guilford Press, pp. 12–31.

Greenberg, L., Watson, J. and Lietaer, G.(1998) *Handbook of Experiential Therapy.* New York: Guilford Press.

Hendricks, M. (1986) Experiencing level as a therapeutic variable. *Person Centered Review,* 9, (2), pp. 141–162.

Levinas, E. (1989) Martin Buber and the theory of knowledge. In S. Hand (Ed.), *The Levinas Reader:* Cambridge, Mass: Blackwell, p. 63.

Mahrer, A. and Fairweather, D., (1993) What is 'experiencing'? A critical review of meanings and applications in psychotherapy. *The Humanistic Psychologist,* 21,(Spring), pp. 2–25.

Prouty, G. (1994) *Theoretical Evolutions in Person-Centered/Experiential Therapy: Applications to Schizophrenic and Retarded Psychoses.* Westport, Conn.: Praeger.

Raskin, N. (1951) In C.R. Rogers *Client-Centered Therapy.* Boston: Houghton-Mifflin, p. 29.

Rice, L. (1974) The evocative function of the therapist. In D. Wexler and L. Rice (Eds.), *Innovations in Client-Centered Therapy.* New York: John Wiley, pp. 289–311.

Rice, L. (1983) The relationship in client-centered psychotherapy. In J. J. Lambert (Ed.), *Psychotherapy and Patient Relationships.* Homewood, IL.: Richard D. Irwin, p. 36–60.

Rogers, C. R. (1942) *Counseling and Psychotherapy.* Boston: Houghton-Mifflin, pp. 115–26.

Rogers, C. R. (1957) The necessary and sufficient conditions for therapeutic personality change. *Journal of Consulting Psychology,* 21,(2), pp. 95–103.

Rogers, C. R. (1959) A theory of therapy, personality and interpersonal relationships as developed in the client-centered framework. In S. Koch (Ed.), *Psychology: The Study of a Science,* Vol. 3. New York: McGraw-Hill, pp. 184–256.

Rogers, C. R. (1961) A process conception of therapy. In C. R. Rogers, *On Becoming a Person.* Boston: Houghton-Mifflin, p. 128.

Rogers, C. R. (1977) *Carl Rogers on Personal Power: Inner Strength and its Revolutionary Impact.* London: Constable.

Rogers, C. R. (1989) A therapist's view of the good life: the fully functioning person. In H. Kirschenbaum and V. Henderson (Eds.), *The Carl Rogers Reader.* Boston: Houghton-Mifflin, p. 412.

Rogers, C. R., Gendlin, E. T., Keisler, J. T. and Truax, C. B. (1967) *The Therapeutic Relationship and Its Impact: A Study of Psychotherapy with Schizophrenics.* Madison, Wis.: University of Wisconsin Press.

Warner, M. (1991) Fragile process. In L. Fusek (Ed.), *New Directions in Client-Centered Therapy: Practice with Difficult Client Populations.* Chicago: Counseling and Psychotherapy Research Center, pp. 41–58.

Key Strategy for the Development of a Person-Centred Paradigm of Counselling/Psychotherapy

Ivan Ellingham

A bare-faced proposition

In a recent article I had the 'bare-faced' effrontery to propose that 'it is the person-centred framework of thought . . . that is set to provide a more adequate base on which to ground a paradigm for the field of c/p [counselling/psychotherapy[1]]' (Ellingham, 1995, p. 4). I am not alone in holding such a view. After I had made the same proposal in an earlier paper, Brian Thorne wrote: 'With Ellingham I happen to believe that it is the person-centred approach engendered by Carl Rogers . . . which has the potential to be developed into a paradigm for the field [of c/p] as a whole' (1992, p. 247).

In the present article, following further discussion of the issue of the development of a paradigm for the field of c/p, I outline a strategy by which I believe the paradigmatic potential of the person-centred approach can be realised. In Part 1, having explained the notion of a paradigm once more, I highlight the current paradigm-less condition of the field of c/p before briefly examining the views of individuals who believe that the development of a paradigm for the field of c/p is an unreal expectation. In Part 2, I point up how the question of developing a paradigm for the field of c/p cannot be divorced from that of generating a paradigm for the domain of psychology as a whole. In Part 3, following comment on the importance of key ideas for the development of scientific paradigms, I lay claim that central to the person-centred framework of thought is an idea capable of serving as the key idea for a genuine paradigm of c/p, an idea which, because it has been employed by non-person-centred theorists, can be honed and refined to form the foundation stone of such a paradigm.

In Part 4, I identify this idea and provide a skeletal description of the strategy by which, on the basis of the person-centred formulation of this key idea and the ideas ancillary to it, real progress can be made towards the development of a person-centred paradigm of c/p.

,First published in *Person-Centred Practice* Volume 4, Number 2 1996.

1. In the present article, in line with the person-centred view that the terms 'counselling' and 'psychotherapy' refer to the same phenomenon, I employ the double-barrelled term 'counselling/psychotherapy', 'c/p' for short.

1. Naked without a paradigm

Leaving aside the much-discussed issue of whether c/p is an art or a science, certainly the great pioneers in the field of c/p — ranging from Freud to Jung to Rogers to Skinner — have been bent on developing scientific understanding of how it is that 'formal talking-centred treatments' enable individuals to overcome their psychological problems.

Bent these pioneers may have been, but the extent to which members of the field of c/p are currently in possession of scientific understanding regarding their professional activities is highly questionable. For, as spelled out by Thomas Kuhn especially (Kuhn, 1970), scientific understanding only properly exists where members of a field of human endeavour are jointly committed to a unitary scheme of thought—committed, that is, to a 'paradigm' by which they define their science's legitimate subject matter and methodological procedures. Within the field of c/p, far from being intellectually bonded by a paradigm, members display instead entrenched rivalries and deep divergences of theoretical understanding: to such an extent, according to Cecil Patterson, that,

> [a]s a person immerses himself or herself in the study of the dozens of theories and approaches to counselling or psychotherapy, he or she . . . develops the feeling of being in a jungle. Differences, inconsistencies, and contradictions appear at all levels, from philosophy to techniques (1986, p. 532).

Confronted, therefore, by a field which Hans Eysenck colourfully describes as a 'mish-mash of theories, a hugger mugger of procedures, [and] a galimaufry of therapies' (1970, p. 145), various commentators advance the view, either explicitly or implicitly, that scientific understanding of c/p in the Kuhnian sense represents an impossible dream — Freud, Jung, Rogers, Skinner, and many others, were victims, so the claim goes, of a futureless illusion.

Take, for instance, the way in which the authors of 'The Counsellor's Handbook' (1994) handle the task of providing a succinct definition of 'counselling'. Aware of differing approaches to 'defining "counselling"', they plump for what is termed 'an integrative process model' (p. 35). That such a model is more mish-mash, than truly integrative and hence more scientific, is made only too plain, however, when the authors openly confess that one of the key assumptions on which the model is based is the premise 'that people are *too complex* to be explained by any *one theory*' (ibid., my emphasis).

Another commentator who takes a similar line is John McLeod. 'Counselling', avers McLeod in his generally excellent 'An Introduction to Counselling' (1993),

> is in many respects an unusual area of study in that it encompasses a set of strongly competing theoretical disciplines. The field of counselling and psychotherapy represents a *synthesis* [my emphasis] of ideas from science, philosophy, religion and the arts. It is an interdisciplinary area that cannot be incorporated or subsumed into any one of its constituent disciplines. An approach to counselling

which was, for instance, purely scientific or purely religious in nature would soon be seen not to be counselling at all, in its denial of key areas of client and practitioner experience (pp. 7–8).

As with the authors of 'The Counsellor's Handbook', McLeod appears to believe it possible to have a 'synthesis' or 'integration' of ideas in the presence of competing theories — a logically puzzling notion if, like me, you consider it proper to define a theory as a 'synthesis' or 'integration' of ideas. Aside from which, McLeod, on a more fundamental level, looks to be suggesting that what for common-sense are disparate aspects of human mental functioning — scientific, philosophical, religious and artistic thought — can never be understood in terms of a single scientific paradigm, a single scheme of mind. This issue of an integral relationship between the development of a paradigm of c/p and that of a paradigm of all aspects of human mental functioning, is a topic I now address.

2. Family nudity

An interesting connection between John McLeod and the authors of 'The Counsellor's Handbook', a connection which I believe applies to many who are critical of the possibility of the development of a paradigm of c/p, is that they, like him, share a background in academic psychology. With this academic discipline generally defined as 'the science of human behaviour and experience' and with members of the field of c/p concerned with generating scientific understanding of a portion of such behaviour and experience, the field of c/p can fairly be said to be a sub-field of the domain of psychology as a whole — which makes it perfectly comprehensible why the generation of scientific understanding of the phenomenon of c/p should be considered the special preserve of psychologists.

So far so good. The problem arises though when, wearing Kuhnian spectacles, we take a closer look at the nature of the discipline of psychology, per se. What we discover when we subject this overarching discipline to such an inspection is that as a science its Kuhnian credibility too is sorely lacking (cf. Kuhn, p. 160 and Gross, 1992, p. 26); and indeed that the entrenched rivalries and theoretical divergences of its daughter discipline of c/p have their roots in the disparity of ideational perspectives intrinsic to the parent (viz., the physiological, cognitive, behavioural, developmental, humanistic, and psychodynamic psychological perspectives). In spite of such theoretical divisions, the discipline of psychology is nevertheless mainly marketed as a 'science' — its status as such having initially been proclaimed not much more than a hundred years ago. Standard introductory psychology textbooks invariably tag the discipline a 'science', even as they demarcate and individually elaborate the various theoretical approaches which go to make it up.

In general, therefore, psychologists are schooled (a) to gloss over the scientific significance of the diversity of theoretical perspectives within their discipline, scientific knowledge assumed to be being generated even so; (b) to make sense of their subject matter from within the conceptual straitjacket of a particular perspective.

Thanks to such schooling, psychologists are not in the habit of developing cross-connections between their own ideas and those of members of other schools; nor do they find it easy to entertain alternative interpretations of the significance of their work; whilst most extremely, the idea that it is 'in principle possible to create a universally acceptable framework of human behaviour [and experience]' (McLeod, 1993, p. 99), i.e. a scientific paradigm of psychology, tends to be beyond their comprehension, if not literally inconceivable.

It is this malady of 'psychologist tunnel vision' that appears to infect McLeod's discussion of the nature of c/p. When he affirms that 'the field of counselling and psychotherapy is currently involved in an important debate' over issues related to extending the scope of individual theories and of combining those which are different, McLeod rightly, in my view, links this debate to the issue which confronts the discipline of psychology as a whole: that of whether the creation of a paradigm, 'a universally acceptable framework', of human behaviour and experience is 'even in principle possible' (ibid.). However, if we accept such a linkage, it is vital, as far as I am concerned, that we be clear concerning its implications. For if we say, as McLeod does, that the field of c/p can never possess a paradigm on the grounds that it 'represents a synthesis [better "mish-mash"] of ideas from science, philosophy, religion, and the arts' (ibid. p. 7), we need to be mindful that what is true for the daughter discipline of c/p is just as true for the parent domain of psychology — given that the daughter is part and parcel of the parent, that the field of c/p is a sub-field of psychology. In short, therefore, if we support McLeod's position, we assert that both the field of c/p and the overall domain of psychology will for ever remain quasi-religious realms made up of rival and competing schools or 'cults', a state of affairs in which, with no paradigm, there is no accepted yardstick for judging whether one school's ideas, explanations and therapeutic procedures are in any way better than another's.

In contrast to such a viewpoint, it is my belief that both with reference to the field of c/p and to the domain of psychology as a whole, it is possible to develop a paradigm generative of genuine scientific understanding. It is also my belief that such a paradigm can be developed on the basis of the current framework of ideas of the person-centred approach. I move on now to consider how this might be done.

3. The bare essential

In their bestselling *Person-Centred Counselling in Action* (1988), Dave Mearns and Brian Thorne concede that 'in some academic quarters the person-centred approach to counselling currently receives scant attention' (p. 5). They postulate that one of the reasons for this is because the approach 'travels light as far as theoretical concepts are concerned' (ibid.) — a judgement underlined by McLeod who, in contrasting the person-centred and psychodynamic approaches to c/p, makes the point that, 'compared to the massive edifice of psychodynamic theory, the conceptual apparatus of the person-centred approach is an insubstantial scaffolding' (1993, p. 67).

Such charges of lightness and insubstantiality can, I admit, freely be granted with respect to the present framework of person-centred thought; not so much, though, *apropos* the *quality* of the concepts involved, but rather in relation to their *quantity*. Here the point is not *how many* notions currently make up the total theoretical edifice (on such a basis, the person-centred framework is certainly heavily outscored by the psychodynamic); but rather the power and fecundity of the key concepts on which that edifice is based. For, as Susanne Langer emphasizes, we should think of 'the sciences' as 'born under quite special conditions — when their key concepts reach a degree of abstraction and precision which makes them adequate to the demands of exact, powerful and microscopically analytic thinking' (1962, p. 13). 'Newton's concept of gravity', she elucidates, 'was such a concept; so was the concept of evolution which Darwin's *Origin of Species* sprang upon the world (though he was not the sole originator) to transform the whole study of natural history from pure taxonomy into a science of biology' (ibid.). It is 'generative' ideas of this kind which foster a new paradigm, 'the reconception of facts under a new abstractive principle, in a new intellectual projection', and so bring into being 'a young, exciting, it may be blundering, science' (ibid.) — although at first, admittedly, the new conception of facts, the new world-view, is likely to be comprehended in only a dim and diffuse fashion. Nevertheless, as a paradigm's central and generative idea becomes increasingly honed and refined and as those ideas which are its offshoots are further elaborated, so the vision projected becomes ever more sharply focused and clearly determined.

With respect, therefore, to the development of a person-centred paradigm of c/p, even of psychology itself, my basic claim is this: that at the heart of the person-centred theoretical framework lies an idea so defined as to be capable of serving as the nub and generative source of such a paradigm. My further claim is that given that Rogers and other person-centred theorists are not alone in seeking to make sense of the world on such a basis, the quality of the present framework of thought of the person-centred approach, and *ipso facto* the sharpness and scope of the vision it promotes, can be enhanced by fusing and interweaving the person-centred formulation of such a visionary idea with the comparable formulations of others.

4. Clothing the scantily clad

The idea central to the person-centred framework of thought which, in my view, is capable of serving as the generative source of a future paradigm of c/p, and beyond to psychology itself, is the notion of 'growth'. Evident in Rogers' writings throughout his life is 'an almost religious reverence for growth' (Van Belle, 1990, p. 47), a notion whose definition in Rogerian/person-centred terms seats it at the heart of a world-vision variously labelled 'holistic', 'organismic' or 'process'. In an academic career devoted to scientific understanding of c/p, Rogers early posited that:

> Therapy is not a matter of doing something *to* the individual, or of inducing him to do something about himself. It is instead a matter of freeing him for normal growth and development (1942, p. 29).

Seeking to specify the character of such 'growth' more precisely, Rogers initially drew parallels between psychotherapeutic 'growth' and the growth of all living organisms (particularly plants); thereafter between psychotherapeutic 'growth', the growth of living organisms and the evolutionary 'growth' of the universe as a whole (see Rogers 1980, ch. 6). Thus, just as Newton apprehended an analogous relationship (i.e. a common logical pattern) exhibited in the motion of 'heavenly' and earthly bodies, so Rogers discerned a common pattern in the self- 'growth' of the counselling client, the growth of living organisms, and the evolution of the universe. However, whereas Newton formulated a single concept, the concept of gravity, to define the character of the analogous relationship he had detected, Rogers came to deploy two interrelated concepts to define his: the common growth pattern shared by the counselling client and all living organisms he characterized in terms of 'the actualizing tendency'; that shared by counselling client, living organisms and the universe as a whole he conceived to be the expression of 'the formative tendency' — the actualizing tendency being part and parcel of the formative tendency (see Rogers, 1980, pp. 118 & 124). According to Rogers, then, these two hypothetical concepts, specifically the formative tendency, are what 'definitely forms a base for the person-centered approach', and possibly 'could be a base upon which we could begin to build a theory for humanistic psychology' (ibid. p. 133).

In identifying the origin of these concepts, Rogers freely acknowledges that not only is his conception of the actualizing tendency influenced by the views of others (e.g. Andras Angyal, Kurt Goldstein and Abraham Maslow, Albert Szent-Gyoergi), but so too is his conception of the formative tendency (e.g. Albert Szent-Gyoergi & Lancelot Whyte — ibid. pp. 119 & 124). In addition Rogers points up connections between his two basic concepts and the formulations of both Jan Smuts (1926), the philosopher of 'holism', and Alfred North Whitehead, the individual who has provided the most definitive expression of 'organismic' or 'process' philosophy (ibid. pp. 113 & 132; cf. Emmet, 1966 & Scruton, 1994, pp. 371ff.).

Thus, in that person-centred theory and its conceptualization of 'growth' constitute but one of a number of concordant attempts at making sense of reality — all of which share a 'holistic/organismic/process' world-vision — I would propose the following three-pronged strategy as a means to further developing the present framework of person-centred thought and so realizing its paradigmatic potential. Overall this strategy involves comparing and interrelating person-centred ideas with ideas formulated by individuals who although not specifically identified with person-centred thought nevertheless espouse the same underlying philosophical world-view. The strategy thus involves:

(1) defining further and with greater precision and abstractness the logical pattern of the central notion of growth.

(2) examining the ideas in person-centred theory ancillary to the notion of growth and considering their relative merits with respect to comparable ideas of non-person-centred theorists — this with a view to (a) reaffirming the present worth of individual person-centred ideas; (b) enriching other person-centred ideas by linking them to non-person-centred ones; (c) replacing certain person-centred ideas with those developed by a non-person-centred thinker.

(3) applying ideas of non-person-centred thinkers in areas where person-centred thought has not previously ventured.

By means of this three-prong strategy, I believe, real progress can be made towards the development of a person-centred paradigm for the field of c/p, even for the discipline of psychology as a whole. It is a strategy I have already attempted to implement (see Ellingham, 1992), a strategy I aim to pursue further in future articles.

References

Bayne, R., Horton, I., Merry, T., and Noyes, E., (Eds.) (1994) *The Counsellor's Handbook*. London: Chapman & Hall.

Ellingham, I. H. (1992) On the conceptual development of a person-centred paradigm for the field of counselling/psychotherapy. Unpublished manuscript.

Ellingham, I. H. (1995) Quest for a paradigm: person-centred counselling/psychotherapy versus psychodynamic counselling and psychotherapy. *Counselling*, Vol. 6, No. 4, pp. 288–90.

Emmet, D. (1966) *Whitehead's Philosophy of Organism*, 2nd edn. London: Macmillan.

Eysenck, H. J. (1970) A mish-mash of theories. *International Journal of Psychiatry*, Vol. 9, pp. 140–6.

Gross, R. D. (1992) *The Science of Mind and Behaviour*, 2nd edn.. London: Hodder & Stoughton.

Kuhn, T. (1970) *The Structure of Scientific Revolutions*, 2nd edn. Chicago: Chicago University Press.

Langer, S. K. (1962) *Philosophical Sketches*. New York: Mentor.

McLeod, J. (1993) *An Introduction to Counselling*. Buckingham: Open University Press.

Mearns, D. and Thorne, B. (1988) *Person-Centred Counselling in Action*. London: Sage.

Patterson, C. H. (1986) *Theories of Counseling and Psychotherapy*, 4th edn. New York: Harper & Row.

Rogers, C. R. (1942) *Counseling and Psychotherapy*. Boston: Houghton Mifflin.

Rogers, C. R. (1980) *A Way of Being*. Boston: Houghton Mifflin.

Scruton, R. (1994) *Modern Philosophy*. London: Sinclair-Stevenson.

Smuts, J. C. (1926) *Holism and Evolution*. New York: Viking Press (1961).

Thorne, B. (1992) Psychotherapy and counselling: the quest for differences. *Counselling*, Vol. 3, No. 4, pp. 244–8.

Van Belle, H. (1990) Rogers' later move toward mysticism: implications for client-centered therapy, in G. Lietaer, J. Rombauts, and R. Van Balen, (Eds.) *Client-Centered and Experiential Psychotherapy in the Nineties*. Leuven: Leuven University Press, pp. 47–57.

The Logic and Practice of Counselling Skills

John Pratt

The term 'counselling skills' seems to have originated in an ad hoc way to define (and fairly loosely at that) counselling-type activities which served to supplement, strengthen or add further, and perhaps complementary dimensions to the roles of a variety of professional helpers or managers. It seems probable that counselling skills once meant simply, 'the skills of counselling'. Possibly because these skills were seen to be applicable to other professional practices, 'counselling skills' is now strongly associated with non-counsellor users of this kind.

But as long ago as 1981, Margaret Morgan writing in *Counselling* talks of professional training courses having specific teaching on 'how to listen and "tune in" to clients . . . and about the specific skills of counselling in general . . . As a result some professionals will understand and practise counselling skills, others will not.' On the other hand, in one of the earliest British publications in the counselling arena, Gaynor Nurse (1975) saw '"counselling" . . . as an integral part of the care which nurses give to patients and relatives'. In the same book she refers to 'counselling skills' only to identify 'listening' and 'empathic responding'. Moreover, she uncompromisingly describes the nurse as 'counsellor'.

Some years later (1984), in an article entitled *Counselling and Health Visiting*, Pauline Wilks uses the terms 'counselling' and 'counselling role' throughout; but the Editor's footnote inviting further contributions in this area refers to 'the possibilities for employing Counselling skills as part of one's normal working life'. (Note the capital 'C' and lower-case 's'.)

In spite of these early associations with the workplace, counselling skills has, in some writers' views, also retained its more independent status in the sense that counselling skills = the skills used in counselling, as though these skills were somehow separable from counselling itself. For example, in 1989, as the then Deputy Convenor of the BAC's Standards and Ethics Committee, Tim Bond wrote an article for *Counselling* titled: 'Towards defining the role of Counselling Skills'. This seemed partly to reflect membership views of themselves, partly the Standards and Ethics Committee's views and partly his own thinking. It proposed 'three formulations of counselling skills':

1. that counselling skills are like communication skills and as such are value-free.
2. that counselling skills, plus other elements = counselling. (He doesn't say what these other elements are but I assume he means the learning about human

First Published in *Person-Centred Practice*, Volume 6, Number 2, 1998.

nature, attitudes and values which he specifies but excludes under (1).)
3. that counselling skills equal counselling.

He goes on to argue for the rejection of formulation (3). And an acceptance of either of formulations (1) or (2). The latter of which appeared to be more in favour. Logically, then, counselling skills are seen either as different from, less than or equal to counselling. Although there are one or two further important and historic statements in the debate about the meaning of counselling skills, I want to deal with formulation (1) from the Bond article at this point, partly so that it can be excluded from this discussion hereafter and partly because the argument paves the way for what I think is a more valid approach to a definition of counselling skills.

Counselling skills as 'value-free'
In response to the Bond article (Pratt, 1990), I put the case that, within psychology, skills of any description are inextricably related to an aim or a goal, that is to some higher order motive — linked to purpose or intention, attitude and value. Skills can only be identified as such in so far as their use moves their user towards achievement of the intended goal, etc. Therefore the idea of aimless, free-floating or value-free skills is a contradiction in terms, a myth, an impossibility. Skills are always manifestations of purpose; a skill cannot be recognised independently of a particular purpose. What follows from this is that the skills of counselling (e.g. listening or communicating understanding, describing feelings, that might represent an empathic attitude toward the client) are probably counselling skills only if they are employed in the pursuit of counselling aims and reflect counselling attitudes and values. For example, it is probably true to say in general that counselling aims to maximise the client's capacity for self-determination; by the same token, the counsellor does not have goals for the client which are different or separate from what the client himself is seeking.

If, on the other hand, such verbal skills are used as a means of obtaining information from a patient so that a better medical diagnosis can be made, or if they are used by a mediator to resolve a conflict between two parties in dispute, or if they are used to clarify or endorse student contributions in a group teaching session or, yet again, if these verbal skills are used by a residential social worker to calm an angry resident, then in each case they are being employed to further the professional's own agenda, albeit that agenda is still to help the individual client or patient or group member. The important difference here is that the means of helping is *authoritative* (as contrasted with *facilitative* (Heron, 1985)). Because the helper believes she knows what is best for the client, the group or the community etc. and is employing skills which superficially resemble counselling skills within that framework. The verbal skills, say of paraphrasing or reflecting feelings, are being used for a different purpose. In such a context they are not counselling skills, but doctoring or nursing skills, mediating skills, teaching skills or social work skills. Counselling skills, however else one might wish to define them, cannot exist independently of a counselling attitude, counselling values and counselling aims. They are inseparably connected to counselling. Within counselling in general, though, it might be thought acceptable to consider counselling skills as having some kind of independent identity which is what I want to deal with next.

Counselling skills as generic counselling activity

Barbara Pearce (1989) in a chapter on 'Counselling skills in the context of professional and organisational growth', from the *Handbook of Counselling in Britain*, refers to counselling skills as 'basic skills which are common to counselling as a generic helping skill and to professional counselling'. Here the 'counselling skills' are firmly embedded in 'counselling' and 'professional counselling' and notwithstanding the variety of theoretical approaches to counselling, Pearce identifies counselling as one of a number of 'strategies' that can be used to help others and therefore lists the skills which are used in this way. In fact, this counselling skills 'strategy' is similar to the three-stage-model of counselling (and specified skills that implement the model) offered by Egan (1975) and others subsequently; as such it implicitly adopts a theoretical position which, to some degree, runs counter to other approaches to counselling and therefore is not properly 'generic'. Nevertheless, the notion that there are skills common to a variety of approaches to counselling does attract support and an extension of this kind of application is represented in the diagram below (Fig.1) which appeared in the Summary Report of a study made by the Lead Body for Advice, Guidance and Counselling by Julie Janes Associates published in 1992. In this context counselling skills are seen to underpin the work of practitioners in each of the four types of professional helping under consideration: giving advice or guidance, counselling and psychotherapy. Again, I have reservations about so qualifying the more directive of these modes of helping in that they do not seem fundamentally to adopt a counselling attitude in the way that has already been explained above.

The conclusion that has ultimately to be drawn from these examples of 'generic' counselling skills is that they, too, cannot bridge the gap between different theoretical approaches to counselling or between different kinds of 'counselling-like' activities. If skilful practice exists then the skills directly and accurately reflect the values and beliefs of that practitioner. For example, fly-on-the-wall observation of psychodynamic and person-centred counsellors at work might, for a few minutes, persuade one that generic skills were being used; a longer look reveals that they

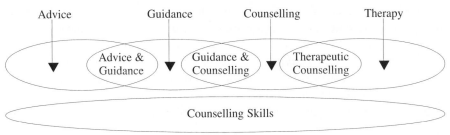

Figure 1

represent different intentions and therefore are not comparable. This difference is illustrated even in the most obvious responses, a client's statement such as: 'You're a man and you wouldn't understand' could well be responded to by 'You feel men don't understand you'. To the psychodynamic counsellor this is a step in the direction of raising awareness of transference and may be followed up at some point. To the person-centred counsellor the same response attempts to communicate an empathic understanding of the client's experience and will not be 'followed up' by her as part of her broader agenda.

The position we have reached so far in the argument, therefore, is that skills as such are inextricably tied to intentions, even to relatively small differences in intention (from an extra-counselling perspective) between theoretical positions in counselling. We have also rejected two definitions of the term 'counselling skills' (viz., as value-free, existing entirely independently and as generic skills underpinning counselling-like activities) as failing to meet psychologically-based criteria for their existence. The next question to be asked is, perhaps 'What are we left with?' We are left with the problem of stating what counselling skills are since, up to this point, we have only said what counselling skills *are not*. We are also left with thousands of people who are described, or who describe themselves, as counselling skills users and whose practice embraces in some degree counselling values and a counselling attitude crystallised into specific intentions. Intentions are the key elements in recognising skills, as I have argued so far and will pursue this assumption to its logical conclusion.

Intentionality and counselling skills

In Section B of the *Code of Ethics and Practice for Counselling Skills,*[1] the BAC discusses the meaning of counselling skills. It says 'What distinguishes the use of "counselling skills". . . are the intentions of the user which is to enhance the performance of their functional role as line manager, nurse, tutor, social worker personnel officer, voluntary worker, etc., the recipient will, in turn, perceive them in that role'. The difficulty with this role-based definition of counselling skills is that it is too general. The statement of intention 'to enhance the performance of their functional role' does not tell us whether 'counselling skills' are being used in pursuit of 'counselling' intentions or some other more authoritative intentions based on the helper's training and experience as an individually titled professional. If the latter is intended then, as has been argued, this has nothing to do with counselling and everything to do with the pursuit of another discipline for which, in my view, the BAC has no responsibility, nor could it possibly have. To make the point in a different way. If the use of counselling skills to 'enhance' is in some way to permeate all the activities that the professional carries out, so that she is, say, more sensitive to or shows understanding of her client in general, this should not be a concern of the counselling world. If, on the other hand, the professional helper's intention is to adopt a counselling attitude towards her client and if she

---

1. This has since been revised. *Ed.*

sees this as an additional and alternative way of working with the client, probably in contrast to her other ways of functioning with that person, then this should be and is jointly the concern both of her own profession and of the counselling movement. This, however, is not what the existing code of ethics and practice seems to imply by the use of the term 'counselling skills'. It goes on (para. 1.2):

> Ask yourself the following questions:
> a) Are you using counselling skills to enhance your communication with someone, but without taking on the role of their counsellor?
> b) Does the recipient perceive you as acting within your professional/ caring role (which is not that of counsellor)?

These are leading questions which predetermine the answers by forcing the counselling skills user to accept the conditions laid down for them. The conditions are unacceptable and the assumptions behind them untenable. I think many who use counselling skills would want to answer the first question by saying: 'No, I am not using counselling skills (merely) to enhance my communication with someone, but yes, I am on particular occasions, which we agree between us, taking on a counselling role with them, but yes again they would probably not perceive me as their counsellor because I do not have or use that title'. They might also go on to say (and I would agree with them): 'I call myself a counselling skills user because it would be inappropriate and misleading to call myself a counsellor even though I may be as well qualified as many counsellors and for some of my time am doing the same work in the same way'.

And in this we have what for me is the heart of the matter. The intentions of the counselling skills user parallel those of the counsellor. I cannot, as the present Code of Ethics and Practice for Counselling Skills can, see counselling skills as having a place on 'a continuum' somewhere between 'listening' and 'counselling', or between 'communication skills' and 'counselling' (Bond, 1989). For this to be valid there must be elements of each activity that are directly comparable and therefore amenable to 'more than' and 'less than' statements. For example it might be argued that, at present, counselling skills users spend less time training or practising than counsellors, or that they do less formal contracting of their counselling work with clients than do counsellors. It is evident that counselling skills is less publicised than counselling and its concerns less published than those of counselling. All of these claims, though, are *peripheral* to the practice of counselling skills and the principles behind it. The core activity of both counselling and counselling skills are directly comparable.

Having taken some pains to reject the ideas that counselling skills are either: (a) a free-standing entity applicable to other enterprises, (b) have some generic role in underpinning various kinds of counselling or counselling-like modes of helping, or (c) are usefully described as appearing on a continuum implying a judgement of their position as 'less than' counselling, in order to affirm more positively what counselling skills are, I now want to abandon the logical or psychological position for a more pragmatic one which acknowledges what counselling skills users actually do as being the core activity of counselling directly comparable to that of a counselling interview carried out by a counsellor. Whether the counselling skills approach is primarily person-centred, behavioural, or is more eclectic, the therapeutic attitude and intention are common to both disciplines. It is not this that differs but the context in which the two types of practice are set. The table in Fig. 2 identifies such similarities and differences.

In order to clarify the nature of counselling skills further I will examine some of the brief descriptions tabled above and in doing so establish the main difference between the counselling skills approach and counselling itself.

Values
That the counsellor, within her contracted working time, puts her client before almost anything else (and there are exceptional circumstances even here) is practically beyond question. The counselling skills user whilst striving towards the same ultimate valuing of her client finds this is threatened and sometimes prejudiced by other professional and organisational influences, particularly by the social fabric of her workplace, as we shall see below. However the counselling skills user at least sets out with the attitude that her client has the personal resources and potential to understand and manage his life and circumstances more satisfactorily and the belief that her own interventions in the 'talking' mode will facilitate this process.

Intention
In the table, both the counselling skills user and the counsellor are described as offering a 'supportive relationship' and opportunities for psychological growth or change. Within such general descriptions, though, there may be developmental processes or experiences (from the client's point of view) ranging from relief from unburdening at one end of the scale to deep-seated personal changes (in whatever theoretical language these may be described) at the other. It is tempting to associate the former with the counselling skills and the latter with counselling or psychotherapy and this may sometimes be the case. Formal counselling, I assume, offers the whole range of opportunities but it would be short-sighted to preclude longer term and more intensive work for the counselling skills user, especially when she is located in a residential setting and has the opportunity to spend regular sessions with an individual client perhaps extending over months or years.

Role conflict
There are two obvious potential conflicts of expectations. One is the client himself, who may not understand the counselling skills user's implicit change of attitude from a directive to a facilitative approach especially where this has been carried out in the midst of his own distress or confusion and there has been no opportunity to put the counselling on some agreed conditions. The second is in the counselling skills user's work colleagues who, unless they clearly understand and value her counselling function, may express their uncertainty, mistrust or even hostility towards it. More important still in this respect is that her employing organisation understands and is fully supportive

	COUNSELLING SKILLS	COUNSELLING
VALUES	The client before all else The client's autonomy The counselling process	The client before all else The client's autonomy The counselling process
INTENTION	A supportive relationship Psychological growth/change	A supportive relationship Psychological growth/change
SKILLS	As implied by theoretical approach	As implied by theoretical approach
ROLE CONFLICT	Potentially yes	Potentially no
CONTRACT	Implicit or explicit may be called 'counselling' or not.	Explicit only Is called 'counselling'.
USE OF TIME	Variable or fixed, but contractable	Fixed, regular
PHYSICAL RESOURCES	May be in question	Assured
THEORY	Person-centred, behavioural, eclectic (mostly)	Wide variety
SUPERVISION	Includes interface of counselling with other nominal role functions and boundaries between these.	Does not include interface of counselling with other nominal role functions & boundaries
TRAINING	Nominally 60–180 hours — may lack self-awareness training, mandatory supervised counselling	Longer, more inclusive

Figure 2

of her counselling function, thus providing appropriate facilities, allowing her flexibility within the role and proper resources, including regular independent supervision.

Contract
Counselling skills users may need to move towards contracting time and other boundaries with clients in order to protect the relationship and its proceedings. However, although such an agreement would happen as soon as is feasible it may not necessarily precede the counselling as would be the case in a formal counselling situation.

Also, some counselling skills users do not use the term 'counselling' to their clients perhaps referring instead to a 'support session', an opportunity to 'talk things through' etc. Others see no stigmatising effect, raising of anxiety or other disadvantage in describing their counselling activity with the client as 'counselling'.

Use of time

Taking on the function of counselling means that the helper has to balance her giving of time for this purpose against other commitments she has. Depending on these and her perception of her client's needs the allocation of time ranges from perhaps ten minutes offered in an ad hoc way, to an hour or longer agreed in advance. Some counselling skills user/client relationships are established much like those in regular counselling, e.g. weekly, of an hour's duration. In particular crises, for example, following a traumatic incident, longer periods are given without prior formal agreement with the client.

Physical resources

The physical setting, the shared residence, the hospital, the client's own home, school or other institution may not provide accommodation which offers privacy, space and comfort suitable for counselling, whereas these might be taken for granted in formal counselling, establishing, as they do, an appropriate ambience for intimate conversation. Nevertheless, the counselling skills user seeks to achieve the safest and most comfortable environment for this work with her client.

Theory

In principle, almost any theoretical stance is possible for the counselling skills user. In practice counselling skills users are likely to have been trained in Gerard Egan's Skilled Helper model of counselling or perhaps in Carl Rogers' person-centred approach to the client or again in some mixture of these with an emphasis on the understanding and performance of basic skills whilst appreciating some of the theoretical assumptions behind them. In my own counselling skills courses there is a strong and ongoing emphasis on person-centred counselling. Course members are expected to understand the principles (including the main theoretical assumptions) and demonstrate the practice of person-centred counselling. It is not appropriate to detail this or further to speculate on the theory of counselling skills here. It is enough to state that theory must be an integral part of counselling skills training programmes.

Supervision

Again, in principle the counselling skills user is just as much in need of regular supervision as the counsellor; in fact, it would be easy to make a case for proportionately greater amounts of supervision to support and develop the counselling skills user's work. In practice there may be less recognition of the need for external supervision, especially if managerial supervision is already provided. In some places supervision is divided between internal provision for 'work' concerns and external supervision for personal support/development. It is difficult to see how the two can be separated, but the recognition of the need for external supervision when resources are limited makes one inclined to accept whatever can be obtained. The case here, though, is for separate supervision of the counselling skills function of the worker's broader role although this supervision will necessarily require the supervisor to be informed and understanding enough to help the counselling skills user to manage her counselling skills function and to deal with the interface between this and other aspects of her work.

Training
All this, in turn raises further questions about training counselling skills users and the function of counselling skills courses. At present they seem to serve two purposes: (1) To provide a first-level qualification in counselling; (2) As a preparation and qualification to use counselling skills as part of a work role in the way I have already described. The second of these requires a broader and more complex programme than the first since it must provide for the management of the counselling process within the work situation as well as of the actual process itself of counselling the client. However, if the counselling is to be of a quality that bears comparison with that of formal counsellors, then counselling skills training will need to include supervised practice and longer opportunities for development of self-awareness. This would put counselling skills courses on a par with counselling courses and simultaneously create the need for a different title for introductory courses in counselling.

To illustrate and support these ideas about the nature and scope of counselling skills I give two examples of counselling skills interventions from different settings and with different content, nonetheless each important in their own way.

> Angela, who is a residential care worker talks to Fred, a resident. Fred is unhappy about the way he always seems to be landed with domestic chores.
> *Angela*: You're looking a bit down in the mouth, Fred, what's going on?
> *Fred*: It's George, he should be laying the table but he's left me to do it again.
> *Angela*: So George has left it for you to do, has he?
> *Fred*: Yeah, and it's not the first time either. I'm fed up with it.
> *Angela*: It's getting you down because it keeps happening.
> *Fred*: He knows if he leaves it long enough someone else will do it; usually me.
> *Angela*: He's taking advantage of you, it feels like he's manipulating you almost.
> *Fred*: That's right; he knows I'm a soft touch . . .

In this exchange, Angela has adopted a counselling attitude using a person-centred approach. The conversation might have continued for a few minutes in this way giving Fred the opportunity to become clear about how he responds to George and the housework. It might even get as far as him seeing himself as playing 'victim' and the consequences of that. The exchange might have come to an end when he had finished laying the table. There was no explicit declaration of the time spent as 'counsellor' or similar, no agreement at the start about any specific content although it may be that this conversation was one of several between these two people discussing Fred's dissatisfaction with the other residents, some of these being during more formal and regular 'talk-time' sessions. (Adapted from Pratt, 1994.)

By contrast, Frank has just arrived in coronary care. He has been to two other hospitals in the region which were unable to alleviate his many problems caused by his failing heart. He is breathless, weary and in low spirits. For the third time in ten days he is confronted by a ward full of strangers and his now sinking hopes for living much longer. This is his last chance — a heart transplant, if in the next two weeks a donor heart should become available. The improbability, indeed the futility of it all suddenly strikes him. He is overwhelmed and, despite himself, begins to cry. A nurse comes over to him and draws the curtain around the bed. His sobbing can be heard up and down the ward. Eventually another person from outside the ward, a Cardiac Support Nurse called Diane comes to him and they converse quietly for forty minutes. After that she arranges with him to meet in her office the next day. So far she has not used the word counselling nor has she said that she has trained as a counsellor (but does not use that title). They meet the next day for an hour and arrange a further appointment. During the second meeting issues of confidentiality of information were discussed and agreed between them. In this instance, Diane is able to act very much like a counsellor in many respects, providing a readily available and supportive service where it is needed. She, herself is supported by regular non-managerial supervision although counselling is only one of her functions which include the re-education and rehabilitation of those in cardiac care.

Both of the above illustrative accounts are based on real experiences. I believe they, and what I have argued for in this article, make the case for treating the counselling skills user with more concern and understanding than we in the counselling business have done up to now.

References

BAC (1989) *Code of Ethics and Practice for Counselling Skills.* Rugby: BAC.

BAC (1998) *Code of Ethics and Practice Guidelines for those using Counselling Skills in their Work.*Rugby: BAC.

Bond, T, (1989) Towards defining the role of counselling skills, *Counselling,* 69.

Egan, G. (1975) *The Skilled Helper: A Problem Management Approach to Helping.* Brooks-Cole.

Heron, J. (1985) *Six-category Intervention Analysis,* University of Surrey.

Janes, J. & Associates (1992) *Summary Report of Lead Body for Advice, Guidance and Counselling,* March.

Morgan, M. R. (1981) Counselling skills and professionals working with people with disabilities and their families, *Counselling,*38.

Nurse, G. (1975) *Counselling and the Nurse,* Aylesbury: Heyden, HM+M Publishers.

Pearce, B. (1989) Counselling skills in the context of professional and organisational growth, in *Handbook of Counselling in Britain.* London: Routledge.

Pratt, J. W. (1990) The meaning of counselling skills, *Counselling,* 1, (1).

Pratt, J. W. (1994) *Counselling Skills for Professional Helpers.* London: Central Book Publishing.

On Being There

Pam Janecka

> *When I am at my best . . . when I am closest to my inner, intuitive self, when I am somehow in touch with the unknown in me . . . then simply my presence is releasing and helpful* (Rogers 1990, p.137).

Rogers' account of 'One more characteristic', from which this is abridged, stirs me greatly. The image here of man's potential runs close to my deepest values. I find it beautiful in its simplicity. I also know that sculpting one's growth to develop this capacity requires committed willingness and courage to draw upon one's full humanness, over a lifetime.

I think what Rogers meant by Presence lies along the same continuum as what I am going to call Being There. My current thinking is that Presence is an *ascendant* of Being There (or more correctly of Being There-ness). By this I mean that for the therapist, Presence is a developmental refinement of the ability to Be There. However, I shall attempt to define what I mean by Being There. Being There is an elusive something I have glimpsed and I want to use this paper to try to pin it down, and to explore how this way of being — which for me has deep personal significance — fits with the Person-Centred Approach.

In the 'Why of Being There' I shall explore why for me Being There is a valid and valued goal in human endeavour, drawing on past personal and professional experiences which have been formative.

The 'How of Being There' looks briefly at what I see as my personal development needs and how I may work towards these.

Being There

I attempt my first definition of Being There thus:

> Being There is being really open to the flow of our experience of
> self and client, such that we can be fully available and committed —
> in the moment — to using all our faculties to feel and understand
> our client's experience and world as if we stood in his shoes.

The first part of this definition is about congruence (C). When I use the term 'open' I mean that *everything* I experience in awareness is available to me, immediately and in unadulterated form. In using the phrase 'open to the flow of our experience of self and client' I mean to convey both the sense of standing still

First Published in *Person-Centred Practice*, Volume 6, Number 2, 1998.

in the moment as living experiences flow through consciousness and also being a participant in the flow of relationship between therapist and client; this is about communication, about sharing (appropriately) our nowness. Rogers' (1980) statement about congruence, which for me explains the choice of word 'congruence', is helpful.

> By this I mean that when my experiencing of this moment is present in my awareness and when what is present in my awareness is present in my communication, then each of these three levels matches or is congruent. *At such moments I am integrated or whole, I am completely in one piece* (p. 15, my emphasis).

And I would add: 'I am completely in the now'.

I would like to call this integratedness and nowness of lived congruence *Being Here*. In my view this sharpened ability to Be Here is the basis for a deepened empathic understanding (EU). For if I cannot fully live in my own now, how can I fully share in my clients now? I like to conceptualise EU as a process which starts with the therapist bringing her 'now' alongside the client's now. I see congruence as a prerequisite — 'such that we can be fully available and committed in the moment' — to developing EU. This view has also been put forward by Tudor and Worrall (1994) and Bozarth (1996).

The last part of my definition of Being There (from 'using all our . . .') relates to EU, more clearly enunciated in Rogers' (1980, p.142) redefinition. However, a significant omission from my definition is the need to *communicate* my sensings of the client's world. This relates to an old blind spot of mine; my reluctance to check my understanding for fear of error led to the belief that I could know without checking! Of course, I can also see that it is not much use Being There if the client doesn't know it!

I am saying, then, that I regard Being Here (mostly about congruence) as a necessary prerequisite for Being There. I now see Being There as mostly about EU, but with congruence maintained; congruence anchors EU in the now.

I remember a discussion in my training group about the impossibility of attending to congruence and EU simultaneously. Thus even a therapist relatively fluent at Being There will need to shift her attention between congruence and EU. I have a visual paradigm for this process. It is as if the therapist's reality (the totality of her experience of the world) and the client's reality dwell on separate focal planes. Thus, in shifting her attention between congruence and EU whilst Being There, the therapist's sight remains in a unidimensional nowness, but a shift in focus moves her attention from therapist's now to client's now. I like this conceptualisation of Being There at a metalevel — it is a dynamic and flowing process. A notion in which one could *arrive* at Being There has a fixity at odds with person-centred theory and life.

The final part of exploring Being There is to look at the link with unconditional positive regard (UPR). Bozarth (1996) presents the view that '. . . empathic understanding is the vessel for maximising the probability of the therapists experiencing of unconditional positive regard towards the client . . .' (p. 49). I would go further, suggesting that Being There embraces UPR in that UPR in some sense falls out of or is a natural consequence of fully Being There. I have struggled to get a clearer handle on this. In the moment-to-moment experience of Being There there is something about the therapist's connectedness self-other-universe that makes it impossible to condemn or judge. It is as if this closeness does not leave enough gap or space across which the therapist could measure/compare/ judge the client against personal beliefs, values etc. The client simply *is* and the therapist *is* alongside. But note that as the therapist shifts her 'focal range' from EU to congruence, there immediately becomes such a gap or space, and the discipline of congruence demands the therapist acknowledge (to herself at least) her genuine response. I cannot at present see how the therapist could avoid, at times, a jarring in her reality as she shifts her attention from EU to congruence, but perhaps this is a mechanism by which the therapist grows and becomes more accepting from her congruent base.

Bozarth (1996), reviewing Rogers' (1959) work puts forward the view that UPR is the primary change agent in client-centred therapy. This view fits my experiential understanding of the process. For as I develop my unconditional positive self-regard (UPSR) I am increasingly able to be aware of, and own, all aspects of my being, so that I can safely be as I am. I think it is the therapist's UPR (particularly) which fosters UPSR in the client, enabling him to move from incongruence towards congruence.

Some of the above ideas are summarised in Fig.1 below.

The why of Being There
A recurring thread in my childhood is that of not being heard, of not having a voice that merited attention. I experienced frustration, rage, disappointment and loneliness, for I took this as a profound non-affirmation of my self. So, out of my unmet needs, I began to learn the value of Being There, and to discern its rudiments. It also made me confront, at an early age, the issue of our existential aloneness and, because I fought for my survival and integrity alone, there grew my belief in human inner resourcefulness, the innate ability to find and follow our own paths. It did not occur to me to choose a path that would develop these earlier learnings until as a young adult I was nourished by the gift of my first therapist Being There for me.

Later I came to nursing, where one of my formative experiences was of *not* Being There. As a junior student nurse I was assigned to care for a mature middle-aged man, whom I shall call George, after his heart attack. Full of zeal in my new role and enthusiasm for my newly acquired knowledge, I explained his illness and the necessary care for recovery. The contrast between his maturity and my naive inexperience was marked but we developed a good relationship. I believe he valued my evident care and freshness (genuineness). But when George's condition worsened and it was clear he would not recover but die, his care was taken over by senior nurses, and, fearful, I passed by his bed, tending others. One day George

THERAPIST'S EXPERIENCE   **RELATIONSHIP**   **CLIENT'S EXPERIENCE**

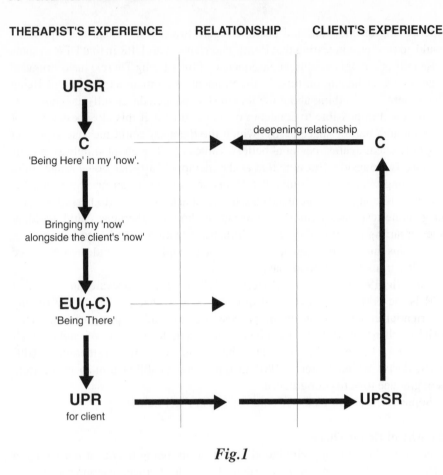

Fig.1

called me over and said 'I miss you, why don't you come and see me any more?' Until this day I have only heard half his message: his plea for my companionship — to which in my fear and uncertainty (I had no answers) I could not and never did respond. But now I see he was making me a gift; he was also saying 'I can handle this, don't be afraid, I just want you to Be There with me on my journey.'

Afterwards I came to understand that Being There was not about providing answers, but having the courage to face with patients what they were obliged to face, and spurred by my debt to George, I began to wade in. My three main discoveries were these:

First, the intrinsic worth of Being There to the client. When I was able to enter into this kind of relationship it seemed patients found such moments restoring, healing, freeing, even sublimely stilling. I remember well a man whom I shall call David, who was dying of motor neurone disease. David bitterly regretted his behaviour in his life and saw no way to atone in the time left and with the immense communication difficulties he faced. David's pain was almost too much to bear witness to, yet I believe that Being There, as best I was able, with him in his agony of despair, lessened his burden and strengthened his courage to work towards his final task of integrating his life.

While the first discovery is of the therapist's gift to the client, the second is of the client's gift to the therapist. I'm struck by my sense of awe, of privilege and of humility at being *allowed* to Be There. For in this allowing, my client permits me to enter the inner sanctum of his vulnerability, the core of his uniqueness. This is an act of profound trust. In that moment we touch perhaps the deepest level of human communication. Then it seems as if my life-stream joins briefly with that underground torrent of all those who have gone there before. I believe this potential — the experience of continuity and shared communion with the past through communication now — to be a mislaid human birthright.

The third concerns transcendence. At times my experience of Being There has coincided with a peak experience. Rowan's (1988) work has been helpful in enabling me to own such experience as 'ordinary'. At best in Being There I feel deeply connected — self-other-universe — such that the feeling of being aligned with the flow of life/creation persists afterwards, giving rise to a profound sense of release, of being effortlessly afloat in an eternal moment. At such times I know that love is the centre nub of the universe, the wellspring of creation.

I certainly prize this experience and so I see here a potential danger of my using clients for my own spiritual gratification. But, this aside, here lies another dimension of my valuing of Being There. I have a deep-seated belief in the self-actualizing tendency of all life *as the primal drive in creation*, and therefore, any benign activity compatible with spiritual development (seen as part of the self-actualization continuum) is intrinsically good. If I were able to work in a way that uses all of myself in enabling others to move towards self-actualization and in a manner that also enhances my own growth and spirituality, then this seems to me the highest good.

The how of Being There

I have proposed that in order to Be There I must first be able to Be Here. Being Here is the ground on which Being There stands. At this point in my life and development I see that most of what I must learn concerns Being Here. And, although practising skills plays an essential part, this is quintessentially about inner growth. The path is shown by the flow of the diagram (above), starting with UPSR. Some ideas for each part of the journey follow:

• *Developing UPSR*

As a starting point I need to identify and dissolve my own conditions of worth. This requires the courage to shake myself free from restraining roots. It also requires a preparedness to *own* my experience fully in the moment. Then there is no gulf across which to measure or judge, I just *am*. This may be scary, it can be magnificent. This process appears to me to be one of self-validation, and needs to be guided by listening to myself, to the voice of the still centre. Here meditation and personal therapy will prove invaluable.

• *Developing congruence / living in the now (Being Here)*

The quiet confidence and stillness arising from UPSR forms a necessary backdrop for Being Here. I need to clear away facades and habitual responses, confronting the transient emptiness, as I discard a repertoire of behaviour I had identified as self. In the practice of responding actively and freshly, I would hope to rediscover self, not now as a fixed concept but as a centre of awareness that flows with the flux of life's experience. There is a spiritual dimension here which I need to explore and develop; personal therapy, meditation and selective reading will help.

To develop immediacy (living in the now) a useful exercise is to observe the bubbling into consciousness of thoughts, feelings and experience, and to touch each briefly for what it is without judgement, analysis or preference. This is in essence to practice the rules of 'epoche', 'description' and 'equalisation' of the Phenomenological Method (Spinelli, 1989).

Parenting provides a unique opportunity for vicarious learning through the empathic following of a child's natural immediacy and congruence.

Finally, since congruence includes *communication* of awareness, with due regard to the *appropriateness* of the communication, I need to develop my skills in both these areas.

• *Developing EU*

I think the therapist's capacity for EU is deepened by her fluency at Being There. While practice and skills development through further training form the mainstay for progress, broadening my life experience through contacts, literature and art, will also help. Looking at my current life, I see that adequate, consistent self-care must be a priority if I am to be fully available to clients. It is also needed to help avoid seeking unmet needs through clients.

Earlier I described my experience of transcendence at times when I am best able to be there for my client. For me, at present, spiritual matters are entwined with aspects of therapy, and I have but a rudimentary understanding of the connection. I need a separate avenue for spiritual development to clarify the issues here and to avoid the pitfall of my using my work with clients as a means of accessing spiritual experience. I find this link between therapy and spirituality deeply fascinating. I think it is possible that there are 'ways of being', embedded in states of altered consciousness, that the therapist could deploy to facilitate therapy. This may be closer to what Rogers describes as 'presence'.

Conclusion

In this paper I have defined and explored what I mean by Being There and how this links with person-centred theory and practice. In so doing I have clarified and deepened my understanding of some aspects of the Person-Centred Approach, and developed a model in diagrammatic form of how person-centred therapy works, as I currently see it. I have also done some work on integrating person-centred philosophy with my own philosophy of life, and created a cohesive whole that both inspires and pleases me. Finally, I looked at where I might go from here in order to grow more able to Be There.

References

Bozarth, J.D.(1996) A Theoretical reconceptualisation of the necessary and sufficient conditions for therapeutic personality change. *The Person Centered Journal*, 3, (1), pp. 44–51.

Kirschenbaum, H. and Henderson. V. L. (1990) (Eds.) *The Carl Rogers Reader*. London: Constable.

Mearns, D. and Thorne, B. (1988) *Person-Centred Counselling in Action*. London: Sage.

Rogers, C. (1951) *Client-Centered Therapy*. London: Constable.

Rogers, C. (1959) *A Theory of Therapy, Personality and Interpersonal Relationships, as developed in the Client-Centered Framework*. In Kirschenbaum and Henderson (1990), pp. 236–257.

Rogers, C. (1961) *On Becoming a Person*. London: Constable.

Rogers, C. (1980) *A Way of Being*. Boston: Houghton Mifflin Co.

Rogers, C. (1990) A client-centered/person-centered approach to therapy. In Kirschenbaum and Henderson (1990), pp. 135–152.

Rowan, J. (1988) *Ordinary Ecstasy*. London: Routledge.

Spinelli, E. (1989) *The Interpreted World*. London: Sage.

Tudor, K. and Worrall, M. (1994) Congruence reconsidered. In *British Journal of Guidance and Counselling*, 22, (2).

Congruence: A Confusion of Language

Sheila Haugh

Understanding of the concept of congruence within person-centred theory and practice is at best blurred and at worst misinterpreted. This is due, in large part, to confusion concerning the meaning of the words 'genuine', 'authentic' and 'transparent' — all words that have been used in attempts to describe the condition of congruence. It is a confusion of language that has a direct and powerful impact on therapeutic practice.

This paper considers the theoretical formulation of congruence and its place within person-centred theory, and briefly examines the hypothesis that congruence is a necessary condition of the therapeutic relationship of other orientations including Jungian Analysis, Transactional Analysis and Gestalt therapy. There is an attempt to clarify the concept of congruence with reference to the theory and practice of person-centred counselling. How congruence is communicated is explored and it is suggested that genuineness, authenticity and transparency are outcomes, rather than definitions, of congruence within person-centred theory.

In 1980 Rogers wrote, concerning congruence in the therapist:

> As for the therapist, what he or she is experiencing is available to awareness, can be lived in the relationship, and can be communicated, if appropriate. Thus, there is a close matching, or congruence, between what is being experienced at the gut level, what is present in awareness, and what is expressed to the client (Rogers, 1980, pp. 115–6).

Congruence means that therapists' internal processes can be accessed at any given moment. Additionally, it means their experience is not denied to awareness or distorted in awareness and can be communicated to another person if appropriate. In earlier writings Rogers had clarified this point. Not only does congruence mean a 'close matching' of experience with what is present in awareness, but this experience would also be one where a person is 'freely, deeply, and acceptantly himself (sic), with his actual experience of his feelings and reactions as they occur and as they change' (Rogers, 1961, p. 283). The therapist's symbolisation in awareness should be accurate.

Congruence is an integral component of person-centred theory and practice in terms of outcomes and process. It is explicit in the theory that successful therapy leads to increasing congruence in the client even if it is not an aim of the therapy.

First Published in *Person-Centred Practice,* Volume 6, Number 1, 1998.

In Rogers' seven stages of process, the seventh stage includes the state where internal communication is clear, with 'feelings and symbols well matched' (Rogers, 1961, p.154). Further, when functioning more fully, a person 'is able to experience all of his (sic) feelings, and is less afraid of any of his feelings' (ibid. p. 191). Developing congruence, matching experience with awareness, is seen as development towards fully functioning.

In therapy, congruence is one of the six well-known necessary and sufficient conditions (Rogers, 1957) which, when present, release the directional flow of the actualising tendency. This flow is the 'constructive directional flow of the human being toward a more complex and complete development' (Rogers, 1986, p.199). In a relationship characterised by these six conditions a person's inherent actualising tendency, hitherto subsumed by conditions of worth and an external locus of evaluation, will move in a positive and life-enhancing direction.

The function of congruence within the core conditions (of empathy, congruence and unconditional positive regard) is elucidated by Watson and Bozarth. Watson (1984) writes that 'congruence on the part of the therapist is a pre-condition for the therapist's experience of unconditional positive regard and empathy toward the client' (p. 19). Bozarth emphasises this point stating,

> I (Bozarth, 1992) have suggested that Rogers' (1959) major theoretical statement poses the conditions of congruency, empathic understanding and unconditional positive regard as theoretically highly interrelated but that the importance of therapist congruency or genuineness is primarily that of enabling the therapist to better experience the other two conditions [empathy and unconditional positive regard] towards the client (Bozarth, 1995, p.13).

Therefore, whilst congruence may mean that the therapist is experienced as real and genuine, the function of congruence lies in facilitating the therapist's ability to be empathic with, and hold unconditional positive regard towards, the client.

The six conditions were hypothesised by Rogers as being necessary and sufficient for constructive personality change, ' . . . no other conditions are necessary. If these six conditions exist, and continue over a period of time, this is sufficient' (Rogers, 1957, p. 221). If congruence is taken to mean, in its simplest of definitions, that experience is available to awareness then it would appear that many other orientations of counselling see such a concept as at least necessary in the therapeutic relationship.

In Jungian Analysis the intended outcome of therapy is that 'the internal world . . . become available for the use and . . . enrichment' (Carvalho, 1990, p. 76). Carvalho writes that, 'It is to be assumed that the therapists themselves have undergone a thorough-going analysis and have made use of it' (ibid. p. 77). It can be understood, therefore, that it is expected that a Jungian analyst should have experience — their inner world — available to awareness. Likewise in Transactional Analysis, 'It follows that you need to enter counselling or psychotherapy yourself whenever you become aware of unresolved personal problems' (Stewart, 1989, p. 8). Whilst this is not so strong a call for experience to be available to awareness, it is only if they become aware of an 'unresolved personal issue' that therapists need enter counselling, implicit is the idea that the therapist does need to be aware of their internal processes and to act upon that awareness.

Gestalt therapy 'demands considerable awareness, self-knowledge and responsibility from the counsellor' (Clarkson and Pokorny, 1994, p. 21). This is a process where the therapist becomes 'more continuously aware of own actual experiencing of sensing, feeling and thinking on a moment-by-moment basis' (Parlett and Page 1990, p. 184). Again, experience being available to awareness is deemed as a necessary attribute of the therapist. Indeed 'Gestalt therapy is not an approach which can be applied . . . by people who are themselves not capable of being aware of their own processes' (ibid. p. 187).

Gestalt therapy also has the requirement of therapists that they 'need to be open to sharing some of their own feelings and reactions' (ibid. pp.185–186). This is also true of person-centred counsellors. As noted above (Rogers, 1980), experience can be communicated if it is appropriate. This begs the question of when such a communication may be appropriate. Bozarth offers what may be considered a guideline:

> It is a functional premise [client-centred/person-centred therapy] that includes wide differences, unique ways of doing things, and 'idiosyncratic' ways of responding . . . *as far as they are dedicated to the client's direction, the client's pace and the client's unique way of being* (my emphasis, 1984, p. 63).

Any experience may be communicated to the client within these parameters. I would also add that each relationship with a client is unique, increasing the range of differences, and therefore the range of responses, made by any one therapist.

To be concerned with when it is appropriate to communicate experience is something of a red herring. For to know *when* to communicate, it is necessary to have a clarity concerning *what* is to be communicated. It is at this point I believe a confusion of language has played a significant role in the mis-undertanding of the concept of congruence. The passage cited above (Rogers, 1980) is preceded by a definition of congruence, 'Genuineness, realness, or congruence . . . this means that the therapist is openly being the feelings and attitudes that are flowing within at the moment . . . The term transparent catches the flavour of this condition'. Here Rogers links together the words 'genuineness', 'realness and 'transparency' with the concept of congruency. Another word often used in this context is 'authentic' (Merry, 1995) and, as a result, there is confusion concerning *what* is being communicated. Lietaer (1993) attempts a clarification of this point:

> Genuineness has two sides: an inner and an outer one. The inner side refers to the degree to which the therapist has conscious access to, or is receptive to, all aspects of his flow of experiencing. This side of the process will be called 'congruence'; the consistency to which it refers is the unity of total experience and awareness. The outer side, on the other hand, refers to the explicit communication by the

therapist of his conscious perceptions, attitudes and feelings. This aspect
is called 'transparency': becoming transparent to the client through
communication of personal impressions and experiences (p. 18).

At first reading, this passage appears helpful. It offers the definition of congruence as
an 'inner' experience and also offers an explanation of differences between
'transparency' and the concept of congruence. However, closer investigation suggests
two difficulties. Firstly, 'genuineness' has replaced congruence as the functional
condition — congruence had become a part explanation of genuineness. Secondly, it
would seem possible to be outwardly transparent, communicating, for example,
conscious access to 'all aspects (of his flow) of experiencing'. In this formulation,
transparency can exist without congruence. Theoretically, therefore, to be transparent
would not necessarily meet the condition of being congruent in the relationship. Lietaer
does caution, 'the distinction we made between congruence and transparency should
not be understood in absolute terms' (p. 31). Nevertheless, I believe the juxtaposition
is misleading and has consequences for practice which I consider below.

The exploration of the use of the word 'transparency' leads to consideration of
the other words that are used in the context of congruence; namely 'real', 'genuine'
and 'authentic'. The meanings for these words, as defined by the Collins Concise
Dictionary (1983) include, respectively, 'not artificial or simulated, genuine'; 'not
fake or counterfeit, original: real: authentic'; 'genuine, trustworthy, reliable'. These
words, for the most part, imply a way of *being* rather than a way of *doing*. What
can a person 'do' to be not artificial or not simulated? I suggest they can only 'be'
not artificial or simulated. Perhaps it is possible to 'do' things to show
trustworthiness and reliability, for example, in the therapy setting being on time
for sessions (as the therapist); not forgetting sessions, etc. In the main, however,
the words imply attributes of a person rather than acquired mannerisms. It is easier
to see this point if one considers how therapists may be if they were *not* these
descriptions. They would be artificial, simulated, not genuine, fake, counterfeit,
not original, not real, not authentic.

A consequence for the practice of person-centred counselling is that the therapist
may be encouraged to engage in behaviours and responses that are informed by
their (the therapist's) intention to be experienced by the client as transparent, as
genuine, as authentic. The condition of congruence is more truly met with an
intention to match awareness to experiencing. I believe this lack of clarity to be,
in part, a consequence of the confusion of language in descriptions of congruence.

There is something of a paradox in the definition and expression of congruence.
At an optimal level *all* experience should be available to awareness. Fortunately,
as Rogers clarifies:

> It is not necessary (nor is it possible) that the therapist be a paragon
> who exhibits this degree of integration, of wholeness, in every aspect
> of his life. It is sufficient that he is accurately himself in this hour of
> this relationship, that . . . he is what he actually is, in this moment of
> time (Rogers, 1957).

The paradox lies in the fact that therapists may not have all experience available to awareness *and* if there is some quality or state of correspondence and agreement between experience and awareness they will, in all probability, be experienced as genuine. At this juncture it is possible to enter the very confusion of language I believe has clouded the condition of congruence. I hope to avoid that confusion by stating that genuineness, authenticity, realness and transparency are *outcomes* of congruence rather than *definitions* of congruence. The more fully experience is available to awareness the more fully the therapist will be experienced as genuine, authentic, real and transparent.

An implication of this misunderstanding in the practice of person-centred counselling is a danger that the focus of therapeutic responses become one of communicating the outcomes of congruence rather than congruence itself. Owing to this confusion of definitions, therapists try to communicate their authenticity, genuineness and realness rather than their experience. This can lead to therapist behaviours such as analysing the client's process, directing the client's journey or inappropriate self-disclosure. These are activities not generally associated with person-centred counselling. It is noteworthy that the three core conditions of empathy, congruence and unconditional positive regard are statements of the experience of the therapist in relation to the client. Theoretically, the client does not need to perceive therapist congruence, only empathic understanding and unconditional positive regard. It is also important to remember that person-centred counselling is a unitary approach based on the actualising tendency. Therapist responses include empathy and unconditional positive regard following the client's direction.

Although the therapist does not need to communicate congruence, I suggest that it is in fact communicated to the client and that the client perceives such communication. Verbalisation is only one way in which we tell of ourselves. There are many ways in which we communicate to the world. A most commonly known way is in our body language; how we hold ourselves, our body movements, and eye contact etc. These actions tell us many facts about ourselves even if we are not consciously aware of them doing so. Gestalt therapy sees 'the importance of the body . . . [as] paramount' (O'Leary, 1992, p.53), seeing the non-verbal behaviour of clients as something to be focused upon and worked with. Smith writes of 'Hidden Conversations' (1991) between analyst and patient, explicit narrations telling of unconscious feelings and thoughts. It is not my intent to suggest that these two formulations, when explored in depth, are in agreement with each other, nor even have the same philosophical bases. They simply serve as examples that communication between human beings is often experienced as diffuse and non-verbal.

In consequence, congruence, the state of experience being available to awareness, will be communicated to the client whether or not therapists chooses to make some aspect of their experience verbally explicit. They will be experienced as authentic if indeed they are being authentic — regardless of their explicit responses. Conversely therapists will be perceived as inauthentic if their experience is not available to awareness, or their communication does not match their awareness.

Rogers wrote that 'this concept of congruence is actually a complex one' (Rogers, 1961, p. 282). Some of the complications arise from the nature of the concept. Congruence could be described as the inner journey whereas empathy and unconditional positive regard are an outward journey toward 'another'. The inner journey to the self can be very painful — it is not surprising if it is sometimes avoided. Congruence calls upon person-centred practitioners to explore their own worlds to bring more experience to awareness. It is a state of being rather than doing. In the being they will be experienced as the outcomes of congruence — authentic, genuine, transparent and real.

References

Bozarth, J.D. (1984) Beyond Reflection: Emergent Modes of Empathy. In R.F. Levant and J.M.Shlien (Eds) *Client Centered Therapy and The Person-Centered Approach.* New York: Praeger.

Bozarth,J.D. (1992) Coterminous intermingling of doing and being in person-centred therapy. *The Person-Centred Journal,* 1, (1), pp. 33–9.

Bozarth, J.D. (1995) Person-centred therapy: A misunderstood paradigmatic difference? *The Person-Centred Journal,* 2, (2), pp. 12–7.

Brazier, D. (Ed) (1993) *Beyond Carl Rogers.* London: Constable & Company.

Carvalho, R. (1990) Psychodynamic Therapy: The Jungian Approach. In W. Dryden (ed) *Individual Therapy in Britain.* Milton Keynes: Open University Press.

Clarkson, P. and Pokorny, M. (Eds) (1994)*The Handbook of Individual Therapy.* London: Routledge.

Collins (1983) *The New Collins Concise English Dictionary.* London: William Collins Sons & Co. Ltd.

Kirschenbaum & Henderson (Eds.) (1989) *The Carl Rogers Reader.* London: Constable.

Leitaer, G. (1993) Authenticity, Congruence and Transparency. In D.Brazier (Ed) *Beyond Carl Rogers.* London: Constable.

Levant, R.F. & Shlien, J.M. (Eds.) (1984) *Client-Centered Therapy and the Person-Centred Approach.* New York: Praeger Publishers.

Merry, T. (1995) *Invitation to Person Centred Psychology.* London: Whurr.

O'Leary, E. (1992) *Gestalt Therapy.* London: Chapman & Hall.

Parlett, M. and Page, F. (1990) Gestalt Therapy. In Dryden, W. (Ed.) *Individual Therapy in Britain.* Milton Keynes: Open University Press.

Rogers, C. R. (1957) The necessary and sufficient conditions of therapeutic personality change. *Journal of Consulting Psychology,* 21, pp. 95–103.

Rogers, C.R. (1961) *On Becoming a Person.* London: Constable & Company.

Rogers, C.R. (1980) *A Way of Being.*Boston: Houghton Mifflin Company.

Rogers, C.R. (1986) Client Centered Therapy. In I.L.Kutash and A. Wolf, *Psychotherapist's Casebook.* London: Jason Aronson Inc.

Smith, D.L. (1991) *Hidden Conversations.* London: Routledge.

Stewart, I. (1989) *Transactional Analysis Counselling in Action.* London: Sage.

Watson, N. (1984) The Empirical Status of Rogers' Hypothesis of the Necessary and Sufficient Conditions for Effective Psychotherapy. In R.F.Levant and J.M.Shlien (Eds.) *Client Centered Therapy and the Person Centered Approach. New York: Praeger.*

Pre-Therapy and the Pre-Expressive Self

Garry Prouty

Introduction

The *necessary* condition of a therapeutic relationship is that the therapist and the client be in psychological contact (Rogers, 1957). However, Rogers fails to provide a conceptual or practice definition of 'Psychological Contact'. Furthermore, it is a gratuitous assumption that all clients possess this attribute. Evolving from these issues, Pre-Therapy is a theory of Psychological Contact. It provides a practice description [Contact Reflection], a description of client internal function [Contact Functions] and a description of measurable behaviors [Contact Behaviors]. Its primary application is to 'contact impaired', regressed, low functioning and chronic clients, such as the developmentally disabled, schizophrenic, dissociated or Alzheimer's populations.

Contact Reflections

Contact Reflections are extraordinary literal and concrete reflections to reach the severely withdrawn or regressed client described as contact impaired. Examples of applications with psychotic and retarded persons are to be found in: (Prouty, 1976, 1990); (Prouty & Kubiak, 1988a, 1988b); (Prouty & Pietrzak, 1988); (Prouty and Cronwall, 1990); (Van Werde, 1989,1990).

Situational Reflections (SR) are reflections of the client's situation, environment or milieu. They are a 'pointing toward the world'. Their theoretical function is to facilitate reality contact. An example would be 'Johnny is riding the bike' or 'Mary opened the door'.

Facial Reflections (FR) are reflections of pre-expressive feeling embodied in the face. An example is: 'You look sad' or more literally, 'You are smiling'. Their theoretical function is to facilitate affective contact.

Word-for-Word Reflections (WWR) are reflections of single words, sentence fragments and other verbal disorganization so characteristic of brain-damaged and psychotic persons. Their intent is to develop communicative contact. The client may say 'tree' (mumble), 'horse' (mumble), 'car' (mumble). The therapist reflects the clear language even if meaning is not clear. Occasionally, the therapist may also reiterate sounds.

Body Reflections (BR) are reflections of pre-expressive 'bodying', such as,

First Published in *Person-Centred Practice*, Volume 6, Number 2, 1998.

catatonic statuesque behavior or other bizarre body expressions. Their purpose is to integrate body expression within the sense of self. The reflections are mostly verbal, but can be done with the therapist's own body.

Reiterative Reflections (RR) embody the principle of Re-Contact. If any of the contact reflections are successful, then apply them again. The purpose is to expand the 'island' of meaningful experiential contact.

These reflections, when combined, provide a 'web' of psychological contact for the regressed, isolated and contact-impaired client. Contact Reflections facilitate the Contact Functions (client process) which result in the emergence of Contact Behaviors (measurement).

Contact Functions

The Contact Functions refer to the client process in psychological contact. They represent an expansion of Perls' concept of 'contact as an ego function'. They are awareness functions and are described as reality, affective and communicative contact. The development or restoration of the contact functions are the *necessary* conditions of psychotherapy. Their functioning are the theoretical goals of Pre-Therapy. Reality Contact (world) is the awareness of people, places, events and things. Affective Contact is described as the awareness of moods, feelings and emotions. Communicative Contact is defined as the symbolization of reality (world) and affect (self) to others.

The vignette

Dorothy is an old woman who is one of the more regressed women on X ward. She was mumbling something (as she usually did). This time I could hear certain words in her confusion. I reflected only the words I could clearly understand. After about ten minutes, I could hear a complete sentence.

C   *Come with me.*

T WWR   *Come with me.*

   (The patient led me to the corner of the day-room. We stood there silently for what seemed to be a very long time. Since I couldn't communicate with her, I watched her body movements and closely reflected these.)

C (The patient put her hand on the wall.)

         Cold.

T WW-BR (I put my hand on the wall and repeated the word.)

         Cold.

   (She had been holding my hand all along; but when I reflected her, she would tighten her grip. Dorothy would begin to mumble word fragments. I was careful to reflect only the words I could understand. What she was saying began to make sense.)

C   *I don't know what this is anymore.*

   (Touching the wall [Reality Contact].)

         The walls and chairs don't mean anything anymore.

   (Existential autism).

T WW-BR (Touching the wall.)
> *You don't know what this is anymore. The chairs and walls don't mean anything to you anymore.*

C (The patient began to cry [Affective Contact].)

C (After a while she began to talk again. This time she spoke clearly [Communicative Contact].)
> *I don't like it here. I'm so tired. . . so tired.*

T WWR (As I gently touched her arm, this time it was I who tightened my grip on her hand. I reflected)
> *You're tired, so tired.*

C (The patient smiled and told me to sit in a chair directly in front of her and began to braid my hair.)

This vignette begins to express Pre-Therapy as a therapeutic theory and philosophy. It illustrates the use of Contact Reflections to facilitate the Contact Functions (Reality, Affect, Communication).

Contact Behaviors
Contact Behaviors are the emergent behavioral changes that are the operationalized aspect of psychological contact. Reality Contact (world) is operationalized as the client's verbalization of people, places, things and events. Affective Contact (self) is operationalized as the bodily or facial expression of affect. Communicative Contact (Other) is operationalized as the client's verbalization of social words or sentences. Pilot studies have provided evidence for reliability (DeVre, 1992) and construct validity (Prouty, 1994). Positive effects for therapy have been measured by Hinterkopf, Prouty and Brunswick (1979) and Danacci (1997). Full scientific and theoretical descriptions can be found in Peters (1986), Leijssen and Roelens (1988), Prouty (1994, op. cit.), and Prouty, Van Werde and Portner (1998).

The pre-expressive self
The pre-expressive self is an intuitive and heuristic concept derived from the author's personal experience, as well as clinical and quantitative case studies of Pre-Therapy.

The pre-expressive self. As a young boy, I lived with my mother, stepfather and mentally retarded/psychotic brother. I have long recognized the influence of my brother on the personal formation of Pre-Therapy. One day, when I was eleven or twelve years old, I invited a friend to visit my home. We were talking when I said 'I wonder if he [brother] understands what we are saying?' To my intense surprise, he responded, 'You know I do, Garry' and then lapsed back into a regressed and autistic state. For years the experience 'haunted' me, giving me a feeling there was 'somebody in there'. It was not until *after* the publication of my first book that the importance of that experience became clear. In the foreword of that text, Luc Roelens, a Belgian psychiatrist, arguing against the medical understanding of psychotic states, relates similar case descriptions. I read them and realized the similarity. He describes several cases of clients suddenly expressing contact. One case concerns a woman patient with a chronic and severe catatonic state. When informed that her husband had fallen from the roof and broken both legs, she immediately responded with her intention to go home and take care of everything. There was no relapse. At four and ten year follow-ups she displayed only mild autism. Another reported case concerned a mute male schizophrenic who had been in a dementia-like state. He was being fed by a nurse when he choked and spat all over her. He immediately responded by saying, 'Excuse me, I did not mean to do that', and then relapsed back into his previous state. My brother, and these cases express the presence of a 'Pre-Expressive Self' that underlies the autism, regression, psychosis, brain-damage, retardation, senility, etc. There is somebody 'in there'.

Pre-Expressive Signs. Signs of a pre-expressive self are derived from the verbal process of psychotic expression. Using word-for-word reflections of psychotic content results in movement toward reality. For example, a young, male catatonic expresses himself by saying 'Priests are devils.' By carefully and precisely reflecting this, it eventually processes to the reality of a homosexual overture from a local priest. This highly condensed metaphor 'contained' latent reality content. The movement from a highly condensed psychotic metaphor to the manifestation of latent reality content is called 'Pre-Expressive Process'. The psychotic metaphor is 'Pre-Expressive'. It contains reality in a pre-expressive form.

The semiotic structure of such initial psychotic expression can be characterized in the following way. These pre-expressive forms have *no context* to derive meaning from and they have *no referent* to complete their symbolic function. This means the expressions lack reality sense and appear to be void of a reality source. Without understanding that the latent reality is 'packaged' in a pre-expressive way, the therapeutic potential of psychotic expression is not envisioned.

Further signs of the Pre-Expressive Self are derived from individual case histories and quantitative studies. All of these have the feature of movement from fragmented, incomplete, bizarre, incoherent expression to fuller cogency and congruence-movement from a pre-expressive to an expressive state.

The Pre-Expressive Self refers to a *potentiating* structure of experience and expression. It is characterized primarily by an *organismic, pre-symbolic* thrust toward reality, possibly a manifestation of the self-formative tendency (Rogers, 1978). It is the polar opposite of the Freudian concept of regression. The organismic pre-symbolic thrust toward reality is distinctly opposite to the regressive concept of movement away from reality. The energy is directed forward instead of being a downward fixation as described by Freud. The concept of regression is a *developmental* concept; whereas, pre-expressive is a *therapeutic* concept. These concepts have a different functional context. They also lead to radically different understandings of psychotic process for the psychotherapist. The picture resulting from a pre-expressive understanding senses a 'buried' self, expressing meaning and reality in a *different symbolic structure* capable of being therapeutically processed by more 'primitive' reflections (Pre-Therapy).

Multiple personality

Roy (1991, 1997) describes the use of Pre-Therapy as an adjunctive method in the treatment of multiple personality disorder. Within the context of a Person-Centered/Experiential therapy, she describes the application of Contact Reflections to develop and assist the integration of a dissociated self and repressed memories. According to Roy, such personality fragments often lack in an experiential felt-sense and may be expressed in halting, primitive symbolizations (pre-expressive). As an example, a client would express singular words such as 'face', 'dark', 'window', 'cellar', 'door', 'hurt', 'bleeding', etc., which Roy would reflect contactfully through word-for-word reflections. Roy goes on to describe an important facial reflection: 'You look angry'. According to the client, this helped make contact with important angry feelings. They were embodied pre-expressively in her face. Roy further states: 'Dissociated material, whether it is as distinctive as a separate personality, or much less so, must be experienced and *allowed to live in the world.*' She also points out that a non-directive, non-interpretive approach reduces the possibility of suggestion, one of the major problems in the treatment of repressed, dissociated memories. Coffeng (1995, 1997) describes the application of contact reflections with multiple personality clients, as well as those with severe trauma and sexual abuse.

A non-verbal client

McWilliams (1998) reports the application of contact reflections with a non-verbal, profoundly retarded woman. The contact work was supplied by her stepmother. The stepmother used body reflections involving finger, head and arm movements, as well as non-verbal sounds. She would also literally reflect facial expressions such as happiness. All of these were combined with the principle of reiteration. This contact work was woven into daily living in contrast to a 'session'. Positive results for the 'client' included a sharp increase in contact with the world, self and other. Her increased contact with the world was evidenced through her attention to environmental situations, such as looking out the car window. Her contact with the other was expressed through her being less isolated, being more 'present' with her family, resulting in increased mutuality. Her improved contact with self was evidenced in a shift from a non-responsive mode of seeing herself in the mirror, to a smiling, satisfied mode of looking. The net result of the contact work was a decrease in psychological isolation and an increase in psychological presence-enhancing for 'client' and family.

Hallucinatory voices

Prouty (1977, 1983, 1986, 1991), (Prouty and Pietrzak, 1988, op. cit.) describe the theory and practice of Pre-Symbolic Experiencing as it applies to the integration and processing of visual hallucinations. Often, during lectures on visual hallucinations, people would ask about the application of contact reflections to audio hallucinations. Until Jill Prouty presented this case material, there had been no evidence for this possibility.

The vignette

C	*The voices.*
	(Client puts hands on head.)
T BR	*Your hands are on your head.*
C	(Moves hands to cover face.)
T FR	*Your hands cover your eyes.*
T BR	*You're breathing deeply.*
C	(The client removes her hands from her eyes and looks at the floor.)
T SR	*You're looking at the floor.*
T SR	*There is a green carpet in this room.*
C	(No response.)
T SR	*We're standing here together.*
T BR	*You're breathing easier now.*
C	(The client looks directly at the therapist.)
T SR	*You looked directly at me.*
C	(The client puts her hands on the side of her head and over her ears.)
	I hear voices.
T WWR	*You hear voices.*
C	*The voice says 'You die, you should kill yourself'.*
T WWR	*The voice says 'You die, you should kill yourself'.*
T RR	*You said earlier you heard voices.*
C	(Looking directly at the therapist, the client began her story about an actual sexual abuse.)

Reality Contact had been established and communicative contact about the voices had been developed. The therapist was then able to use classical psychodramatic technique, that is, developing the roles for the drama and setting the scene. Sufficient psychological contact had been established to proceed with therapy. The therapist then asks:

T	*Is it one voice or many?*
C	*One.*
T	*Male or female?*
C	*Male, my brother.*
T	*Choose someone in the group to be your brother.*

The client was able to release rage at her brother for not protecting her from sexual abuse during his presence. In addition, the client was able to process guilt and anger over this, which was the origin of the voices. The vignette illustrates the use of voices as a therapeutic process and the use of Pre-Therapy as an adjunctive method of contact to enable therapy.

Some further thoughts

Lacan: A theoretical observation can be made concerning postulation of a 'mirror stage' of 'I' development (Lacan, 1977). Lacan reports observations of human infants and how they respond to mirrored images of themselves. He starts by describing how monkeys lose interest in their own mirrored image. In contrast, human infants continue to recognize and respond to their own mirrored image. They see themselves. This differentiation, he concluded, reveals a *human* stage of development he calls 'the mirror stage'. He characterizes this as a stage of a primordial integration of the 'I' (self). Pre-Therapy also seems to lead to a primordial integration. Both seem to indicate an integration of self at primitive levels. Perhaps Pre-Therapy facilitates self-integration at a 'mirror stage' of development. Perhaps this may account for the success with non-verbal, profoundly retarded clients (see McWilliams).

Minkowski: Still another interesting observation can be made concerning the theoretical interface between Pre-Therapy and the phenomenological description of schizophrenia offered by Minkowski (1970). Minkowski describes schizophrenia as a lack of *vital contact* between the person and reality. He describes vital contact as the person's *experiential penetration* of the phenomenon. Next, he describes a *relatedness* between the phenomenon and the person as characterized by an ebb and flow, a mutual process of attending and receiving. Another quality of vital contact or the person's involvement with the phenomenon is *sympathy* (empathy). Finally, there is the characteristic of 'horizon' as *infinitely nuanced.* Our meanings are continuous. The last element of vital contact concerns *synchronicity.* Things, as well as ourselves, move forward in time, in a 'parallel' fashion. Schizophrenia, for Minkowski, is the absence of this *vital contact.*

There is a marked parallel between Minkowski's formulation concerning the lack of vital contact as central to the nature of schizophrenia and Pre-Therapy's empathic contact as central to its treatment. What this brings together is a description of treatment (Pre-Therapy) that corresponds to the problem (lack of vital contact).

Summary

This paper has described techniques to develop psychological contact with regressed, isolated, pre-relationship' and 'pre-process' clients. The concept of the 'Pre-Expressive Self' is introduced. The application of these techniques was originally targeted for schizophrenic and developmentally disabled clients. They have been recently expanded to Alzheimer's victims as a tool for communication, as well as, to processing multiple personality clients along with those suffering from severe trauma and abuse. The hallucinatory work has been expanded from purely visual experience to include auditory experiences. Possible interfacing between Pre-Therapy and the observations of Lacan and Minkowski are described.

References

Coffeng, T. (1995) Experiential and pre-experiential therapy for multiple trauma. In U. Esser, G. Pabst & G. Spierer (Eds.), *The Power of the Person-Centered Approach.* Koln, Germany: GWG Verlag.

Coffeng, T. (1997) Pre-experiential contact with dissociation (Video). IVth International Conference for Client-Centered and Experiential Therapy. Lisbon,

Portugal.

Danacci, A. (1997) Ricerca sperimentale sul trattamento psicologico dei pazienti schizofrenic con la Pre-Therapia. Dr G Prouty. *Psychologia Della Persona. 2,(4)* Maggio. Bologna, Italy.

DeVre, R. (1992) *M A Thesis.* Ghent, Belgium: Department of Psychology, University of Ghent.

Hinterkopf, E., Prouty, G., & Brunswick, L. (1979) Apilot study of Pre-Therapy method applied to chronic schizophrenic patients. *Psychosocial Rehabilitation Journal,* 3,(Fall 1979), pp. 11–9.

Lacan, J. (1977) The mirror stage as formative of the function of I, as revealed in psychoanalytic experience. *Ecrits* (pp. 4–7). New York: W. W. Norton.

Leijssen, M. & L. Roelens. (1988) Herstel van contactfuncties bij zwaar gestoorde patienten door middel Van Prouty's Pre-Therapie. [The contact functions of Prouty's Pre-Therapy.] Belgium: *Tijdschrift Klinische Psychologie.* 18e jrg. nr., 1 Februart, pp. 21–34.

McWilliams, K., & Prouty, G. (in press) Life enrichment of a profoundly retarded woman: an application of Pre-Therapy. *The Person Centered Journal.*

Minkowski, E. (1970) Schizophrenia. *Lived Time* (pp. 281–2). Evanston, Illinois: Northwestern University Press.

Perls, F. S. (1969) *Ego, Hunger and Aggression* (p.14). New York: Random House.

Peters, H. (1986) Prouty's pre-therapie methods en de behandeling ven hallucinaties een versalg. [Prouty's Pre-Therapy methods and the treatment of hallucinations.] The Netherlands: *RUIT,* (Maart), (Translated.), pp. 26–34.

Prouty, G. (1976) Pre-Therapy, a method of treating pre-expressive psychotic and retarded patients. *Psychotherapy: Theory, Research and Practice,* 13, (Fall), 290–94.

Prouty, G. (1977) Protosymbolic method: a phenomenological treatment of schizophrenic hallucinations. *Journal of Mental Imagery,* 1,(2), (Fall), pp. 339–42.

Prouty, G. (1983) Hallucinatory contact: a phenomenological treatment of schizophrenics. *Journal of Communication Therapy,* 2,(1), pp. 99–103.

Prouty, G. (1986) The pre-symbolic structure and therapeutic transformation of hallucinations, in M. Wolpin, J. Shorr & L. Kreuger (Eds.), *Imagery,* 4.New York: Plenum Press, pp. 99–106.

Prouty, G. (1990) Pre-Therapy: a theoretical evolution in the person-centered/experiential psychotherapy of schizophrenia and retardation. In G. Lietaer, J. Rombauts, & R. Van Balen, (Eds.), *Client-Centered and Experiential Psychotherapy in the Nineties* (pp. 645–58). Leuven, Belgium: Leuven University Press.

Prouty, G. (1991) The pre-symbolic structure and processing of schizophrenic hallucinations: the problematic of a non-process structure. In Lois Fusek (Ed.), *New directions in client-centered therapy: practice with difficult client populations* (pp. 1–18). Chicago, Illinois: The Chicago Counseling Center.

Prouty, G. (1994) *Theoretical Evolutions in Person-centered/Experiential*

Psychotherapy: Applications to Schizophrenic and Retarded Psychoses. Westport, Conn. : Praeger (Greenwood) Publications.

Prouty, G. & Cronwall, M. (1990) Psychotherapy with a depressed mentally retarded adult: an application of Pre-Therapy. In A. Dosen, and F. Menolascino, (Eds.), *Depression in Mentally Retarded Children and Adults* (pp. 281–93). Logan Publications: Leiden, The Netherlands.

Prouty, G. & M. Kubiak. (1988a) The development of communicative contact with a catatonic schizophrenic. *Journal of Communication Therapy,* 4, (1), pp. 13–20.

Prouty, G. & M. Kubiak. (1988b) Pre-Therapy with mentally retarded/psychotic clients. *Psychiatric Aspects of Mental Retardation Reviews,* 7,(10), pp. 62–6.

Prouty G. & S. Pietrzak. (1988) Pre-Therapy method applied to persons experiencing hallucinatory images. *Person-Centered Review,* 3,(4), pp. 426–41.

Prouty, G., Van Werde, D., & Portner, M. (1998) *Prae-Therapie.* Stutgaart, Germany: Klett-Cotta.

Rogers, C. (1957) The necessary and sufficient conditions of therapeutic personality change. *Journal of Consulting Psychology,* 21,(2), pp. 95–103.

Rogers, C. (1978) The formative tendency. *Journal of Humanistic Psychology,* 18, pp. 23–6.

Roy, Barbara C. (1991) A client-centered approach to multiple personality and dissociative process. In L, Fusek, (Ed.) *New Directions in Client-centered Therapy: Practice with Difficult Client Populations* (pp. 18–40). Chicago, Illinois: The Chicago Counseling and Psychotherapy Research Center.

Roy, B. (1997) An illustration of memory retrieval with a DID client. Paper presented: Eastern Psychological Association, Washington DC.

Van Werde, D., (1989) Restauratie van het psychologisch contact bij acute psychose. *Tijdschrift voor psychotherapie,* 5, pp. 271–9.

Van Werde, D. (1990) Psychotherapy witha retarded schizo-affective woman: an application of Prouty's Pre-Therapy. In: A. Dosen, A. Van Gennep and G. Zwanikken (Eds.), *Treatment of Mental Illness and Behavioral Disorder in the Mentally Retarded: Proceedings of International Congress, May 3rd & 4th* (pp. 469–77). Amsterdaam, The Netherlands: Logon Publications.

The Dance of Psychotherapy

Dave Mearns

An exploration of the intriguing Therapeutic Processes involved in the Client's changing Self-Concept during Person-Centred Therapy, where battles may rage between different parts of the Client's Self and where the Therapist must have good balance to ride the rollercoaster.

Wholeness

In the first exposition of the personality theory which underpinned his work, Carl Rogers included the proposition that: 'The organism reacts as an organised whole to his phenomenal field' (Rogers, 1951, p.486). This proposition goes on to explain and illustrate the extent of integration within the human personality wherein parts which may have been very wounded are supported and protected by other parts in such a way that all can survive, albeit meagrely in some cases.

The person-centred discipline of attending to the client as a 'whole' person follows from this and related propositions. This area is commonly misunderstood as implying that the person-centred therapist should only relate to the *wholeness* of the client and should not attend to the elements and dynamics within the personality. If a person-centred therapist worked from that misconception they would learn that it reduces their ability to work at depth with many clients. This especially applies to the client for whom the forces within his or her personality have effectively cancelled each other out: for example, where a highly controlled part of the personality has developed in order to restrain a more spontaneous, responsive part which, if given freer expression, might make the person vulnerable to the power and 'conditions of worth' imposed by parents.

In therapeutic work it is important to be able to work with the different parts of the client's personality as these emerge and to create a therapeutic relationship, manifesting the so-called 'therapeutic conditions', with each part of the personality.

However, it is vital that the personcentred therapist does not *force* this framework upon the client by pushing for the separation and labelling of different parts of the personality: that would be to overlay an analytic rather than person-centred framework. In working with clients I am careful to make no mention of different parts of the personality until or unless the client makes similar reference. Furthermore, I am studiously careful to use the labels which the client uses to describe these different parts, even though these may only be half-formed and

First published in *Person-Centred Practice*, Volume 2, Number 2, 1994.
First presented as the keynote lecture at the BAPCA AGM 1994.

cumbersome. This strict person-centred discipline prevents the therapist encouraging and enhancing schisms within the personality. Just as important, it also reduces considerably the possibility of the work becoming sidetracked onto the agenda of the therapist and away from the reality of the client.

Introducing 'Elizabeth'

In this chapter I shall use a variety of case material to illustrate the points I am making about person-centred work with different parts of the client's personality. The first such illustration relates to a client whom we shall call 'Elizabeth'.

Elizabeth survived into her early forties before her life began to disintegrate. That disintegration could be traced back to her survival and adaptation to some powerful *conditions of worth* in childhood. These conditions of worth included the following injunctions:

You are good if you are caring.

You are not good if you express dissent.

Crying for yourself is selfish.

You are evil if you hurt your Mother.

You are evil if you hurt your Father.

Your value is in the service you give to others.

Second-best is failure.

Elizabeth survived these conditions of worth and indeed lived a worthwhile life, at least in other people's terms. It was a surprise to all who knew her when she broke down during the early stages of counselling training. She had previously worked for several years as a counsellor in a voluntary organisation but her new professional training quite quickly reached the fragile parts of her personality. She left training and went into therapy where she gradually uncovered competing parts of her personality which she referred to as 'the nun' and 'the little girl'. These two main parts of her personality can be characterised by the way she referred to them during therapy:

Part A: 'The Nun'	Part B: 'The Little Girl'
• I am a caring person	• I don't really care
• I love my clients	• I really despise most of my clients
• I don't do enough as a person	• I despise myself
• I love my husband dearly	• I despise my husband
• I cry for the pain in the world	• I am a sham
• I don't know why you bother with the likes of me	• I am going to leave the whole damned lot of them (her family)
• I am always letting people down	• I am so, so scared
• I do *try* to do the right thing	• Help me to get out
• I am just not good enough	• Don't desert me
• If only I could get rid of that bad little girl inside me	• Help me destroy that pompous Nun!

During the breakdown of the fragile balance held between these parts of her personality, a third, unnamed, part developed. This part can be characterised by other quotes:

Part C
- I am really struggling with all of this
- I am getting so tired . . . so very tired
- I don't know whether I am going to make it
- I am crying for *me* nowadays
- Sometimes I look at myself and it's like watching a boxing match going on inside me
- This depression feels totally different from before. It feels much blacker and I feel fully *in* it rather than fighting it

Although she experienced considerable pain in relation to this third part of her personality as it evolved, it did represent a movement towards integration.

It is important to note that Elizabeth was by no means suffering from 'multiple personality', nor was she even dissociating. Much nonsense is produced nowadays under the label of 'multiple personality', usually by counsellors who are not schooled in psychopathology. Elizabeth simply operated from a personality which contained *conflicts* which to her were best represented in terms of separate entities.

Rogers' personality theory is useful for understanding the dynamics within Elizabeth's personality. The part which she describes as 'the nun' appears largely to be composed of *introjected* elements of her self-structure. (See Rogers, 1951: Proposition 10, page 498.) This largely introjected aspect of her personality helped her to survive the conditions of worth under which she lived, but that part contrasted sharply with 'the little girl' who had largely been *denied*. (See Rogers, 1951: Proposition 11, page 503.) There was no place for 'the little girl' in the normal life of Elizabeth and yet this part of her personality struggled to survive within Elizabeth's experience of herself. This part was not allowed a voice in Elizabeth's normal social living until it received direct attention during counselling training and later therapy.

The pattern of personality dynamics illustrated in the case of Elizabeth is fairly common, with an introjected 'good' part of the personality and another part which contains the ghosts of the denied aspects of self. This second part has never had a chance to discover how far it is 'good' or not: the only way it has been able to survive is by maintaining a position of opposition to the other part of the personality.

Relating with the different aspects of the client's personality

In working with a client who has such different and opposing parts to her personality, the person-centred therapist's task is to manifest the therapeutic conditions in relation to *all* the parts of the personality. This is what is meant by working with the 'whole' person. It is absolutely critical that the therapist *values* each of these parts of the client's personality, *listens* to each of them carefully, and is *congruent* in his relationship with both parts of the personality. A common error in practitioners who are not sufficiently well trained is to *align* more strongly with one part of the personality against the other. The danger in this naive procedure is that the therapist is actually colluding with one part of the personality and implicitly rejecting another part. At the very least this tends to block or elongate the therapeutic process and at worst it might engender psychosis.

It takes some discipline on the part of the person-centred therapist to resist the invitations of the different parts of the client's self because each can put up a strong case for the vilification of the other. And yet, *both* of these parts of the personality have been enormously important in the client's survival. Although Elizabeth may currently despise 'the nun', the construction of that part of her personality would have been extremely important for her survival within the family. Indeed, it is difficult to imagine how the young person could have survived the oppressive conditions of worth laid down for her without the help of 'the nun'. 'The little girl' may be despised and feared by 'the nun' because she is potentially disruptive, if not destructive, to the delicate balance which 'the nun' has worked hard to achieve. And yet, the survival of 'the little girl' carries the potential for Elizabeth to be more than a role-playing caricature.

In work with Elizabeth there were numerous examples where both 'the nun' and also 'the little girl' held out for an *exclusive* relationship with the therapist at the expense of the other part, for example:

Sequence A

The Nun: 'I think I need to stop seeing you.'

The Therapist: 'Can you say more?'

The Nun: 'It's just that . . . well, it's not really helping me . . . I just think that it's stirring things up.'

The Therapist: 'That's what's been happening for you — things have been stirred up . . . what things?'

The Nun: 'Everything really — I'm arguing more — I'm even getting angry at things that don't matter . . . and sometimes I just can't stop crying.'

The Therapist: 'And that makes you want to stop the therapy.'

The Nun: 'Either that . . . or maybe you could help me *control* things better. My psychologist used to do that — he would help me work out ways to control my panic.'

The Therapist: 'My hesitation is that I'm not sure whether that's what *all* of you wants. I can certainly help you to link up with a psychologist if you want that, but can we explore it a bit more right now?'

The Nun: 'I don't want to get upset [tears in eyes].'

The Therapist: 'Like, you can't take much more of that upset — it's been so, so painful — it *is* so, so painful . . . ?'

In this extract the therapist listened carefully to the client and communicated that listening. However, the therapist did not wholly follow the wishes of the client in her desire to focus exclusively on *control*. Already established in the therapy were the different parts of the client's personality and in this extract the therapist seeks to keep the communication open so that *all* the parts of the client's personality might be heard.

A similar process was in operation on another occasion when 'the little girl' endeavoured to attract the exclusive attention of the therapist.

Sequence B

> The Little Girl: 'It feels like you are siding with her [the nun] against me. I need you to be more here for me.'
> The Therapist: 'I thought that I have been *very much* here for you.'
> The Little Girl: 'That's not how it feels — it feels that you have been more here for her.'
> The Therapist: 'I have been wanting to be fully here for both of you.'
> The Little Girl: 'That's impossible.'
> The Therapist: 'Why?'
> The Little Girl: 'Because if you are here for her then you are not being here for me.'
> The Therapist: 'Yes, that's how it feels, doesn't it — you would really want me *just* for you . . . And maybe *she* would want me just for her?'
> The Little Girl: [pause] ' . . . OK . . . So long as you *like* me more than you like her!' [smiles].

This is a delightful extract from therapy because 'the little girl' is actually able to obtain some insight into the competition between the different parts of her personality. Also, there was a rare moment of humour and intimacy as she made the pretended demand on the therapist 'to *like* me more'.

Working with the different, and often competing, parts of a client's personality is almost exactly the same as working with a *couple* in therapy. Just as in the earlier extracts, the couple therapist would take great care not to be over-aligned with one part of the couple to the exclusion and judgement of the other. What the couple therapist would try to do is to use himself as an *empathic mediator* in relation to each of the partners. He would endeavour to empathise as fully as possible with each of the partners. That focus on empathy not only allows each partner to be heard but creates the possibility of each partner hearing the other through the therapist. The way this empathic mediation works is that one partner feels heard by the therapist and therefore is enabled to say more and more. In normal communication between the partners the empathy and consequent elaboration would have been halted much earlier. However, with the pressure off the listening partner, they may be less defensive and able for the first time to hear the struggle of their mate. Exactly the same process happens in person-centred work with different parts of the client's personality. For example, in the work with Elizabeth, the two parts of her personality became more fluid with both taking part and exchanging the limelight in therapy sessions. Increasingly, situations arose where each part was able to hear the other part through the empathic mediation of the therapist, for example:

>The Nun: 'I have really tried *so* hard. I don't know if I can go on.'
>
>The Therapist: 'I see that you have been trying so very hard to hold things together — it brings tears to your eyes, and to mine too, to feel how hard you have been trying . . . it feels quite desperate — *you* feel quite desperate . . . You don't know if you can go on . . .'
>
>The Nun: 'Yes, I'm *really* scared. This feels like the end.'

Sometime later in the same session we find a remarkably similar result coming from the therapist's empathy with the other part of the client's personality:

>The Little Girl: 'I get totally pissed off with that crying nun. Why can't she stand up for herself? When she cries I want to kick her head in. I want to kill her.'
>
>The Therapist: 'It seems like you're not just "pissed off" with her — that it's much stronger than that — you're *more* than angry with her . . . ?'
>
>The Little Girl: 'Yes [eyes filling with tears] — it's more than anger — I'm really desperate . . . I'm really scared that . . . that I won't be able to survive.'

In the course of these two pieces of dialogue both parts of the client were able to hear how much they shared: they were both scared; they were both crying; they were both fighting; they both felt 'desperate' and they were both doing the best they could for the client. This understanding of each part by the other contributed building-blocks to the client's future *acceptance* and valuing of *all* of her parts. That self-acceptance and valuing had been directly facilitated by the valuing which the therapist has shown to both parts of her personality and through the mediating effect of his empathy.

The rollercoaster process of self-concept change in therapy

On the way to the client's increased self-acceptance, the rollercoaster that is the therapeutic process may offer many more unexpected heights and troughs. In order to understand the process of self-concept change which is facilitated by therapy, it is useful to dip into the realms of attitude change theory. The self-concept is an attitude which is learned like any other attitude. Any attitude has numerous elements which may be categorised into three 'components' of the attitude:

• **The cognitive component** (knowledge and beliefs about the attitude object)

• **The affective component** (feelings in relation to the attitude object)

• **The behavioural component** (how we tend to behave in response to the attitude object)

Hence, our attitude towards our Self will contain numerous elements of knowledge or belief about ourselves; various feelings about aspects of ourselves including evaluations of our attributes; and numerous behaviours which reflect our self-concept. For example, a person with a very negative self-concept would likely have a collection of beliefs and memories about his failures with more emphasis being given to these than successes; he would also have a variety of, largely negative, feelings about himself; and also his behaviour would likely reflect that overall negativity, perhaps through him exhibiting a lack of confidence, shyness, anxiety, etc.

Within any attitude there is great *consistency* among the elements with most of them reflecting the same message. 'Dissonant' (or 'inconsistent') elements within the negative self-concept — elements which perhaps reflect successes or positive feelings about self would be fewer, more often denied, and sometimes rationalised to reduce their potency ('it was only really because of luck that I succeeded in that'; 'people must be wrong to think that *I'm* good at that'; 'people sometimes think I'm good but that's only because I'm good at fooling them!'). It is the *consistency* exhibited by the many elements within the self-concept that offers coherence and predictability to the person. Failure to achieve consistency is enormously disturbing and in extreme cases may even result in psychosis. Consistency within the self-concept is so important to the functioning of the human being that a negative self-concept may even be defended with the same agility as a positive self-concept. The effect of therapy is to increase the 'dissonance' within the client's self-concept. Some of the ways in which dissonance becomes increased include:

- *all* the aspects of the personality are given non-judgemental attention by the therapist, even if they are inconsistent with the self-concept. [This works against the conditionality which has thus far restricted the parts of the client which are 'acceptable' to him.]
- the various *introjections* which the client has accepted from childhood are re-examined against the client's experience. [Hence the validity of many of these introjections is thereby brought into question.]
- some of the *denied experiences*, usually implying strengths or positives for the negative self-concept, are rediscovered and examined during therapy.

The increase of dissonance within therapy is not a comfortable experience because dissonance brings its own tension. That tension may be experienced in a variety of emotions which Rogers describes well in his theory as providing a secondary motivational force to assist the actualising tendency (see Rogers, 1951: Proposition 6, page 492). [The disturbance represented by the emotion further motivates change.]

This tension may be relieved by the self-concept *changing* in a direction which accepts more of these new, positive elements. That is the kind of change which is generally sought and experienced in therapy. However, that therapeutic change may be preceded by other efforts to reduce the dissonance. For example, there can be efforts on the part of the old, negative self-concept to fight back against the first rays of hope. This is illustrated in a case which is cited in Mearns (1992), pp.72–73:

The self-concept strikes back

One example was Scott, a man who was prominent and effective in the business community, but almost totally inadequate in interpersonal relationships, particularly where emotions were involved. During the first six months of our work, Scott developed considerable understanding of his self and of his self-in-relationship at work, with his wife, and with his children. Scott was a man who used his brain most effectively and this was exemplified in the counselling room. His way into the whole process was to develop a cognitive understanding of his emotions. His understanding eventually extended to his own history, and what he came to recognise as the emotional abuse he had suffered from his father.

During that first six months, Scott showed nothing which resembled a feeling: neither joy, sadness, or anger. However, in the seventh month, Scott's affect started to loosen. He began to see that he could be a different person from the way he had come to see himself. In his communication with his wife, Scott began to express his feelings: sadness, regret, and tentative, loving feelings. In relation to one of his employees, he communicated uncharacteristic empathy, and with his children he found himself more able to play.

Just as quickly as Scott's changing manifested itself in his behaviour, the process stopped, and indeed reversed.

Within a few weeks, Scott was thoroughly cut off from other people and had begun drinking heavily. He missed three consecutive appointments without making prior contact. When I telephoned him after the third missed appointment, he referred to the fact that he was 'too far gone to really change', and said he wanted to stop our sessions. . . For Scott, the inconsistencies which developed centred on his awakening emotionality. He regarded himself as a 'cold, unemotional, consistent person' (his words in our third meeting). Yet, in the last weeks of his work in counselling, he had seen himself express love, hate, anger, and deep sadness. These emotions had extended to his outside life, thus offering powerful inconsistency with his self-concept.

The last, desperate, effort of Scott's self-concept to maintain its consistency and reduce the dissonance was to extricate himself from therapy and sink deeper into his negative view of himself. Scott's self-concept was 'striking back', but if the therapist could stay on board during this rough ride there was hope.

Following the 'dance' of psychotherapy
The 'dance' of person-centred therapy involves the therapist in a largely 'following' role, being taken through many unusual steps and manoeuvres, often round in circles and seldom with any clear idea of where the dance is going. It will never be possible to predict the nature of an individual client's dance but it may be possible for us to become familiar with some of the sub-routines upon which dances are constructed. While this still will not allow us to predict an individual client's

process, at least it will help us to feel less clumsy and more confident on the dance floor. That confidence will help us to be a more solid support to our clients as they go through a changing process which can have many powerful experiences. For example, the elements in the changing process experienced by Elizabeth included the following:

Summary of the self-concept change process

1. **Constructing a protecting aspect of her personality** ('The Nun') which could exist in the context of the conditions of worth imposed upon her. That construction served as a means of protecting the self and allowing it to function, albeit in a restricted manner.
2. **Domination** by the protecting part of the personality over other, dissonant, parts.
3. **Rebellion** on the part of the dissonant parts ['The Little Girl'].
4. **Conflict** between, or among, the parts of self. This conflict brought with it a dramatic increase in many emotions, particularly **fear, anger** and **depression**. The conflict phase also brought with it times of despairing **'stuckness'** when the self-concept had shown the first signs of beginning to change but that change was arrested and pervaded by immobility. There were also times of **counter-revolution** where the part of self which had shown earlier domination began to reassert itself and drive the rebellious part underground once more (the self-concept striking back).
5. **The emergence of hope.** Hope may arise slowly and very partially at first, perhaps through the effects of becoming able to listen to competing aspects of self; obtaining a partial understanding of these different parts; and an early realisation that all the parts of the self have been doing their best towards the survival of the self at different times of life.
6. **The growth of self-acceptance.** Although early signs of hope may be threatened by further conflict, the first bricks have been laid in what can become a more self-accepting personality construction involving less schism and more acceptance of all its elements. This creates both a broader and firmer base for relating with others (as described in Rogers, 1951: Proposition 18, page 520).

Perhaps a nice way to end this chapter is to turn back to Elizabeth at the time in her therapeutic process when the emergence of hope was beginning. The different parts of her Self had recently become able to *listen* to each other, *understand* each other and to *value* each other. Maybe they were even growing towards loving each other?

During a therapy session, Elizabeth described a 'conversation' which she had had with herself the day before:

The Nun: 'I've been scared of you for a long while.'

The Little Girl: 'I've been scared of *you* for a long while.'

The Nun: 'I thought you might kill me.'

The Little Girl: 'I was sure you were trying to kill me.'

The Nun: 'I couldn't be you when I was young — there was no space to be you.'

The Little Girl: 'I know — I was there.'

The Nun: 'In the background?'

The Little Girl: 'Yes, *always* in the background.'

The Nun: 'And so, you got more and more angry?'

The Little Girl: 'Yes, and scared too.'

The Nun: 'Do you understand why I took control?'

The Little Girl: 'I do now — you thought it was the only way to survive . . . for us both to survive . . . you must have been very scared too?'

The Nun: 'Yes.'

The Little Girl: 'Maybe we did the best we could.'

The Nun: 'Maybe we did.'

References

Lietaer, G. (1984) Unconditional Positive Regard: A Controversial Basic Attitude in Client Centered Therapy, pp.41–58 in R. Levant and J. Shlien (Eds) *Client-Centered Therapy and the Person-Centered Approach.* New York: Praeger.

Mearns, D. (1992) Chapter 6 in Dryden W. (ed), *Hard Earned Lessons from Counselling in Action.* London: Sage.

Mearns, D. (1994) *Developing Person-Centred Counselling.* London: Sage.

Mearns, D. and Dryden, W. (1990) *Experiences of Counselling in Action.* London: Sage.

Mearns, D. and Thorne, B. (1988) *Person-Centred Counselling in Action First Edition.* London: Sage.

Rogers, Carl. (1951) *Client Centered Therapy.* London: Constable.

Storymaking and Storytelling in Counselling

Liz Nicholls

As a trainee counsellor I became interested in stories as part of the therapeutic process, and as a way of understanding the perceptual world of my client. The purpose of this paper is to explore and develop further my ideas in this area, and in so doing to stimulate the thinking and interest of other counsellors. For me this has been a valuable area of study which has impacted on my work, making me more open to both my own and my clients' use of stories.

My belief is that clients are telling 'stories' on several levels in therapy. First, there is their personal history, which is the 'larger story', the story of their life so far, or the edited version told to emphasise the parts they may be struggling with. Second, smaller stories may be told to illustrate particular aspects of experience. These may be in the form of an anecdote, or a traditional story from oral culture or written literature. Clients tell different kinds of stories: factual accounts, imaginative stories, humorous tales. I feel it is important to look behind the story, believing that everything the client brings is significant.

For me the term 'story' denotes a form of narrative; it is self-contained, whether factual or fantasy, has a beginning, middle and end, and has a purpose, conveying a particular interest, or moral. I see metaphors as the building-blocks for stories. Lynch (1995) uses the terms 'narrative' and 'story' interchangeably. He defines narrative as:

> a told sequence of events which are in some way connected, which occur through a passage of time, and which involve one or more characters.

My journey began with an article by Reeler (1993) which introduced me to the intriguing idea that therapy is the investigation of the client's personal story. As a person-centred counsellor, I prefer to use the word 'exploration' rather than 'investigation'. Reeler suggests that storytelling might be therapeutic in itself, that the possibility for change exists in the telling (Reeler, 1993). He speaks of psychotherapists as 'witnesses' to the client's story. As a 'witness' to my clients' stories I am affirming their existence, their importance, their 'acceptableness' to another human being.

Brown, a psychiatrist and psychotherapist (1992) suggests that the purpose of

First Published in *Person-Centred Practice*, Volume 6, Number 1, 1998.

therapy might be the co-creation of a story by client and therapist which will enable the client to make sense of their life, a way of 're-framing' their history. In person-centred terms, I understand this as change being facilitated through attention being paid to the story, or rather to the teller of the story. Stones (1992) develops this idea, suggesting that we define ourselves through the stories we tell, and that in telling a new story, or the same story with a different emphasis, there exists the possibility of forming a new identity. I found a similar theme in transpersonal thinking, that growth is about letting go of the 'smaller story' and becoming aware of the 'larger story' (Rowan, 1993 p. 65).

The more I looked at this, the more I realised that as human beings we are surrounded by 'stories'. As a counsellor, I believe myself to be involved with my clients in a complex process which can include hearing, telling and co-creating stories. I began to wonder whether a counsellor is actually someone who enjoys working with stories. I was particularly interested to read Bohler's (1987) reference to the work of Carl Rogers:

> Rogers did not just hear the last sentence, he remembered the whole
> story. He grasped themes, overtones, undertones and incongruities.
> And he offered many of these back to the client.

I like the idea of working with the whole story as it is this which leads a client towards integration of various aspects of themselves.

I agree with John Rowan (1993) that,

> . . . it is strange that people whose work will largely consist of listening
> to stories are taught so little about how people tell stories.

Some knowledge of the way stories are told in particular cultures, as well as the function and purpose that stories perform in our development, might enhance counsellor training — an idea previously suggested by Mearns and Thorne (1992 p. 27). It is important to note here that each person who comes into counselling is a unique individual; their stories too will be unique, and they will have their idiosyncratic way of telling them. Maybe part of the counselling process entails the counsellor finding out more about why this particular client is telling this story at this time and how it relates to their previous stories. Is it the same or different? Are they 'stuck' with a story that no longer works for them?

McAdam (1985) proposes that stories follow a particular grammatical structure which includes six main elements:

1. the setting;
2. the initiating event;
3. the internal reaction or response of the protagonist;
4. the attempt or action on the part of the protagonist to deal with the situation;
5. the consequences of this action;
6. the reaction to these events, or the moral of the tale.

Research (reviewed by Mancuso, 1986) suggests that this structure enables the reading and recall of a story, with this ability present from the age of three, and across cultures. If these elements are missing from a story or are present in the wrong order, this seems to pose difficulties in recall and retelling. It appears that these elements are necessary to aid effective communication of meaning (McLeod, 1994).

I feel that counsellors could learn more about the process of storymaking and storytelling through reading and writing. Bolton (1993) has used 'Writing as Therapy' workshops with health professionals to help them to access and make use of their experience through writing stories. Gillies (1988, pp. 38–41) has facilitated the use of literature with social work students to encourage sensitivity, increase understanding beyond personal experience and aid the integration of theory and practice.

My own experience of creating a story at a play therapy workshop was that there was a tremendous feeling of my own power in the creation and sharing of my story. This has enriched me in my personal life and in my work, giving me more confidence in responding to images and stories shared by my clients.

There is a growing interest in the relationship of narrative to the counselling process in this country. I attended a workshop at Keele University in 1995, led by Gordon Lynch (1995), a person-centred counsellor who drew on the work of White and Epston (1990), who regard therapy as an opportunity for people to 're-author' their lives — to take control of their stories. We were encouraged to write the ending as we visualised it for one of our client's stories (the 'story' of their particular process). In doing this I was enabled to voice many of the beliefs, values, hopes and expectations that I had for my client within the counselling process, a very simple but powerful way of bringing the process more fully into awareness. It seems to me that this could be incorporated into our repertoire as professionals, both as a form of self-supervision and within the accepted supervisory relationship.

As a member of a supervision group exploring creative approaches, I have found creative writing a valuable means to exploring imaginatively the relationships in which I am involved with clients or colleagues. I have found a way into issues on paper which I had previously found hard to tackle in any other way. For example, I found a change in my relationship with a client whom I shall call Jill, having written the story of how it might be for me to be on a desert island with her. There is freedom to express yourself in a story in which anything is permissible.

As part of my training, it was necessary to complete a small research project — a pilot study. I decided to look at how, as counsellors, we develop our attitude to stories and how this in turn affects our practice. My belief was that the counsellor's experience of stories will affect the 'storytelling' that occurs in the counselling relationship. I enjoyed reading as a child, and also have powerful memories of being told factual, inspirational stories by my father who is visually impaired. I believe these experiences have shaped my attitude to stories. I think of myself as a 'creative' person, enjoying hearing and making stories as well as writing and reading poetry. I take into my work as a counsellor the ability to use my imagination. I see part of my work as experimenting with and expanding on images which the client presents in order to further my understanding of their perceptual world, rather like shuffling the many pieces of a jigsaw puzzle trying them out to see which pieces fit together.

It has been my experience that this is helpful to some clients. For example, one client, Angie, introduced the idea of her future looking like a road with many obstacles and winding turns, which often felt overwhelming. During the session we continued to build on this image and I followed her empathically as she described some of the 'monsters' she met on the way. She suddenly stopped — I could see a visible change in her as she declared, 'Do you know this is just like a game I have at home. I always win that game.'

She had created an image which helped her to feel more powerful in her situation. I feel that images can be powerful resources, helping us to move from despair to hope. I have confidence that Angie can return to this image because it was generated from within her.

My aim was to explore the attitude of two counsellors to stories, both in their personal lives and as part of their professional development, and to see whether they recognised and worked with 'stories' in the counselling process. I wanted to establish their experience of stories, and to gain a sense of their attitudes towards them by looking at the part stories have played in their lives. First, did they read as children? Did they have a favourite story? Was there someone who acted as a storyteller? Second, do they read now? What kind of stories do they enjoy? Do they read for pleasure or for instruction? Third, do they consider that stories play a part in their development, both personal and professional? Do they use stories as part of their work with clients? If so, what is the purpose of using stories with clients? Is there anyone with whom they would not use stories? Would there be a case for including information about the way in which people tell stories as part of counsellor training?

Until recently there has been little research in this area. However, it is a subject that is beginning to receive more attention in Britain, particularly the client's experience of storytelling. John McLeod and Sophie Balamoutsou (1995) are studying the development of metaphors in counselling sessions, within the broader narrative/story of the client. This evolved from a replication of Martin's (1992) work, a quantitative study of the therapist's intentional use of metaphor. They present a detailed case-study exploring narrative processes in a single therapy session. One of the observations from this work was that the client appeared to be weaving stories about himself around a central theme throughout the session.

McLeod (1994) refers to a study of narrative elements in the psychotherapy process by Rennie (1992), the results of which infer that clients are conscious of their 'storytelling' as part of the therapeutic process. Luborsky, et al. (1992) looked at the narratives generated by clients in therapy sessions and found that changes in the pattern of a client's narrative were linked to the outcomes of therapy; for example, more positive narratives were linked to more positive outcomes.

The research

I chose a qualitative approach to explore counsellors' attitudes to stories. It was important to me that the approach was one that valued experience. Interviewing seemed an appropriate way of gathering information about stories, since from the literature it was established that stories are told within the context of a relationship (Gersie and King, 1990). Riches and Dawson (1995) take the view that the narrative interview is a form of storytelling, they speak of the researcher being alongside the 'researched', involved in the process of receiving and co-authoring stories.

I had access to two colleagues who were willing to take part in the study, both counsellors working within the person-centred approach: Debbie, a trainee counsellor, and Anne, a counsellor, trainer and supervisor. I chose them as I felt they might be open to working with stories. I conducted semi-structured interviews following a loose framework of questions. My aim was to provide enough structure to contain the data effectively, while allowing enough freedom for flexibility and exploration.

There were opportunities to experiment with questions with colleagues. Taping the interviews enabled an accurate record of the exchanges to be kept. Transcription proved to be too time-consuming; notes were made immediately following the interview. The questions provided some initial structure with which I could begin my analysis. I chose a middle order approach (Dey, 1993, pp.103–4), developing broad categories — looking for general relationships between the categories of data (Marshall and Rossman, 1989, pp.112–5).

Results and discussion

Both Anne and Debbie talked freely of their experience of stories within the counselling process, linking stories with pictures and imagery. Debbie spoke of using 'metaphor' and stories as a form of illustration with some clients. Anne described the way in which she used 'small stories' as a means of clarifying what a client is saying. Anne saw the concept of counselling as a form of storytelling as an alternative framework in which counsellors might make sense of their experience. She was clear that this was not a framework that she explicitly used, but felt that there might be a place for this becoming a named approach. This is indeed beginning to happen with the development of interest in 'the narrative approach to counselling' (McLeod, 1994).

From the pilot study, there were reservations expressed about the possible effects for clients and the 'general public' of the implications of using the word 'story'. There were fears that for some people the word might imply that the content would be assumed to be fictitious, thereby leaving them feeling that they were not being taken seriously. This issue has been raised by other practitioners (Rowan, 1994; Efran et al., 1990 p. 82), whose conclusion is that what is important is the effect that a client's recollections have on their present life rather than the literal truth of what is said.

Rennie (1994) identified several therapeutic functions fulfilled by storytelling: providing emotional relief, allowing the client to access inner disturbance in such a way as to maintain enough distance to allow the necessary processing to occur. I looked at the purpose that Anne and Debbie felt the stories were performing within the counselling process. Debbie saw stories as a means of conveying feelings, to put in a more 'pictorial' form something that it was hard to find words for, a way of helping clients to experience pre-verbal feelings. She believed a client could take what they wanted from a story, that it was a way of communicating without 'leading'. Both counsellors said that stories helped them to clarify their understanding of what a client was saying.

Anne described the way in which she used what she termed 'mini stories', and gave examples of these — 'it feels like you're in a pit', 'it feels like you're in a tunnel'; she has found these to have furthered her own understanding of clients. She felt that if a client introduced a 'fantasy story' this might be a way for them to communicate a 'truth' which might be too painful to present in factual form. Anne said stories provided space to play with an image and that from this process connections might emerge for the client, so that 'maybe a fuller story, a more connected story comes together for them'. She described this as part of the process of integration within the counselling process.

There were no hard and fast rules about who introduced 'stories' in the counselling. Anne said it was sometimes herself and sometimes the client. She warned of the danger of it being intrusive and unhelpful to introduce a story to a client 'who has difficulty playing', pointing to the importance of working 'at the edge of their awareness'. Although she often had a sense of where a client was up to in the form of a picture in her mind, which she called her 'reflective story', she did not always choose to share that with her client.

Both counsellors were in agreement that there are differences in people regarding their openness to stories. In their view, stories are concerned with imagery and creativity, and are therefore not a form of expression that would make sense to everyone, with some people given to more analytical and factual statements than to using images. Anne referred to the way she thinks as being 'visual', but spoke of other ways of conceptualising experience; for example, some clients think in words.

This difference in conceptualisation may also apply to counsellors, and possibly influences their choice of approach. There may be differences in attitudes to the use of stories between the various approaches. My reading would suggest that cognitive behavioural therapists might use stories in their work in a structured way (Morgan, 1989 p.15) while those from psychoanalytic and psychodynamic traditions might use them as material for projection, identification and interpretation of internal conflicts (Lubetsky 1989; Jacobs, 1988).

Anne described it as being unproductive to introduce a concept (such as that of storytelling) that was foreign to the client, and the importance of asking 'does this fit for this client?' She spoke of 'the ability to play with an image' as an important factor in determining the appropriateness of using stories. Anne spoke of 'different stories', feeling that possibly the 'best' stories are those that are more flexible — 'those with more space between the lines'. In contrast, she gave the example of an 'obsessional' person for whom the story may have to be tightly pinned down; her thinking was that 'simpler stories are the ones that are most healthy'.

Debbie said she used her judgement to decide whether stories would be an appropriate form to use with a particular client in a similar way to how she assesses a client's ability to use an image as part of a relaxation procedure. She believed that stories were not a suitable form of communication for 'analytically minded clients' and felt that a factual account could sometimes mean that a client 'talked about' rather than experienced feelings. She found that stories were more a part of the counselling with 'long-term clients', with what she termed 'sensing stories' more likely to be told in 'the middle phase' of the work. Debbie spoke of these as 'special times' and noted that stories were less of a feature with clients referred for short-term contract work. She wondered if a possible explanation was the difference in time available for exploration of issues. I found this surprising, as from the literature counsellors are using stories as part of their work in 'brief therapy' (McLeod, 1995; White and Epston, 1990).

Debbie gave an example of working with a client with low self-esteem. She told her client a story which illustrated the different responses a parent might make to their child's drawing and the varying effects these might have on the child. I was fascinated to hear that her client then brought to a later session a story that she had written to share with Debbie.

Both counsellors read stories about people, and referred to biography and autobiography. For Debbie it was important that books were 'written with feeling'; she liked 'books that people put themselves into'. She believed stories to be concerned with creativity, particularly 'escapist', fantasy stories, which 'freed the mind' enabling her 'just to let it be'. Her feeling was that the attitude behind this kind of story helped her to be able to let go of the need for solutions and ways forward; she described this as important to her practice. She thought that factual reading informed her work, in terms of giving her information, but she warned of the danger of leading someone down the wrong path in counselling by attaching a particular theory to their individual process.

Anne related her reading to both personal and professional development. She said, 'To be able to play might enrich you both personally and professionally'. She felt that to take more time to play, especially with fiction, would encourage introspection and play. She warned that if a counsellor cannot 'play' then the process may become stifled. Reading was also seen by Anne as a way for a counsellor to take care of themselves — a form of relaxation.

Having established that the two counsellors interviewed did use stories in their work with clients, and that they saw links between their reading and their development, I now wanted to gain a sense of how their attitudes to stories developed — was there any connection between their experience of stories in childhood and their openness to stories as adults?

Both Anne and Debbie eagerly answered my questions about their experience of stories as children. Debbie began without hesitation to tell me of her favourite story, 'Alexander and the Pudding Tree', taken from a book of Eastern European

Folk Tales. The most memorable parts for her were the pictures and noises involved in the story; she remembered her brother used to read the story to her with lots of expression. She experienced difficulties with schooling, being unable to read until the age of 11; this created in her a 'hunger' for books, and she later read a book a day. Reading as a pastime was not valued by the rest of Debbie's family; there were few books in the house. Her grandfather, however, used to make up 'wonderful stories', 'naughty, funny' stories about when he was a child. I could hear the 'child' in her voice as she spoke of this. Debbie enjoys creating stories with her own children.

Anne spoke of her 'very imaginative father'. I could hear the pleasure in her voice as she recounted the way in which as a child she had been encouraged to think of three very different things; it was then her father's task to 'weave these together' into a bedtime story. She felt this was an important experience which has remained with her — she used to practise it with friends as she grew. She regarded some of her work with clients as making connections in her mind between present and past stories, involved in their process of making connections in a way which can help the client to 'weave' it all together and make sense of what is happening. However, she warned of the danger of intellectually making connections that aren't real for the client.

I had expected to find that the context in which stories were experienced was a significant factor. Gersie and King (1990 p. 33) looked at the need for trust and intimacy in a relationship before a person can take the risk of entering into a story. I also expected to find that the value placed on stories in adulthood was closely linked to childhood experience. It was not as clear-cut as being able to say that 'positive experience' of stories in childhood would lead to valuing stories as an adult, since Debbie clearly experienced struggles in relation to written stories as a child; however, it would seem that her experience of storytelling within the family, together with her later 'success' with reading, have enabled her to perceive stories in a way that is helpful to her both personally and professionally.

Conclusion

At every stage in this project people were telling me stories. It was as though I had somehow given permission or made space for stories to be told. The findings suggest that storytelling and storymaking within the counselling process is affected by the counsellors' own experience of stories. If stories are valued as part of everyday life, and in personal development, they are likely to be incorporated into the work of the counsellor. This makes sense to me, particularly with regard to person-centred counsellors who value the 'use of self', which in the case of the counsellors interviewed included their experience of stories as informative, creative, fun.

Childhood experience both of reading and being told stories or involvement in the process of creating stories would seem to have a direct bearing on the formation of attitudes to stories in adulthood. Positive memories of storytelling in particular seem likely to lead to a positive attitude to stories as an adult. It would be interesting to look at whether counsellors with little or no experience of storytelling in a close relationship would differ in their attitude to and ability to use stories in the counselling process.

Further study could take many directions, for example (1) looking at the implications of including information about stories in training programmes; (2) looking at the views held by clients, counsellors and the 'general public' about the connotations of using the word 'story' in relation to counselling; (3) whether attitudes to the usefulness of stories as part of the counselling process differed between approaches. As my work is primarily with clients experiencing an eating disorder, I am interested in looking at the metaphors that these clients bring into counselling, in the hope that study of this kind might further my own and others understanding of this form of 'dis-ease'.

References

Bohler, C. J. (1987) The use of storytelling in the practice of pastoral counselling. *Journal of Pastoral Care.*

Bolton, G. (1993) Just a bobble hat: the story of a 'Writing as Therapy' training workshop. *Changes,* 11, p.37.

Brown, E.M. (1992) Exchanging stories. *Changes,* 10, p. 51.

Dey, I. (1993) *Qualitative Data Analysis.* London: Routledge.

Efran, J. S., Lukens, M. D. and Lukens, R. J. (1990) *Frameworks of Meaning in Psychotherapy.* London: W.W. Norton. p. 82.

Gersie, A. and King, N. (1990) *Storymaking in Education and Therapy.* London: Jessica Kingsley.

Gillies, C. (1988) Reading and insight. In J. M. Clarke, and E. Bostle, *Reading Therapy.* London: Library Association Publishing.

Jacobs, M. (1988) The use of story in pastoral care. *Contact* Part 1: Vol. 95, pp. 14–21; Part 2: Vol. 96, pp. 12–7.

Lubetsky, M. J. (1989) The magic of fairy tales: psychodynamic and developmental perspectives.*Child Psychiatry and Human Development,* Vol. 19, pp. 245–55.

Luborsky, L., Barber, J. P. and Diguer, L. (1992) The meanings of narratives told during psychotherapy: the fruits of a new observational unit. *Psychotherapy Research,* 2, pp. 277–90.

Lynch, G. (1995) *Narrative and the Therapeutic Process.* Workshop, Keele University.

Mancuso, J. C. (1986) The acquisition and use of narrative grammar structure. In T. R. Sarbin (Ed.), *Narrative Psychology: The Storied Nature of Human Conduct.* New York: Praeger.

Marshall, C. and Rossman, G. B. (1989) *Designing Qualitative Research.* London: Sage.

Martin, J. (1992) Therapists' intentional use of metaphor: memorability, clinical impact and possible epistemic/motivational functions. *Journal of Consulting and Clinical Psychology,* 60, (1), pp. 143–5.

McAdam, D. P. (1985) *Power, Intimacy and the Life Story: Personological Inquiries into Identity.* Homewood, Ill: Dorsey Press.

McLeod, J. (1994) The emergence of the narrative approach to counselling and psychotherapy. Paper presented at the Annual Conference of the Counselling Psychology Division of the British Psychological Society, Birmingham, May.

McLeod, J. and Balamoutsou, S. (1995) The identification of narrative processes in psychotherapy. Paper delivered at Psychotherapy Research Conference, University of British Columbia, Vancouver, Canada, June.

McLeod, J. *(in press).Working with Narratives.*

Mearns, D. and Thorne, B. (1992) *Person Centred Counselling in Action.* London: Sage.

Morgan, L.B. (1989) The use of indirect suggestion in counselling. *Counselling.*

Reeler, T. (1993) Psychotherapy and storytelling: a Popperian conjecture. *Changes,* 11, pp. 205–14.

Rennie, D. (1992) Qualitative analysis of the client's experience of psychotherapy: the unfolding of reflexivity. In S. G. Toukmanian and D. Rennie (Eds), *Psychotherapy Process Research: Paradigmatic and Narrative Approaches.* London: Sage.

Rennie, D. (1994) Referred to in McLeod, J. (1994) in press.

Riches, G. and Dawson, P. (1995) Making stories/taking stories: methodological reflections on researching grief and marital tension following the death of a child. Revised version of paper presented at first annual BAC conference on 'Research in Counselling', Birmingham University. February 1995.

Rowan, J. (1993) *The Transpersonal-Psychotherapy and Counselling.* London: Routledge.

Rowan, J. (1994) On believing the client. *Journal for the British Association for Counselling.* 5, (4), p. 263.

Stones, C. R. (1992) Lived stories: critical experiences and changed self-identity (the Rip Van Winkle phenomenon).*Changes*, 10, (4), p. 286.

White, M. and Epston, D. (1990) *Narrative Means to Therapeutic Ends.* New York: W.W. Norton.

Acknowledgement

I would like to acknowledge the encouragement and practical support of my former tutor Paul Wilkins (Senior Lecturer, Manchester Metropolitain University) in the preparation of this paper and to thank him personally for his stories which sparked off this process in me.

Beyond Carl Rogers

David Brazier

Appreciative response to material appearing in the first edition of Person Centred Practice prompted this writer to review past developments in our perception of the Person-Centred Approach and to offer a personal view on where we might be able to go now.

A spirit of caring

Carl Rogers cared about other people. This is not so much a statement of theory as a statement about what he actually spent his professional life doing. A great deal of his time was spent sitting listening to people and his effectiveness was attributable, he believed, to the fact that he sincerely did come to understand and care about them. I am inclined to the view, therefore, that the Person-Centred Approach is essentially about love. There is much said and written about the idea that the PCA is essentially about power, but I do not think this is the central issue. Power only raises its head when love is lacking.

Since Rogers died there has been a need to clarify the theory of the PCA. There is also the question, 'where now?' By getting more clarity about what Rogers was getting at, we may also get a sense of what still remains to be done.

Carl Rogers wrote about being client-centred (Rogers 1951). By this he meant giving total attention to the other person, achieving real psychological contact with the other person, understanding them, cherishing them, and putting one's own concerns aside for a time in order to give somebody else a real listening to. This is something rare and precious.

When I first started working with person-centred groups about twelve years ago, I soon noticed that while there were people who saw caring for others as the prime aim, there were also many who thought that the essence of humanistic growth work was to 'get something for me' and to get other people to 'take responsibility for themselves'. This particular idea seemed at that time to be most closely associated with the Gestalt school of thought. Since then, I get the impression that Gestalt has moderated somewhat. Jan Hawkins' (1993) moving article illustrates, however, that this self-seeking line of thought may have gained ground within the Person-Centred Approach itself.

In the present political climate this is perhaps not surprising. 'Everyone for themselves and the devil take the hindmost' is not a philosophy one thinks would be associated with a caring community but it is currently socially widespread and we should not expect to be completely immune. It does seem, however, that there

First published in *Person-centred Practice*, Volume 2, Number 1, 1994.

is an ambivalence built into the foundations of person-centred theory which is sufficient to allow many people, who all call themselves person-centred, to take very different views on the matter.

Metamorphoses of PCA

Although we know that a rose by any other name would smell as sweet, there is, nonetheless, a great deal conveyed by and implied in names. At first, Rogers called his method a 'less directive approach' (Rogers, 1942). The book he wrote in 1942 is still a very interesting and relevant one. In it, for instance, we find that the first characteristic of a therapeutic relationship is 'a warmth and responsiveness on the part of the counsellor which makes rapport possible, and which gradually develops into a deeper emotional relationship' (p. 87). Rogers was, in a way, trying to steer a middle path between the extremes of 'over-involvement' and 'professional distance'. He did not want the therapist to be an authority figure. This stance was radical in its time. All language is vulnerable to the effects of over-use, however. There is a danger sometimes that non-directiveness now becomes a dogma which immobilizes us. I have heard many students agonize over whether any attempt at all to reach out to the client constituted 'direction'. This is a dilemma which particularly afflicts those who wish to offer creative or expressive methods as part of therapy, but it hampers us all sometimes. There is a danger in over-doing this concern as well as in neglecting it. If Rogers himself did not intend to influence people, he would never have written so many books and papers.

Non-directiveness certainly does not mean and, was never intended by Rogers to mean, that one should refrain from reaching out to another person in distress or from offering something which one has which would be of use to somebody else. For there to arise a consensus within a person-centred group, that it is good form to attack anyone who tries to help somebody else, (Hawkins 1993) is a complete contradiction.

Rogers became aware of some of the drawbacks of the term 'non-directive' and went on to call his method 'client-centred' (1951). This certainly put the emphasis upon concern for the other person. Client-Centred Therapy is obviously a thoroughly altruistic activity. The asymmetry of the relationship which it suggests, however, does give rise to some theoretical difficulties. I have written about some of these elsewhere (Brazier 1993). Rogers certainly asks a lot of the therapist and this is no bad thing. He asks, for instance, 'is the therapist willing to give the client full freedom as to outcomes? . . . Is he willing for him to choose goals which are social or antisocial, moral or immoral?' and asserts 'If not., it seems doubtful that therapy will be a profound experience for the client' (Rogers, 1951, p. 48).

The problem here, is that Rogers is prescribing highly moral and social attitudes for the therapist at the same time as saying that the client should have complete freedom. This is not self-contradictory so long as client and therapist remain separate categories of people. On many of our training courses, however, the student finds him or herself in both roles simultaneously. Students may have come on the course because of a sense of needing the freedom rather than because of a commitment to the discipline involved in providing it. If self-actualization can involve experimentation with anti-social activities and if becoming a therapist means conforming to a highly socialized (and nowadays increasingly regulated) role, considerable inner tension may arise. A person who really follows their self-actualizing tendency may learn a great deal about him or herself and about others as a result of getting into escapades for which their professional colleagues may be unwilling to forgive them.

Rogers reconciled this contradiction by his faith in the self-actualizing tendency. As Irene Fairhurst (1993) points out 'An acceptance of the Actualising Tendency is central to person-centred personality theory' (p.25). Again, however, there is less than complete clarity what is meant by the actualizing tendency. Is a tendency the same as an instinct, for instance? Presumably not. Fairhurst expresses a common view in saying that belief in the actualizing tendency 'offers an optimistic alternative to Freud's death instinct, and notions of the "savage beast"' (p.25). However, if a tendency is not an instinct, there may be less of a gap between Rogers and Freud than is commonly assumed since the latter writes:

> There is unquestionably no universal instinct towards higher development observable in the animal or plant world, *even though it is undeniable that development does in fact occur in that direction* (Freud 1920, p. 314, my italics).

The actualizing tendency may allow us to believe that the social and caring aspect of people will come to the fore eventually, even if life takes a variety of twists and turns along the way. Rogers often talks about the 'fully functioning person' and thereby reveals his own idea of where the actualizing tendency leads. Rogers is saying that if people are given complete acceptance they naturally tend toward such a condition. Does this not boil down to saying that if we give caring to others, they will become caring themselves?

Since these principles could be extended to life well beyond the consulting room, Rogers subsequently adopted a further change of name for his philosophy, calling it the Person-Centred Approach. Person-centred does not have the same asymmetrical implications as client-centred. In a group, I may relate to you in the same way as you relate to me. We may care for each other. We may even find that 'at a deeper level' between us 'there is a fundamental connectedness' (Bryant-Jefferies 1993, p. 23). This last assertion does seem to go beyond Carl Rogers.

A person-centred theory is rooted in notions of what it means to be a person. The term person-centred, sounds thoroughly humanistic and while individualistic humanism may have seemed self-evident to many in Rogers' day, the notion that what is human should always come first has taken quite a bit of criticism from the ecological perspective in recent years. Are we to actualize ourselves as individuals or as parts of something greater than ourselves? The spiritual implications of this question may be unsettling for many who have been at home in the person-centred approach for a long time, but they were not entirely alien to Rogers himself, who conceptualized the self-actualizing tendency as simply a special case of a greater 'formative tendency at work in the universe' (Rogers 1980, p. 124).

Related to this point is the question of what we mean by self or person. I do not wish to get involved in complicated discussion at this point but there is ample evidence that the western individualistic notion of what constitutes a person is not shared by many other cultures (Holdstock, 1993) and if we were to reconsider what 'becoming a person' (Rogers, 1961) meant, this would recast much of our thinking about what therapy means.

Directions

The paradox is, that Carl Rogers was so liberal and open to new ideas and often expressed the wish that we should all become creative and innovative, and yet we now find ourselves in considerable difficulty in imagining how to go on beyond him.

There has been some tendency in the PCA to move on from, rather than resolve, issues. The question of what is really meant by non-directiveness is still not entirely clear and remains a minefield for beginning practitioners. Then the question of how overtly congruent to be, when one is being client-centred, is a question about which there is a wide variety of opinions. Again, the question of what is really meant by a self-actualizing tendency has never been pinned down sufficiently for one to be able to say whether it really does coincide with or contradict the views of other theorists or for one to put it to the test of research. Changing the name of the approach has been an important device for getting across an important message at a gut level. It has not, however, really resolved the problems of definition which still beset us. In fact it has probably compounded them.

The question of the meaning of the actualizing tendency is clearly crucial. In practice, it remains an article of faith. Perhaps this is as it should be, but, if so, we might then have to face up to the idea that the PCA is a faith, not a science, and this would sit very uncomfortably with many. Should all person-centred graduates sign a declaration: 'I believe in the actualizing tendency'? We get into considerable confusion by denying that we have a creed of dogmas when, in fact, we do. On the other hand, there are a good many who are attracted to the PCA for the very reason that it does seem to offer the possibility of encompassing many of the elements of a spiritual path without the necessity of commitment to a traditional faith. Whether this is trying to have one's cake and eat it, however, remains arguable. The fact remains that one way beyond Carl Rogers lies in the direction of some kind of spiritual understanding and commitment and there is some evidence that Rogers himself was heading in this direction.

Another path beyond Rogers has been opened up by the people interested in 'focusing' (Gendlin, 1981), and, to some degree, those involved in expressive therapy and multimedia work. They have attempted to see a way ahead by concentrating upon what the client needs to do rather than upon what the therapist should attempt. This, however, leads them immediately into conflict with those who hold the nondirective principle supreme since it takes us directly into teaching the client what to do. We do now have people who call themselves 'focusing teachers'. On the other hand, do we not teach students what to do, and do Rogers' books not also tell us what to do? As in many debates within the PCA the dilemma becomes: are we prescribing one thing for therapists and something completely different for clients? Such asymmetry would not bother many approaches in which clients are done-to by professionals and the two castes never meet, but we are not like that, are we?

Another attempt to find a way ahead lies in the contribution from cross-cultural studies. Looking at what other cultures mean by some of our basic terms may yet force us into a fundamental reevaluation of what we are doing and dislodge us from the western, protestant, individualistic framework within which Rogers grew up.

Then there are attempts to find a way ahead by looking into the theory and philosophy which underlies Rogers' ideas — theories about experiencing and phenomenology, or, alternatively, theories about systems and information processing. Each adds something important to our comprehension.

A personal resolution

Although what Rogers wrote looks like science, what really matters about it to me is the spirit which he tried, in different language, at different times, to convey. I do not think that Rogers' message changed much over the period of his career. Only the words he used changed. What we have to do is somehow to appreciate the essence that these various words tried to convey. If we can do this we will be able to go on beyond Rogers safely because we will be able to go on expressing the heart of the matter in many different tongues but still be saying what is important

This spirit, as I understand it, had much to do with caring for each other and creating conditions for each other in which we all can grow to our fullest potential. And if we are to avoid hopeless self-contradiction, 'potential' in this sentence is going to have to mean 'potential to care about each other'. It cannot be that the approach is concerned with caring for others only in order that they start to care about themselves because this would lead to its early extinction. We need a way beyond Carl Rogers which can liberate the essential message from the language of an individualistic culture.

We have to find a way to reconcile the prescription for the therapist with the prescription for the client. To say that there is no such prescription, that it is all non-directive, is just to dodge the issue. I think we certainly need somehow to clarify the message sufficiently that people no longer think that it is good person-centred practice to attack people for caring about or 'rescuing' others, though there is also no doubt that there is a great deal for us all to learn about how best to care.

We need to find an interpretation of the actualizing tendency which does not seem to imply 'everyone for themselves' and which recognizes the interconnection between people and the personal satisfaction that comes from loving as well as from being loved.

References

Brazier D.J. (1993) The necessary condition is love: Going beyond self in the person-centred approach. In D.J. Brazier (Ed.) *Beyond Carl Rogers.* London: Constable.

Bryant-Jefferies R. (1993) A personal exploration of person-centredness. *Person Centred Practice.* 1,(1), pp. 19–24.

Fairhurst I. (1993) Rigid, or pure? *Person Centred Practice.* 1,(1), pp. 25–30.

Freud S. (1920) Beyond the pleasure principle. In *Penguin Freud Library volume 11.* London: Penguin, pp. 269–338.

Gendlin, E. (1981) *Focusing.* New York: Bantam Books. Revised Edition.

Hawkins J. (1993) Person-centred or self-centred? *Person Centred Practice.* (1), (1), pp.12–18.

Holdstock L. (1993) Can we afford not to revision the person-centred conception of self? In D.J. Brazier (Ed.) *Beyond Carl Rogers.* London: Constable.

Rogers C.R. (1942) *Counselling and Psychotherapy.* London: Constable.

Rogers C.R. (1951) *Client-centred Therapy.* London: Constable.

Rogers C.R. (1961) *On Becoming a Person.* London: Constable.

Rogers C.R. (1980) *A Way of Being.* Boston: Houghton Mifflin.

The Therapeutic Clinical Interview — Guidelines for Beginning Practice

Barbara Temaner Brodley

Clinical interviews can be distinguished into two general types — the therapeutic clinical interview and the diagnostic/assessment clinical interview. The guidelines that follow are an introduction to the practice of the therapeutic interview for the beginning clinical student. They are based on client-centered psychotherapy theory (Rogers, 1957; 1959; 1986a) and emphasize an empathic and non-directive way of conducting a therapeutic interview.

The empathic understanding interview is applied in the context of many contemporary therapeutic theoretical orientations. It is fundamental to client-centered work, but it is an essential process in Kohut's psychodynamic approach (Kohut, 1959; 1981) and it is an important aspect of psychoanalytic therapies (Josephs, 1988) as well as gestalt, cognitive, behavioral, hypnotherapy, relationship, and other, therapies.

Psychotherapy is an art enlightened by wisdom, theory and research. As a practiced art, it cannot be done by consciously following rules. For effective practice most, if not all, therapeutic approaches require the therapist to have incorporated, or assimilated, their relevant philosophy of humankind and their conception of how and why therapeutic personality change occurs. The attitudes and inexplicit, or non-conscious, mental activities of experienced therapists are more frequently involved in determining their responses than their explicit, conscious cognitive activity. The beginning clinician must, however, <u>behave</u> with clients as much as possible as an experienced therapist, long before having had the hours and the years of practice required to become experienced and 'intuitive'. Guidelines are intended as a means to help students enter into atherapeutic clinical interviews before they have committed themselves to any particular therapeutic approach and before development of the chosen theory's mental set and attitudes.

The Situation

The student will either (a) be taking turns as therapist and client with another student or (b) will have enlisted a volunteer from among acquaintances to function as a practice-client. A time frame for the interview should be established of, at

---

First published in *Person-Centred Practice,* Volume 1, Number 2, 1993.

least, one half-hour in length to as much as one hour. The setting should be private and comfortable and free from interruptions.

After each interview, clients should be asked for their feelings and reactions to the interview and in the case of co-counselors it is desirable for both persons to discuss their reactions to the interview.

Practice interviews should be tape-recorded, so they may be reviewed. Counsellors should make sure that clients have given their permission (in writing if possible) for tapes and transcripts to be used in supervision.

Counsellors, when functioning as clients and practice clients, should be asked to talk about a personal concern, about something that has recently been upsetting or worrisome or a source of anxiety or other feelings. The client may be given a simple initial instruction such as the following: 'Tell me anything that is of concern, or bothering you, these days.' The practice-therapist might also say: 'You can start anywhere you choose. I am going to be trying to understand what you tell me as best as I can.' The therapist might want to add: 'If any questions occur to you to ask me during our interview, would you try to postpone asking them until we have finished the interview?' If the therapist does not choose to defer questions, then answer them directly and honestly during the interview and follow the answer with a question to the client such as: 'What is your reaction to what I said?' In beginning practice it is best to defer questions and this approach is recommended.

Practice interviews are confidential except for consultation and transcription that disguises identities.

The Procedure
The procedure of the empathic therapeutic interview requires the student to inhibit, or put aside, any and all assumptions concerning their clients, and to attend to them as unique individuals with their own particular manner of expression, manner of relating interpersonally and their own personal situations, stories and concerns. A manner of respect and courtesy towards the client is fundamental to the procedure.

The therapist listens attentively to the client and *attempts to understand*, maintaining an acceptant attitude towards whatever the client is describing, explaining or expressing. The therapist *attempts to understand*, specifically, whatever the client is attempting to communicate, *from the client's internal frame of reference*, or perspective. The therapist, thus, is attempting empathically to understand the client in the immediate moments of the interaction.

Empathic understanding is a subjective experience, not an overt behavior. Empathic understanding is a sense, or feeling, of understanding that develops in the mind and feelings of the therapist. It is an experience of taking into oneself the ideas, meanings and feelings that clients have been expressing as their own in the immediate moments of the interaction.

This kind of understanding necessarily involves a therapist's mental processes that are associative, interpretive and emotive. There is no grasp of meanings or experiences of one person by another person without such processes. Nevertheless, in empathic understanding, the therapist is striving to achieve representation in her own mind, feelings and experience — into the therapist's own subjective verbal symbol system — an accurate grasp of whatever the client is expressing in the interaction. The therapist's subjective understandings should be as free as possible from her/his own assumptions, beliefs and evaluative attitudes.

Empathic understanding is fundamentally a subjective experience on the part of the therapist. However, the only way in which the accuracy of such understanding of the client can be verified is by its coherent communication to the client. Thus, in the therapeutic interaction, it is necessary, from time to time, for the therapists to speak, to verbalize, and expressively communicate, what they have immediately understood from the client. This permits the client an opportunity to verify its accuracy or correct it (Rogers, 1986b). The client is the only expert about what it is she was attempting to communicate in the immediate moments or minutes before the therapist speaks to check her subjective empathic understandings.

In addition to the quality of acceptance and the checking to determine the accuracy of empathic understanding, another crucial feature is the neutrality of the therapist in respect to the realities, values, feelings and attitudes that are expressed by the client. The over-all impact of the therapist's communicated empathic understandings is usually experienced by clients as supportive of them. Nevertheless, empathic understandings and the responses that express those understandings are always neutral in respect to the frame of reference of the therapist. The evaluative neutrality of responses in an empathic and non-directive interview is intrinsic to this type of therapeutic interview. The therapist tries acceptantly, non-critically and non-judgmentally to understand the point of view, and specific feelings and meanings expressed by the client. A therapist's response is not a true empathic understanding response if it conveys or signals an evaluative stance of the therapist, regardless of whether the evaluative stance is positive or negative.

The most general point about the empathic therapeutic clinical interview that the student needs to keep in mind is that it is a form of *following*. Both the concept and the practice of empathically understanding a client's internal frame of reference, as well as communicating specific understandings, is a form of *following* the client. True empathic understanding, however, *is not a technique* of restating or mirroring the client's intended communications and is almost never experienced as a technique by clients. Instead, it is perceived as *being understood*, as having one's personal meanings grasped by the other person. This usually feels like an authentic interaction wherein the listener has genuinely paid attention and tried to understand. And it feels good to clients and stimulates further exploration and disclosure.

Empathic understanding is a form of following the client and does not involve trying to get ahead of the client. Occasionally, however, when a therapist has been closely attuned to a client, and closely following the client's expression, the client may experience the therapist's empathic response as accurate to the client's inner experience, but also as a new idea or new realization. This occurrence of seeming to be somewhat ahead of the client, is a therapeutic and valued experience, but it is not something for the therapist to *try* to achieve. It arises out of the understanding and trusting relationship created by the means of the therapist closely, respectfully and accurately following the client.

In summary, the therapist feels empathic understanding as she follows the client's narrative. This empathic understanding is a subjective experience on the therapist's part. From time to time, the therapist feels the need to articulate empathic understanding responses (based on subjectively felt understandings) in order to find out from the client whether or not those understandings are accurate or in need of correction. The empathic understanding responses are usually articulated in the form of statements that imply the question, 'Am I understanding you?' Their tentativeness is communicated by intonation and by the therapist's acceptance of corrections. Empathic understanding responses are always offered for the client to confirm, reject or qualify (Rogers, 1986b).

Most of the guidelines that follow indicate what the therapist student should avoid or *not* do. If all the 'do nots' are adhered to, and the students' efforts have been focused upon empathically understanding as well as they are able, it is quite possible that the process that ensues will be productive for the client. It may result in the client's increased emotional openness and willingness to disclose further. It may show a development in the client's themes of concerns, and some movement towards new self-understanding. It may result in more positive feelings as well as other signs of therapeutic change.

The Guidelines

When you are attending and listening to your client, try to do the following:

1. Absorb the meanings which the client is expressing to you. What is the client succeeding at 'getting at', or what is s/he trying to 'get at'?

2. When you express your tentative understanding, think of yourself as trying to check whether or not you have, in fact, understood. You may express this tentativeness simply by your intonation, or you might preface your empathic response with an introductory statement that communicates your tentativeness and your interest in the client's assessment of the accuracy of your understanding. Examples of such introductory statements are: 'Is this right?' or 'Are you saying . . . ?' or 'Is this a correct understanding right now?' or 'I think I understand. Is this what you mean?' You might use a declarative form of introduction to your empathic response, although it should be in a tentative spirit, such as 'You are feeling . . .', 'You want to . . .', or 'You are telling me that . . .'

3. Avoid introductions to your empathic responses which suggest you are trying to interpret the client or that your task is to discover or elicit 'deeper' meanings buried in what the client is expressing. Introductions which sometimes create such misunderstanding are 'I sense you are really feeling . . .'; 'I sense you are feeling . . .', or 'You sound like you . . .'. Try to avoid these introductions to your empathic responses.

4. While making responses which are intended to express the client's point of view, frame of reference, perspective, perceptions and feelings, *stay completely*

within the client's frame of reference. As you are listening, try to grasp the client's viewpoint together with the meanings and feelings that are the client's at that time. Try to absorb those things into yourself — without the reservations and interferences of skepticism or criticism — in order to reach a feeling of understanding. Put aside any doubts or critical feelings about the client's statements and *try to understand the client's point of view and feelings.*

5. If you don't understand what the client has been expressing to you — perhaps your thoughts were distracting you, or perhaps the client's communication was eluding you at the time — simply say you haven't understood yet, and then ask the client to repeat or state in a different way what was being expressed.

6. After you make an empathic understanding response, allow your client to initiate the next response. Allow silence. Relax and give yourself and your client a chance to think and feel further — to reflect upon the experiences that are being expressed between you.

7. Do not ask leading or probing questions. Examples of typical leading or probing questions are: 'How do you feel about that?'; 'Tell me more about . . . '; 'What do you think he would feel about that?'; 'Can you tell me more about your relationship to . . . ?'

8. Do not ask your client questions that involve assumptions or theories that are not part of those directly expressed or clearly implied in what your client has been saying. Examples of such interpretive-probing questions are: 'Do you find yourself waking up early and not being able to go back to sleep?' 'Do you remember how you felt about things when your brother was born?' 'How do you feel when someone has authority over you?' etc. Of course, many empathic understanding responses may be literally in the form of a question because you are wanting to find out if your subjective empathic understanding is correct or not. And sometimes you will find you need to ask a question for simple factual clarification. For example, 'Did you say that was your sister or your cousin?' or 'Did you say you got home late or that he got home late?' or 'Did you mean "now" in the sense of "these days" or in the sense of "right now" here with me?' These types of questions are called 'questions for clarification' and are a form of empathic following.

9. Do not volunteer interpretations of any kind.

10. Do not volunteer comments upon what the client has expressed.

11. Do not volunteer agreement with what the client is saying.

12. Do not abstract feelings or emotions from the content or situation that the client is expressing, unless the client's point is the feelings or emotions.

13. Do not volunteer suggestions or guidance of any kind.

14. Do not volunteer praise or criticism of the client or of the client's behavior.

15. Do not turn a specific statement into a generality or a generality into a specific — unless that is what the client seems to be intending that you understand.

16. If your client indicates feeling 'stopped' and doesn't know how to proceed and asks for your help, a relatively non-directive response that is often helpful is

to say something such as 'Sometimes, if one gives oneself a bit more time, some thoughts or direction will come to mind.' Or 'I feel there's no hurry, so if you can, try to let yourself relax to give yourself a chance to see if something comes to you.'

17. If your clients say they don't have anything more to say about a topic and don't know what to do now (and you have already tried the approach above), and they ask for more help — then you may suggest they give themselves time to consider if there is some other topic they feel concern or worry about. Or say 'Sometimes it helps to think back over the concerns that brought you in.' We do not intend to avoid giving guidance or help in proceeding in the interaction when the client requests it, but the best guidance is usually the encouragement to take time and search the client's own experience and thoughts.

18. If clients lose their train of thought or forget what they were saying, do not prompt or remind them — unless they ask for help. Scattered thoughts and discontinuity of theme should be accepted in the same manner as developed and coherent thought.

19. Do not integrate for the client, e.g., 'That sounds like it may be related to the problem you have with your mother.' Empathic interviews often result in integrations, but it is not the therapist's responsibility to find or direct such connections.

20. Do not volunteer comments about the client's apparent feelings, state or other experiences, e.g., 'You seem to have a lot of emotions about that topic,' or 'It seems you have an issue with abandonment or loss,' or 'You are feeling pretty angry at me right now.' Of course, these examples may be similar to empathic responses, if the client has been expressing any of these ideas.

21. If your client asks you a question, (a) give yourself a chance to absorb the question, (b) ask for further clarification of the question if you need it, (c) respond to the question in a direct, person-to-person manner. This can mean different things, depending upon the nature of the question, your own knowledge and expertise in the arena being inquired about, your own personal feelings about self-disclosure and your personal feelings about expressing opinions. In any case, to respond to a question in a direct, person-to-person manner means one does not avoid the question or treat the client as the issue for asking a question. Depending on factors such as those mentioned above, you may literally answer the question, you may say you don't know the answer to that question, you may say you don't feel comfortable revealing such personal things, or you may say something that is a general answer to the question but also demur because you do not know the general answer applies in the present situation. After responding in some direct way to the client's question, you may want to check the client's satisfaction or dissatisfaction with your response. It is also possible to respond to questions directly and, in addition, express an empathic response with respect to the feelings, concerns or perspectives that seemed to have sparked the question. Responding to the

feelings behind a question, however, should not be a means of avoiding the question.

In general, try to remember that the therapist's interest is in the client as a whole person. The whole person is primarily represented in the therapy relationship by the client expressing a personal point of view, personal meanings and reactions to things. Respect for and trust in clients is communicated by the therapist's interest in the clients' representations of their inner world and inner perspective and reactions to their world. Speaking to check the accuracy of empathic understandings is the therapist's basic medium for communication of empathy and acceptance towards the client. Empathic following responses, embodying the therapeutic *attitudes* of empathy and acceptance, stimulate constructive processes in the client.

References

Josephs, L. (1988) *A comparison of archeological and empathic modes of listening.* Contemporary Psychoanalysis, 24, pp. 282–300.

Kohut, H. (1959) I*ntrospection, empathy and psychoanalysis.* Journal of the American Psychoanalytic Association, 7, pp. 459–83.

Kohut, H. (Producer) (1981, October 4) *Remarks on empathy (film).* Filmed at Conference on Self Psychology, Los Angeles.

Rogers, C. R. (1957) *The necessary and sufficient conditions of therapeutic personality change.* Journal of Consulting Psychology, 21, pp. 95–103.

Rogers, C. R. (1959) *A theory of therapy, personality and interpersonal relationships as developed on the client-centered framework.* In S. Koch (Ed.), Psychology: A study of a Science. Vol. III. Formulations of the Person in the Social Context. New York: McGraw Hill.

Rogers, C. R. (1986a) *Client-centered therapy.* In I.L. Kutash and A. Wolf (Eds.), Psychotherapist's Casebook, San Francisco: Jossey Bass, pp. 197–208.

Rogers, C. R. (1986b) *Reflections of feelings.* Person-Centered Review, 1, pp. 375–7.

Guidelines for Student Participants in Person-Centred Peer Groups

Barbara Temaner Brodley and Tony Merry

Person-centred peer groups are group-structured and group-directed, and function without formal facilitators or leaders. They meet to develop the participants' understandings of person-centred psychology and to develop capabilities for implementing person-centred theory in individual, couple, family and group therapy situations.

Student peer groups are created primarily for students to explore person-centred psychology and practice, but they also function to foster the personal development of participants, to serve individual and group-determined goals and, at times, may function to provide individual therapeutic experiences. The aim of all person-centred groups is to create the facilitative climate of Rogers' therapeutic attitudes (Rogers, 1957) in the group. The therapeutic climate promotes individual and group goals by facilitating constructive relationships among participants and open sharing of experiences and ideas so they can learn from each other.

Person-centred peer groups involve all the participants in the attempt to create an optimal interpersonal and psychological climate, based on Rogers' therapeutic attitudes, within the group. Participants experience this optimal climate as one of freedom and safety.

Freedom and psychological safety in a group setting, conceived and brought about by means of person-centred attitudes, are necessarily qualified or approximated freedom and safety. This is so because the pursuit of individual freedom cannot ethically involve an 'attempt to deprive others of theirs' (Mill, 1859). In person-centred groups, freedom is further qualified by the pursuit of psychological safety for all participants. In order for such a climate to be perceived and experienced by participants in the group, each participant's freedom must ideally be expressed without producing threat, hurt or insult in the experience of the others. Regardless of the care taken by participants, it is very unlikely, if not impossible, to prevent all experiences of threat, hurt or insult.

Consequently, absolute freedom and safety are not realistic expectations for person-centred groups. When a participant is speaking (or whatever way his or her behaviour is in the foreground of the group), he or she may be being very mindful of the feelings of others in the group and be behaving self-expressively within limits dictated by that mindfulness. Nevertheless, mistakes, misjudgements,

First published in *Person-Centred Practice*, Volume 3, Number 2, 1995.

insufficient information about others, and insufficient *art* in combining self-representation with mindfulness of and consideration for the feelings of others inevitably result in experiences of threat, hurt or insult among persons in the group from time to time.

The person-centred group is necessarily a *process of attempts* to contribute to a climate of freedom and safety for all participants. Because of the natural imperfection of a group situation, corrective processes employed by participants contribute towards the experience of an optimal climate. Corrective processes (which include apology, and rephrasing a statement better to represent a respectful and considerate attitude, etc.) can bridge the discrepancy between absolute safety and the flawed situation by correcting for specific injuries and misunderstandings and by showing that people are intending to respect and express care for each other even when failing to succeed in that intention.

The primary values of person-centredness — respect for persons and trust in their capability to be self-directed, self-regulating and constructive — are maintained as attitudes and reflected in participants' behaviours as consistently as possible. These primary values function as guiding and shaping attitudes for each participant in the group. The values, transformed into *attitudes* of respect and trust, inform and shape the implementation of the person-centred attitudes of congruence, unconditional positive regard and empathic understanding among the persons in the group both when they are self-representing and when they are assisting the group or particular individuals in the group.

The Guidelines
These guidelines introduce the concept of 'courtesy' as a practical and guiding idea that may help participants maintain the attitudes of respect and trust, along with the therapeutic attitudes, while in the group. 'Courtesy' is a familiar concept in our culture and it has commonly understood behavioural associations and implications. Definitions and synonyms for 'courtesy' and 'courteous' include, 'considerate of others . . . attentive . . . respectful . . . politeness connected with kindness . . . civility' (Webster, 1979, p. 420). The English-speaking concept of 'courtesy' is very close in meaning to the person-centred values of respect and trust, but courtesy also suggests familiar forms of behaviour that express consideration and respect. Commonly understood behavioural associations to the idea of courtesy may give some immediate, in-the-moment guidance when self-representing and when assisting in the group. The thought, 'I am trying to act courteously', or, 'I want to act courteously' may help people choose their words in ways that have a likelihood of resulting in perceptions and experiences of psychological safety in the group.

The guidelines that follow do not cover all types of behaviour that may occur in peer groups, but are meant to serve as examples of behaviour that are likely to promote freedom and safety. The guidelines will be presented under three categories — (1) general guidelines, (2) guidelines for self-representation and pursuit of personal goals including self-disclosures, expression of wants and desires, self-reflective and therapeutic process, emotional expression, reactions to and observations about other persons in the group, expression of ideas, etc., and (3) guidelines for assisting in the group, including interactions to assist exploration of conflicts and misunderstandings among other participants, acts of acknowledgement or invitation towards others, assisting in the sharing of time during sessions, time-keeping, etc.

(1) General Guidelines
1. Allow silences and try to relax and reflect inwardly during periods of silence.
2. When you speak, take time to centre yourself, and take your time as you speak to help yourself remain centred.
3. If you begin to feel that your remarks are taking too long, stop and ask the group if they are still willing to listen.
4. Ask for responses if you particularly want them, and make clear whether you want validation of being understood or you want reactions from the frame of reference of other participants.
5. If you make a mistake, or you realise you have misunderstood, or you lose control, you can, when the opportunity presents itself, make corrections.

(2) Guidelines for self-representation and pursuit of personal goals
1. When you start, give the group an idea of what kind of thing you are going to say (offer a suggestion, ask for something, express an idea or point of view, tell something of a very personal or emotional nature, etc.).
2. Ask the group if they are willing to attend to the kind of thing you are going to be saying at that time.
3. If you want to express thoughts or feelings to another person, ask for consent before you begin.
4. If your remarks are a reaction to something the other person has said or done, before stating your reactions, describe the behaviour or summarise what has been said. Then ask if you have observed or understood accurately. Be open to corrections.
5. If your remarks are reactions to another person, be careful to discriminate your feelings and emotions in reaction to that person, from your observations and interpretations. Make your observations and interpretations explicit as *interpreted* by you. Avoid accusational language. Avoid blaming language. If your reactions are complex, go slowly through your separate points and ask if you are being understood. When finished, ask for the kind of responses you want and from whom you want them.
6. When self-revealing or self-disclosing, pause from time to time to give others who may need to check their understandings an opportunity to do so. When you have completed your disclosures, let the group know what kinds of responses you particularly want and from whom.
7. Make empathic responses to find out if you have accurately understood other persons when you are *quite unsure* of understanding.

(3) Guidelines for assisting in the group

1. Keep the therapeutic attitudes in mind as you listen to and respond to other participants.
2. Attempt to clarify when the interaction between others seems to involve misunderstandings. For example, you may say you have the impression that there is some misunderstanding, or request restatements, or may ask the interacting persons whether or not they feel understood by each other, or may ask the others in the group if they feel the communication has been understood, or may summarise the misunderstanding as you perceive it.
3. Attempt to find out if the focus of the group is satisfactory to participants.
4. Attempt to support participants' desires to speak in the group. For example, ask if there is someone who has so far in the session not spoken who wants to do so, or ask a specific person, or comment that a specific person had earlier started to speak but may not have finished, or if someone is interrupted, when possible, ask if they had finished.
5. Assist in the timekeeping and sharing of time in the group. For example, ask if there is anything any participant wants to be sure to talk about during the present session, or remind the group that a participant had stated a wish to talk about something but has not done so, or remind the group of the amount of time left before the end of the session.
6. Try to respond to requests from others. Seek clarification for yourself from the person making the request if it is not clear to you.
7. Try to contribute your point of view if someone is seeking group consensus about matters of group structure or group goals.
8. Try to remain aware of people in the group who come from a different culture or background from yourself. Different people have different experiences and expectations of groups, and behaviour within groups; misunderstandings can sometimes occur because of this. If you think this may be happening, you can check it out and clarify it with the person or people involved.

Although these guidelines do not cover all possible group situations or ways to participate, we hope they convey our intention to provide some guidance, especially to people new to person-centred philosophy and theory, that might help them to participate in peer groups in ways that promote freedom of expression while attempting to promote psychological safety and trust in the group. We hope it is understood that the guidelines are not intended to be treated as demands or rules. They should be open to challenge and change and additions. *Courtesy* and *responsiveness*, within your own limits, are being suggested as ideas that may contribute to your participation in the group in ways that may bring about good interpersonal and psychological conditions for you and your group. It is a hypothesis to be tested.

References

Baldwin, M. (1987) Interview with Carl Rogers on the use of the self in therapy. In *The Use of The Self*, M. Baldwin and V. Satir (Eds). New York: Haworth Press, pp. 45–52.

Mill, G.H. (1859). On Liberty. In M. Lerner (Ed) (1961), *Essential Works of John Stuart Mill*, New York: Bantam Books.

Rogers, C.R. (1957) The necessary and sufficient conditions of therapeutic personality change. *Journal of Consulting Psychology*, 21, (2), 95–103.

Rogers, C.R. (1959) A theory of therapy, personality and interpersonal relationships as developed in the client-centered framework. In *Psychology: A Study of a Science, Vol 3, Formulations of the Person and the Social Context*, S. Koch (Ed), New York: McGraw Hill, pp. 184–256.

Rogers, C.R. (1980). The foundations of a person-centered approach. In C.R. Rogers, *A Way of Being*, Boston: Houghton Mifflin, pp. 113–36.

Rogers, C.R. (1987) Client-centered? Person-centered? *Person Centered Review*, 2, (1), pp. 11–3.

Webster, N. (1979) *Webster's New Universal Unabridged Dictionary*. New York: Simon and Schuster.

A Person-Centred Approach? —
Working with Addictions

Mike Farrell

I am writing this article as a reflection of my own personal struggle with a question: Is there such a thing as a person-centred approach? I understand the principles of client-centred therapy and I believe I work with them within my counselling practice, but what about my other job?

I work for a small charity providing specialist help for homeless people to find and keep housing. Most of my clients have serious 'attendant' problems of one kind or another in addition to their homelessness, e.g. mental health problems, alcohol problems, drug dependencies, learning difficulties. Ironically, I have been recently redeployed as the charity is in imminent danger of financial collapse. It may be too late for any learnings from doing this to benefit those clients, but there is always the future, isn't there?

The last two and a half years of doing this work has raised a lot of questions for me. I worried less about whether what I was doing was 'person-centred', and more about whether it worked. That is still the case, but I am interested in whether each side has something to learn from the other.

As part of my work, I was attached to a day centre for homeless people aged over 25 in the Marylebone area of central London. The centre sees 50 to 70 clients a day and is designed to meet their primary needs. There is a cheap cafe, a nurse and visiting GP, a counsellor, showers, a washing machine, a day room and an advice service for help with money and temporary accommodation. Many of the clients have been regular users of the centre for a long time (up to 10 years) and many, perhaps 70per cent, are heavy drug and/or alcohol users. My role was to provide a specialist housing advice resettlement service for the clients, in particular those with alcohol problems.

The work involves close liaison with the staff to take referrals and to make contact with clients in more informal ways. I offer to work on finding appropriate housing and arrange to work with clients over a period of time to build up the necessary information and relationship to do the work.

There is a serious housing shortage in London which means that the work is usually going to take three months to a year to find housing. I also make a housing needs assessment, which means identifying the preferences of the client, making an assessment of the appropriateness of a referral and working with clients to

First Published in *Person-Centred Practice*, Volume 4, Number 1, 1996.

bring them to a position where they are ready for 'independent living'. Finding housing is only ever part of the equation. Most long-term homeless people have had some form of housing in the past which has broken down, so part of my role is to provide a safe space in which they can develop the skills and insight to manage and maintain their accommodation. Referral to another specialist agency is always an option, but only 2 out of my 54 clients from last year took up this option. It is not necessary for a client to be abstinent for them to find accommodation, but many housing providers are suspicious of drinkers/drug users, believing that they will present management problems (e.g. cause neighbour complaints) and they will not pay their rent and might deal drugs on the premises, etc. So having a dependency problem does present problems in finding housing, but it also presents problems in terms of managing accommodation.

Living on the streets or in B&B Hostels, etc. means living without bills, neighbours, decorating to be done, repairs to be done, etc. It is possible for clients to lose or fail to develop the skills needed to defer gratification and to invest now for the future, not to spend money on drink this morning but to pay the rent instead. Unfortunately, when clients are not ready or able to take these responsibilities or are not supported enough (sometimes it is all three), we have found that tenancies can break down and, following a familiar pattern, clients sometimes abandon their homes and return to the streets or the simpler life among others who are living on the edge of society. The worst possible result is that clients who have ostensibly had what they were searching for, and lose it, can end up feeling much worse than they did in the first place, having lost even the belief that finding a flat would sort out all their problems.

Clients were perceiving that they had very little agency in their situations. Some common statements were:

It's because the Councils don't care, that I'm in this position.
If they'd stop giving all the houses to Black people there'd be some left for us.
They evicted me for no reason.
Worker X did nothing for me, she offered to help but she didn't do anything.

They were also not perceiving their drinking as a problem despite the financial, social and medical difficulties they were facing, e.g. they had very little personal money, they often had experienced relationship breakdowns, couldn't get work, etc. It seemed to me outrageous that the alcohol agencies had, in effect, 'washed their hands' of these clients. The predominant attitude seems to be, 'When you're ready to give up drinking, come back and see us'. Alcoholics Anonymous has a rationalisation for this position which is that clients need to reach 'rock bottom' and may have an enlightening, possibly spiritual experience which will set them on the road to recovery. I know some people who have experienced this, but I also knew many people who have died through drug and alcohol abuse and homelessness, so 'it ain't necessarily so'.

I went back to the PCA literature and found very little to help me. I could give the work up and become a full-time counsellor, thus avoiding my advice/assessment and outreach role, or I could develop new strategies and better empathy. The former was appealing, but we know that heavy drinkers are 8 times more likely to die prematurely than normal (Fingarette, 1985), and that the life-expectancy of a homeless person may be as low as 45 (Keyes and Kennedy, 1992). For these reasons the 'laissez-faire' attitude should, I believe, be a last not first resort.

Rogers' model of the seven-stage process of counselling was useful. In discussing clients who are operating at Stage 1, at a low level of personal insight, Rogers says, '. . . [the client] . . . tends to see himself as having no problems, or the problems he recognises are perceived as entirely external to himself' (Rogers, 1961, p. 133). This certainly seemed to fit, but his conclusion that for these clients counselling may not be effective left me wondering what would be effective.

I also had another question: why were my clients drinking and using to such an extent? Again, I did not find much guidance from the person-centred literature (that I knew). In order to know what approaches might be more effective I felt I needed more clarity on what was going on. I wondered if other PCA practitioners had a coherent view on why people developed dependencies but it seemed that the prevalent view was that providing the climate of empathy, etc. was necessary and sufficient and anything else was a distraction (and possibly, heresy). It struck me that if medical science had taken this view and solely concentrated on treatments and completely ignored causes we would not have made the discovery that sterilising surgical equipment prevented infections, thus revolutionising the effectiveness of medical treatments.

If people develop strong dependencies because the substances they are using have highly addictive properties (as is the case with Benzodiazepam) then we need to be aware of this, *and we need to tell our clients if they are not.* For instance, a client who sets her own goal to go 'cold turkey' is in serious danger of inducing a possibly fatal medical reaction. If we assume (as some do, e.g. Jellinek, 1960) that some clients have a genetic predisposition to drinking being a problem, it is unlikely that the client will be able to influence their behaviour by working at a controlled drinking programme, and the only treatment goal that will be successful will be total abstinence. Do we need a theory?

Merry (1994) says, 'we cannot know in advance what . . . [the clients] . . . experiencing might contain, or what meaning it has for this person'. He argues that getting the counselling skills right is the important thing.[1] I agree, but I would argue that it is as important to understand the evidence about alcohol and drugs to be a truly effective practitioner. For the same reason it is important to have supervision actively to monitor the quality of your practice. Otherwise, why bother with supervision? Why not relax and be content with your listening as it is at the moment? If we believe, as I do, that it is possible to extend our empathic and other abilities, then I would argue that it is important to know the evidence, even if you never deliberately have to act as a 'teacher' to your client. I believe our emphasis

---

1. I have never argued this position, and certainly not in the editorial of Vol. 2, No. 2. Quite the opposite, in fact. *Ed.*

on empathy is holding the impact of the PCA back, the rest of the world beyond the counselling room need it demonstrated to them in clear terms *how* the PCA personality theory and practice can be applied in other settings effectively. For example, it seems to me that part of the power of a person-centred approach is to be clear that any goal setting must remain in the client's power. However, that does not mean that the counsellor cannot help the client clarify his goals, bringing whatever skills and experience they have to do so. It is relatively unimportant whether the counsellor has suggested a strategy for controlled drinking that others have found useful, e.g. drink as slow as the slowest person in your group, *if that is the client's goal*. The mistake a lot of alcohol agencies have made is in crossing this boundary and imposing goals on the clients, e.g. abstinence, which is partly why none of my clients are currently using alcohol services.

The evidence shows that the most effective interventions with clients with dependency problems are those which match them with a treatment approach that suits their needs (Fingarette, 1985; Velleman, 1992). My concern has been to try to throw my understanding of the PCA around the work I am trying to do with clients, and see whether it can contain elements of reaching out and to contain the experiencing my clients are bringing. I am struck mostly by the importance of the condition that two persons 'need to be in contact' (Rogers in Kirschenbaum and Henderson, 1990) and some of what I am talking about is developing that contact.

But why are they drinking so much, and why so much denial? A model first developed after researching smokers and their behaviour called the Cycle of Change (Prochaska and Di Clemente, 1983) broke down the cycle of change into four stages: **precontemplation**, when the problem is either not identified as a problem, or changing the use is not under consideration; **contemplation,** when changes are being considered; **action**, when there is an attempt to put changes into practice and **maintenance** of the changes. I immediately realised that the problem I was facing was related to working with clients in the precontemplation stage of the model — 'When drinking fulfils very important needs, when the individual believes these needs cannot be fulfilled elsewhere, the drinking will come to be seen as the solution, not the problem' (Tobler, 1991).

Learnings from the drug-counselling field on harm minimisation techniques seem to be proving more effective with working with precontemplators. (Incidentally, it is interesting to consider why drug counsellors seem more likely to have an acceptant attitude to illegal drug use, than alcohol counsellors have to legal drug use.) Research indicates that providing information to clients can be a very effective intervention, almost as effective as any other form of treatment (Fingarette, 1985). So I will provide clients with information on being healthy. For example, heavy drinking causes vitamin deficiency (particularly Vitamin B) and vitamin supplements can help prevent more extensive organ damage, if clients want to continue drinking. I will also offer to help clarify the nature and extent of 'the problem' with a client as this is an area in which there is often poor information. For example, one client mentioned that he drank a few cans a day, but as he was drinking a premium strength lager this constituted 21 units a day (approx. 100

units a week); his daily intake represents the recommended weekly maximum for men and drinking at this level is likely to cause a wide range of critical medical problems (see Royal College of Psychiatrists, 1986). He knew it was bad, but didn't realise how bad.

The second strand was to clarify the *why* of addiction. Alice Miller says, 'The causes of addiction . . . always lay hidden in childhood' (Miller, 1987, p. 18). I was struck by this idea. Certainly it is my experience that many clients transfer their dependency from one substance, e.g. heroin, to another, e.g. alcohol. Also, the nature of dependency is that it is of a driven nature which often seems preconscious in intent. I have formed a view unsubstantiated by scientific evidence that many of my clients are in a state of trauma as a result of their life experiences; that they are self-medicating with drugs and alcohol to keep their distressing feelings at bay and as such there is a tremendous investment in maintaining this way of being. One client recalls being sent to bed alone in a house without lighting from as young as he can remember, aged five or younger. He recalls being frozen rigid with fear in bed throughout his childhood but his fear was unacceptable to his parents. Their condition of worth (or the precondition under which they would continue to love him) was that they would only accept him if he didn't feel fear. As a consequence he began at the earliest of ages to label his feelings of fear as 'stupid'. Many other things happened to reinforce this view throughout his childhood. Not surprisingly he now feels, even at the age of 49, that his feelings of sadness or fear are 'wrong' or 'stupid'. An 'incongruence between self and experience' has arisen (Rogers, 1959, p. 247). But not being able to have his feelings exacts a toll, according to Alice Miller, 'Depression and inner emptiness are the price they must pay for their control' (1987, p. 45). By self-medicating we have an alternative to going to therapy, 'We bury that out-of-sorts feeling with the artificial energy of our addiction . . . [but] . . . it is still gnawing at us' (Lee, 1993, p. 31). In this client's case his self-medicating means he is drinking an average of 140 units a week.

Addictions such as: alcohol, exercise, child abuse, drugs, vandalism, cigarettes, food, sexual exploitation of others, dieting, work, TV, caffeine, masturbation, sex, criminal behaviour, sleep, pornography, compulsive thoughts and suicidal thoughts, can all be used to block pain sensations. Similar arguments can be, and often are made against the use of prescribed psychotherapeutic drugs, but that is another article. Physiologically, the kinds of activities listed above can trigger hormones which act as keys to block receptor sites in the brain (Boddy, 1981, p. 408) from pain messages. For example, Morphine (heroin) is used in palliative cancer treatment usually for terminal cases. The Morphine does not stop the pain messages which are being triggered from the action of carcinogenic cells, it simply stops the brain from registering the pain. The addict is self-medicating in exactly the same way to block out pain even though the pain arises as a result of stored-up trauma which can be re-experienced by the body in a very similar way to pain resulting from external causes. An example of this phenomenon which is gaining wider acceptance is the effects of post-traumatic stress disorder (Scott and Stradling, 1992).

Another related reason for the use of substances, etc. is the search for 'highs'. 'People who as children successfully repressed their intense feelings often try to regain at least for a short time their lost intensity of experience with the help of drugs and alcohol' (Miller, 1987, p. 98).

The artificial 'high' then is used to escape from actual feelings to a realm of artificially induced feelings which cannot be sustained (because the drug wears off) and which cannot be genuine (because physiologically the act of taking the drug has blocked the actual bodily feelings). This is why there is such a consensus that it is usually unproductive to work with clients either as a counsellor or other practitioner if they are currently 'under the influence'. The problem here is that whilst we can experience some of our feelings whilst we are drunk or stoned, they will not be truly conscious because we are, after all, deliberately attempting to alter our state of consciousness by using the drug. Work (such as counselling) concerned with raising our levels of consciousness is likely to have reduced effect and therapeutic value. My own view is that the more a client's state of consciousness is altered, the less productive the work is likely to be. Alcohol, for example, physiologically reduces inhibition (Royal College of Psychiatrists, 1986). Real progress, however, is being made when the therapeutic relationship is of a quality where reduction of inhibition occurs at a truly conscious level.

Finally, a word on congruence, or genuineness. Rogers (1959) argues, as one of his six conditions for a therapeutic relationship, that it is the therapist's communication of congruency within a climate of empathy and acceptance which enables the client to develop their level of insight and overcome their defensiveness in an area. This enables the client to become more congruent and therefore promotes personal growth. It seems a valid interpretation of this statement that part of the therapist's congruency may be to offer a challenging view of the client's situation, e.g. about the impact of an addiction, or to offer information that seems important. It needs to be said, however, that reduction of inhibition is unlikely to occur if the counsellor's interventions or offerings are of a judgemental or shaming nature.

It is interesting that, as this particular work seems to be drawing to a close for me, I have finally finished the article about it. Perhaps my own process will be of interest to others who are involved in the world of work beyond the counselling room. The PCA is certainly not the dominant model being used by alcohol and drug agency counsellors. However, a person-centred approach in this field might include a congruence or genuineness on the part of the counsellor to enable clients to increase their consciousness about their behaviour while holding on to the importance of goal-setting remaining firmly with the client. If person-centred therapists could embrace this, in my view, the PCA might begin to have a real impact on the future of drug and alcohol counselling.

References

Boddy, J. (1981) *Brain Systems and Psychological Concepts*. London: Wiley.
Fingarette, H. (1985) *Heavy Drinking: The Myth of Alcoholism as a Disease*. University of California Press.

Jellinek, E. (1960) *The Disease Concept of Alcoholism*. New Jersey: Hillhouse.

Kirschenbaum, H. and Henderson, V. (1990) *The Carl Rogers Reader*. London: Constable.

Keyes, S. and Kennedy, M. (1992) *Sick to Death of Homelessness*. London: Crisis.

Lee, J. (1993) *Experiencing and Expressing Anger Appropriately*. London: Bantam.

Merry, T. (1994) Editorial. *Person Centred Practice*, Vol 2, No. 2.

Miller, A. (1987) *The Drama of Being a Child*. London: Virago

Prochaska, J. O. and Di Clemente, C. C. (1983) Transtheoretical therapy: toward a more integrative model of change. *Psychotherapy: Theory, Research and Practice*, 19, pp. 267–88.

Rogers, C.R. (1959) A Theory of Therapy, Personality and Interpersonal Relationships, as Developed in the Client-Centered Framework. In S. Koch (Ed.) *Psychology: A Study of a Science. Volume 3. Formulations of the Person and the Social Context* (pp. 184–256). New York: McGraw-Hill.

Rogers, C. R. (1961) *On Becoming a Person*. London: Constable.

Royal College of Psychiatrists (1986) *Alcohol — Our favourite drug*. London: Tavistock.

Scott, M. and Stradling, S. (1992) *Counselling for Post-Traumatic Stress Disorder.* London: Sage.

Tobler, G. (1991) Helping the precontemplator. In Davidson, Rollnick, S. and McEwan, B. (Eds) *Counselling Problem Drinkers*. London: Routledge.

Velleman, R. (1992) Therapeutic Approaches (Chapter 2). *Counselling for Alcohol Problems*. London: Sage.

Survivors of Childhood Abuse — The Person-Centred Approach: A Special Contribution

Jan Hawkins

Introduction

For survivors of childhood abuse, the therapeutic arena can be a minefield where, at best, more damage can be avoided and, at worst, there may be more harm done (Masson, 1988). It is essential that people who are attempting to heal from the legacy of childhood abuse can find suitable support and/or therapy if they are to move forward. I feel that the PCA offers a particularly potent contribution to Survivors in their healing, because of the central philosophy of trust in the person, and the emphasis on the core conditions. The essential, fundamental source of healing comes from the (attempt at) equalising of power which separates person-centred therapy from almost any other type of therapy.

Definitions of abuse vary, and there is currently some controversy around the word, particularly by those seeking to diminish or minimise Survivors' experiences. For clarity in the present discussion, abuse is discussed in the context of the Chambers Twentieth Century Dictionary definition: 'to use wrongly'; 'to pervert'; 'to revile'; 'to violate'. The focus of attention in the media, and support offered by statutory agencies mostly falls on sexual abuse; here the focus is on all types of abuse: sexual, physical, emotional and neglect.

The PCA — The approach for Survivors

The PCA offers all clients something special, the core conditions when present providing a safe and nurturing environment for growth. For Survivors of childhood abuse this may be the first safe environment they have encountered. The unconditional acceptance of the therapist gives permission for the client to explore the most unacceptable parts of themselves and their experience, and also models acceptance. Survivors of childhood abuse are experts in reading others' reactions. They have had to develop this skill in order to survive. Sometimes this skill is overdeveloped leading to more fear and insecurity. This is a natural part of the process, and because the therapist is able to be 'real' in the relationship, this can be explored without leaving clients feeling more insecure about themselves.

The therapist's empathic response to the client again values their experiences,

First published in *Person-Centred Practice*, Volume 4, Number 1, 1996.

and encourages and allows the client to explore further, knowing they have a companion on their journey to self (see Bass and Davis, 1994). This journey may be horrific, and the impact on the therapist must not be underestimated.

Because the therapist is able to be congruent, clients may begin to trust themselves and to be so too, exploring the most painful material gradually dropping the defences they needed to protect them for so long.

None of the above is new or surprising, given what we know about the person centred approach to therapy. However, with so many approaches to therapy to choose from, it can be a minefield for people looking for help in healing. Firstly, the general public do not usually realise that there are choices in approach, and what the implications of these choices are. The major difference between the PCA and other approaches to therapy is the power base. For Survivors of childhood abuse, this is a critical element to healing. These are some of the most disempowered people, who as children, were denied their basic human rights to decide who, how and when they would develop their own sexual identity and expression. Physical abuse, often in the form of sadistic torture, frequently leads to dissociation where the child splits from their body in order to survive the pain (Herman, 1992). The same process occurs with sexual abuse. They have been given the message that anyone can beat them, humiliate or otherwise use them, and that this is all they can expect from the world. Adequate parenting promotes a sense of self-empowerment in children, whereas abusive parenting strips children of their power on a daily basis.

Any approach which keeps the therapist at an expert distance simply reinforces the client's sense of inadequacy and disempowerment. Many Survivors of childhood abuse define their own locus of control externally and 'when the client perceives the locus of judgement and responsibility as clearly resting in the hands of the clinician, he is, in our judgement, further from therapeutic progress than when he came in' (Rogers, 1951, p. 223).

Case histories (identifying facts removed)
Mr. A had spent 25 years in psychoanalysis, mostly for 5 days a week. His first therapist finished the therapy after 17 years, and the second one after 8 years, the latter saying he should not seek therapy again for at least a year. Mr. A began person-centred therapy having learned the language of psychoanalysis which he was convinced I would use to judge him. Many months went by before this impasse was crossed. I was then the worst he had ever seen, because I did not take notes, display certificates and was also 'warm'. This barrier gave way to discussion of sexual abuse in early childhood which he had never discussed in therapy before, as he was afraid of the effect it might have on the therapist.

Ms. B had seen an eclectic therapist for four years, and this therapy had finished about five years before she began seeing me. A number of very clear indicators of her history were not empathically received, and she was given homework to do on specific problems, for example on excessive house-cleaning (in the client's terms). Other examples are of repeated door-locking, and complete man-hatred which caused difficulties in working relationships. That therapy ended with the client feeling more abnormal than when she had started, and inadequate because the 'homework' had failed to relieve her of the difficulties she had discussed in therapy. Very early in our sessions she threw out hints, which I responded to gently and empathically (sensing that any immediate clear naming response would be overwhelming — this was later verified by the client). I was aware of the hypervigilant look of her terror. Gradually, she was able to tell her story, and began her healing. She had always known about the physical and sexual abuse she had suffered, but had never told anyone about it before.

Ms. C had seen a variety of therapists over a number of years. The first was a psychiatrist who told her that she 'wanted to sleep with her father'. She spent a year trying to defend herself. Her next therapist was very supportive and reflective, but still she felt unsafe and confused, and the focus on the 'here and now' (a phrase used by this therapist) made her feel inadequate and confused because she was plagued by memories from her childhood. In first coming to a person centred therapist, she experienced acceptance and empathy and began to trust. This led to beginning to focus on the legacy of her history. Her male therapist was warm and supportive, but said, 'I feel guilty because I am a man'. This congruent response meant that Ms. C was unable to explore further (she was concerned not to hurt her therapist), though she tried for a while , believing it was her own inadequacy that led to the problem. It reinforced her feeling of alienation and of being too much for people (see below). Her therapist had told Ms. C that he found it difficult to believe how bad she described herself as feeling sometimes, because he found her such a bright, articulate woman. This indicates two possible problems for the therapist (and therefore for Ms. C); (a) that the therapist could not fully accept Ms. C in all her experiencing, and/or (b) the therapist was not familiar with a common feature of the legacy of childhood abuse, that of fragmentation and dissociation (not to be confused with multiple personality disorder). Ms. C was never able in that relationship to discuss her own self-abusive feelings and behaviours.

Discussion

A number of participants in our groups and workshops for Survivors of all types of abuse, tell us about previous therapy experiences where they have been told that they are 'fantasising', that they must 'take responsibility' for the abuse, or that they are 'very powerful to have seduced all these men'. Some who have tried to explore what has happened to them have been met with nods and silence, which left them feeling alone. We have heard about terrible things happening to vulnerable people who seek support in their healing. Some of this may be attributed to lack of training or experience, but some I feel is because of the approach to therapy. For example, many of the post-Freudians still adhere to the seduction theory, and we hear often of therapists who tell their clients that it was all a fantasy.

For many survivors, a recurrent theme in their healing is the idea that they are 'making it up', they 'feel guilty for maligning parents', that they are 'exaggerating'.

It is painful to admit to oneself that the people who should have loved, comforted and protected us, in fact betrayed and abused us. Even when the client has always remembered the abuse, they may still go through this process. Survivors of childhood abuse have often kept their secret for many years because there was no one they could trust to tell. However, oftentimes they have told, only to be disbelieved, punished or to have their experiences minimised by people who have a vested interest in keeping the abuse quiet. Occasionally, when the child tells about the abuse, the sexual abuse stops, but the child has been made to continue living with the abusive parent, and has been ostracised by both parents for disclosing. Some children could not have survived their abuse without repressing the trauma altogether. In one study, 200 women who were hospitalised as children because of abuse, were followed up 20 years later. 38% had no memory of the abuse (Accuracy About Abuse, 1994).

It can be terrifying for the adult suddenly to remember traumatic incidents of abuse, often associated with the intensity of fear experienced as a child. When Survivors tell their stories to therapists they will be extremely sensitive to any feeling (verbally expressed or not) of disbelief or shock. This is why we need to explore for ourselves what we understand about all types of abuse, and the impact on development and later lives. Likewise, the impact upon ourselves as therapists, listening to sometimes graphic and harrowing experiences. Without exploring these issues we may subtly convey to our clients our own possibly ambiguous feelings, and thereby impair their healing.

I have argued that the person-centred approach to therapy has a special contribution to make to the healing process of Survivors of childhood abuse, because of the centrality of trust in the actualising process, and because I believe that the core conditions are 'not necessarily necessary, but always sufficient' for change (Bozarth, 1993). The case of Ms. C, above, demonstrates what Rogers said: 'you can only go as far as your therapist has been', and the fact that the therapist, perhaps, had not given time to this area, had created a block for the client. This, despite being warm, empathic, congruent and accepting (however, the acceptance was conditional — see above). Those of us who agree about the necessary and sufficient nature of client-centred therapy must humbly accept that our own process needs constantly to be developed, and our issues with particular areas (i.e. death, disability, abuse, culture, etc.) can contaminate the client's process.

Similarly, if we have not fully explored our feelings about phenomena such as self-harming and dissociation we may be in danger of assuming that our client is mentally ill, or suffering from a psychotic episode or multiple personality disorder. We may prevent them from talking about these issues because we find them too distressing to hear, and become selectively empathic. These feelings and fears may be subtly communicated to the client who will feel even more alienated and frightened, or give up their struggle for healing in therapy.

It is important to be open to extra exploration and/or training always, as there is always something new to learn. This does not imply that training or personal development would lead to dilution or contamination of client-centred therapy, which is a concern expressed by many client-centred practitioners. Personal development/training and experience should lead to deeper empathy, and in the case of Survivors of childhood abuse, a deeper sense of 'prizing' due to discovering the enormous courage Survivors need to come to therapy in the first place. Even 'experienced therapists often fall short of being empathic' (Raskin, 1974).

In my own early work as a counsellor, I am sure that in very subtle ways, I blocked clients in the journey to self. This was because my empathy was not deep enough. I had not fully explored my own issues around child abuse. When I had (and the more I learn, the more I realise there is to learn), clients seemed to move on in ways I found extraordinary. It was as if I had sent out telegrams to all my clients, current and future, saying it was safe to bring this issue to therapy (Rogers, cited in Bass and Davis, 1994, p. 17).

The PCA has a special contribution to make to the healing process of Survivors of childhood abuse. The trust in the actualising tendency, and the way of being of the therapist provide a facilitative environment in which the horrors of traumatic experiences may be explored (sometimes re-experienced). Because this will all be at the client's direction and pace, healing can occur, and changes will be made.

We know that for many clients, this is the first opportunity they have encountered to be listened to and accepted. This is an especially powerful experience for those who have been abused. The scars of emotional abuse are invisible yet profound. To be listened to, without judgement or undermining, to have feelings matter — simply to have airspace, can challenge the life script enormously. Because person-centred practitioners do not seek to analyse or interpret, they are less likely to reinforce the client's own lack of faith in their worth. Because of the emphasis in person-centred therapy on the relationship between client and therapist, there is the opportunity to learn (for many this is for the first time) what it is like to be received. David Brazier (1993) points out that, for abused children, it was not so much that they were not loved that caused harm, but that their love was not received. This poignant clarity is borne out time and again by clients who have been abused. For one client, one of the most positive things I gave throughout the therapy (I was told in an ending session) was that I 'allowed her to give me' a Christmas present — and liked it.

Memories and feelings about abuse can surface at any time, at any age and the person of the therapist provides a companion through what R.D. Laing describes as the 'authentic stage of madness'. So often a recurrent theme for Survivors who are actively healing is the idea that they are going mad, and all the coping strategies and survival defence mechanisms are challenged and left behind. Healing from childhood abuse is not going mad, it is going sane.

References
Accuracy About Abuse, PO Box 3125, NW3 5QB.

Ainscough, C. & Toon, K. (1993) *Breaking Free. Help for Survivors of Child Sexual Abuse.* London: Sheldon Press.

Bass, E. & Davis, L. (1994) *The Courage to Heal. A Guide for Women Survivors of Child Sexual Abuse*. (3rd. edition) Harper Perenniel.

Bozarth, J. (1993) Not Necessarily Necessary, but Always Sufficient. In Brazier, D. (Ed) *Beyond Carl Rogers*. London: Constable.

Brazier, D. (1993) The Necessary Condition is Love: Going beyond self in the Person Centred Approach. In Brazier, D. (Ed) *Beyond Carl Rogers*. London: Constable.

Herman, J. L. (1992) *Trauma and Recovery: From Domestic Abuse to Political Terror*. Pandora.

Laing, R. D. (1959) *The Divided Self*. London: Penguin.

Masson, J. (1988) *Against Therapy*. Fontana.

Raskin, N. (1974) Studies on psychotherapeutic orientation: Ideology in practice. Cited in Rogers, C. R. (1980) *A Way of Being*. Boston: Houghton Mifflin.

Rogers, C. R. (1951) *Client-Centred Therapy*. London: Constable.

Person-Centred Counselling in a Primary Health Care Setting: A Personal Perspective

Ruth Reid

Introduction

Working in general practice as a trainee counsellor has made me aware of the conflicts posed by the Person-Centred Approach. Carl Rogers' central hypothesis — that each person has within him or herself the capacity for growth and self-enhancement, provided certain conditions exist — has continued to be tested in psychotherapy practice with a vast amount being written on the subject. Person-centred theory has had a significant impact on education, group work, play therapy and on individuals who have been influenced by the personal and theoretical writings of Carl Rogers. However, there is very little written in relation to therapeutic work in conventional health-care settings, particularly time-limited work. The practical implications of offering person-centred counselling within the financial and time constraints of the National Health Service has presented a dilemma for me, as the whole concept appears to contradict person-centred philosophy as it is widely viewed.

Crucial to therapy is the achievement of a healthy relationship between the counsellor and the client based on mutual respect and power sharing, the belief being that it is the client who knows what hurts and where the solution lies, and that he or she also holds the power to determine the duration of therapy.

The idea that it is clients who possess the knowledge about what is troubling them and are relied upon to seek out their needs is in conflict with other more 'medical' models of therapy where the counsellor is seen as the expert 'prescribing' a treatment for the client. Thorne (1992) states that the term 'non-directive' is interpreted by critics as 'doing nothing'. He writes: 'The radical belief that it is the client who knows what hurts and how to find healing throws a mighty spanner in the works for those who see it as their task to evaluate "conditions" and set up programmes to remedy problems and to alleviate pain'(pp. 64–5).

What I have found is a general downplay of person-centred therapy in primary health-care settings. Some of this stems from a belief that person-centred therapy is not compatible with time-limited work, and stems from a general disregard of the work of Carl Rogers, which is seen as fine for teaching basic counselling

First Published in *Person-Centred Practice,* Volume 7, Number 1, 1999.

skills but inadequate as a therapeutic orientation in its own right.

It is because of its perceived simplicity that the Person-Centred Approach is generally regarded as appropriate for training purposes or basic skills, but is somehow insufficient for real therapy. The idea that the counsellor is an equal in the relationship, that he or she does not diagnose, interpret, direct or assume a role, is difficult for those who believe in a more directive approach, i.e. that a person suffering some psychological distress requires first a diagnosis and then a cure. The assumption is that the therapist knows best how to treat the ailment and knows what solution or technique is most appropriate.

Issues concerning power and expertise are significant. Rogers (1978) wrote:

> It has taken me years to recognise that the violent opposition to client-centred therapy sprang not only from its newness, and the fact that it came from a psychologist rather than a psychiatrist, but primarily because it struck such an outrageous blow to the therapist's power. It was the politics that was threatening (p.16).

Person-centred therapy is not full of preconceived beliefs about a person's unconscious processes, which require the therapist's interpretation and direction towards their conscious minds; nor about changing cognitions and behaviours. It is a natural process that occurs within the client and is led by the client, provided the core conditions exist in a mutually accepting relationship. The expertise is in the ability of the counsellor to provide these conditions and for them to be perceived as present by the client.

Many clients come into counselling with a range of behaviours that help to maintain a conditioned self-concept. If these conditioned responses are broken down too quickly by inopportune questioning and unravelling, the client may feel more threatened and vulnerable. The unconditional acceptance of the person-centred counsellor reduces that threat by allowing the client to decide how much to reveal or explore. The counsellor's role is foremost to help build a relationship of safety and trust.

There are many times when I have felt stuck as a counsellor, and have wondered whether another technique would help me and my client to progress, only to find that, if I trust the process and scrutinise my ability to offer the core conditions effectively, the outcome appears to be facilitative to my client.

Patterson and Watkins (1996) wrote: 'the concept that the relationship is the essence of psychotherapy is threatening because it places responsibility on the person of the therapist. He or she has no place to hide' (p. 221).

Merry (1996) discusses the difficulty of remaining person-centred at those times when therapeutic movement seems to be slow:

> What was going on in me that urged me to provide an empty chair, or make some suggestion to help the client out? What I found was my insecurity and my anxiety. It certainly did not belong to the client (p. 508).

I am not trying to convey a dismissal of other forms of therapy, but I have a strong belief in the essence of the Person-Centred Approach. There appears to be an undercurrent of general disregard in health care settings, as if it might usurp the power base of more traditional therapies. Rogers (1978) in his time was aware of this when he wrote:

> The very effectiveness of this unified approach constitutes a threat to professionals, administrators and others, and steps are taken consciously and unconsciously . . . to destroy it (p. 28).

Health-care settings are normally understood to refer to health centres, clinics and surgeries usually situated in the community, rather than larger hospital units. The work in these settings, whether relating to mental or physical health, is usually of a primary nature. This can be because it is often a first point of contact for those in need, or there is a preventative aspect to the work.

Thorne (1992) commented that 'certainly the Person-Centred Approach does not align itself easily with the spirit of the age'(p. 64) in terms of perceived quick and cost-effective solutions.

Woolfe et al. (1989) consider Rogers' work 'dated' with the interest in 'short-term crisis-orientated counselling' (p. 11). Continuing on this theme, they say: 'we would suggest, therefore, that the person-centred strand within the world of counselling, though still strong and important, is less absolute than many counsellors might suppose . . .'(ibid.)

Dryden and Feltham (1995) suggested that 'Humanistic therapies are probably unlikely to be found or offered in the National Health Service or other conventional institutions, but Person-Centred counselling is being practised widely in student counselling services' (p. 67).

Yet in a recent paper in the *Lancet* (Friedli et al. 1997), discussing, among other issues, the increased popularity of brief psychotherapies in general practice over the last twenty years, the authors stated:

> Brief psychotherapy is provided by a range of different professionals in general practice, and has generally taken the form of a non-directive intervention based on the theories of the American psychotherapist Carl Rogers (p. 1662).

Rogers (1951), in a rare reference to his theoretical hypothesis in relation to health problems, refers to the 'famous Peckham Experiment in London' (p. 60). The Peckham Centre was organised for family health and recreation by a group of biologists. Rogers refers to the work of these biologists, who wrote: 'we try not to give advice and refrain from assuming the authority of special knowledge'. Responsibility is placed with the family. They went on to comment:

> It was found in practice that when examinations were conducted in a spirit which led up to conclusions which were bits of advice, often no action was taken; whereas by leaving it to the spontaneity in the individual and to his own sense of responsibility, action is taken in

the overwhelming majority of cases' (p. 60).

Time for What? Time limitation and experiences in practice

I realised that working as a counsellor in general practice had both advantages and disadvantages. The advantages were very significant. People generally had trust in their general practitioner and therefore a measure of trust in the environment of the practice and the people working there. As a more local facility, it was perceived as less threatening and more familiar and accessible than a hospital setting. There was no stigma attached, as the counsellor was seen as a part of a whole team offering support and care. Services, too, were free and usually available on request.

There was always the possibility, however, that the patient, when seeing the counsellor, was carrying out the doctor's suggestion and saw it as part of his or her treatment plan. The doctor was seen to be the expert and the patient felt obliged to attend.

In my experience, attendance at another's instigation rarely works, and sessions can be doomed from the start. I found it valuable and essential to be very clear about what counselling could and could not achieve if I sensed from my client any misunderstanding in this area. Publications such as *Counselling and Psychotherapy: is it for me?* (BAC, 1995) and *Understanding Talking Treatments* (MIND, 1998) proved useful at times.

In earlier counselling work with clients in the surgery, I had become fixated with offering six sessions and found that we never moved beyond this point. The six sessions was an arbitrary number, but it had become lodged somewhere in me, and, as my supervisor pointed out, had clearly also permeated my client's awareness. I therefore started working with clients offering open-ended sessions, which proved initially to be mutually satisfactory. This was until I recognised a 'stuckness' (Mearns and Thorne, 1988, pp. 96–7) in a long-term relationship which I realised was coming from my pressure to conclude it. A waiting-list was growing. I was being drawn away from my client's issues and attending to my own. Perhaps this had something to do with being productive and efficient, but it certainly was not conducive to effective person-centred counselling. As Mearns and Thorne (1988) wrote, 'The therapeutic process may become stuck through the influence of the counsellor's values, fears or deep-seated needs' (p. 98).

One of my concerns when working in general practice was about how I would cope with the number of referrals. I felt sure that I would eventually need to restrict the number of sessions offered. This was unsafe ground, and the idea conflicted with person-centred ideology. I did not want to be prescriptive in the number of sessions on offer, neither did I want to be open-ended. I felt that I wanted to be open to anything my client brought, to work to their agenda. This, I believed, did not exclude being able to negotiate a mutually convenient settlement or clarification of important information. I began offering my clients more of a dialogue about the number of sessions and a request to be able to review mutually how we were feeling and working together. To some extent I felt more comfortable with this issue, which was about mutual respect and openness.

Little by little, I realised that there were some counsellors who were expressing similar concerns about time. Inskipp (1993) wrote:

> *On Becoming a Person* still moves me. However, I've always been driven by time . . . the efficient use of time, and the large number of sessions often used by Rogers when he worked with clients did not seem to equate with the resources available to work with college students; as I saw it, though his core qualities of empathy, unconditional positive regard and congruence became my guiding light to counselling and teaching (p. 91).

Thorne (1994) wrote about having, 'dared to think the unthinkable' when faced with an 'ever-escalating waiting-list' in the university counselling service. 'Could it be', he wrote, 'that there were some prospective clients for whom short-term counselling was not only a possible option but the most desirable and potentially most effective?' (p. 61).

Rogers commented (Lewis et al. 1959) on two cases of time-limited client-centred psychotherapy, the limit being apparently imposed 'because of the practical necessity to meet our long waiting list' (Shlien, in Lewis et al. 1959, pp. 312). Rogers wrote:

> It is of interest to me that though each of these clients was limited in the hours he could spend in therapy, as is explained by Dr Shlien, the process seems very similar to that of unlimited therapy, except that certain aspects become intensified (Shlien, 1959 p. 311).

Patterson (1985) acknowledged the problem of time:

> Where time is limited, either by pressures upon therapist time, or by client factors such as resources and mobility, it is felt to be necessary or desirable to resort to methods to speed up the process. It is assumed that client-centred or relationship approach is too lengthy . . . [He commented that] Giving the decision of when to terminate to the client does not lead to interminable therapy. Yet it must be realized that clients need therapy of varying duration (pp. 215–16).

Yalom (1989) pondered whether his client, Betty, would have taken longer to achieve the inner resolve needed to work on her weight loss if she had not known that her time in therapy was limited. He commented, 'There is a long tradition in psychotherapy going back to Carl Rogers and before him Otto Rank, which understood that a pre-set termination date often increases the efficiency of therapy' (p. 113).

I had devised a plan for myself that, within the four places that I could then offer, two would be without limit and two would have a limit imposed of six to ten sessions with a commitment to find further support if needed. I began to find that some clients wished to continue with sessions, while others wanted to terminate earlier. I began to realise that, by worrying about the effect of limited time on my work with my clients, I was in essence taking away responsibility from them and also my trust in their power of self-direction in the therapeutic process: I could only offer what was possible for me in practice. I gradually felt a release and a greater freedom in my work, which I think represented itself in a heightened ability to be present with my clients on their journey of discovery.

Personal learning
What is of interest to me as I have begun to read more widely is that Rogers was in no way prescriptive in his use of time, and that duration of therapy could be flexible depending on the situation and needs of both the client and the counsellor. Perhaps my assumption of the meaning of client-centred being 'client decides' in this respect reflects much of the misinterpretation of Rogers' work generally. There is a difference between working within a client's frame of reference in therapy and acquiescing to all the client's wishes on a practical level.

In terms of Rogers' description of the process continuum in therapy, I have found that most clients move, even in a short space of time, from discussing symptoms to discussing themselves; from discussing their environment to exploring themselves; and from discussing others to becoming more aware of themselves. Rogers commented:

> Is change on the continuum rapid? My observation is quite the contrary: the client might start therapy at about stage two and end about stage four with both client and therapist being quite legitimately satisfied that substantial progress had been made. It would occur very rarely, if ever, that a client who fully exemplified stage one would move to a point where he fully exemplified stage seven. If this did occur, it would involve a matter of years (Rogers, 1961, p. 155).

What I have learned in practice is that, when I am able to be congruent with my clients and trust their own actualizing tendency, the process of therapy can move forward. The client knows what he or she requires at that moment. It may be that a shorter period marks only the beginning of a process of exploration, as Rogers suggests. I find I no longer need the rigidity that I first found necessary. Corey (1991) wrote: 'As clients increasingly assume an inner locus of control they are in the best position to assess the personal meaning of their therapeutic venture' (p. 20).

This loosening permeated other areas of my work as well. I realised that formal assessment was an external way of understanding a client and that more could be learnt from the client's own subjective reality. Corey (1991) sums up my emergent feelings and experience in this area while discussing perspectives on assessment in person-centred therapy:

> Focusing on gathering information about a client can lead to an intellectual conception about the client. The client is assumed to be the one who knows the dynamics and behaviour, and for change to

occur, the client must experience a perceptual change, not simply receive data. Thus, therapists listen actively, attempt to be present, and allow clients to identify the themes that they choose to explore (p. 10).

Over a period of five years working as a counsellor, I have seen people suffering from a wide range of psychological distress. Unfolding in the sessions have been difficulties with relationships, low self-esteem, bereavement, loss, eating problems, panic attacks, depression and anxiety, to put labels to a few. At the core of their distress there seems to be an incongruence between their real selves and the selves evolved to meet the approval of others. Time and again, I have found that Rogers' hypothesis is proven in practice, confirming my belief of its place in health care at least on a par with other forms of therapy.

Horton (1996) considers the therapeutic relationship as 'the strongest evidence linking process to outcome' (p. 288). Patterson (1985) wrote:

There is another element in client-centred or relationship therapy that creates resistance, and that is its revolutionary nature. This has become increasingly evident, especially with the recent proliferation of so-called innovative methods and techniques or strategies of intervention, all of which seem to have in common an active, directive, and controlling view of psychotherapy . . . No array of techniques, no matter how skilfully practised, can lead to a real therapeutic relationship (p. 222).

Ashurst (1993), in an evaluation of counselling in general practice, suggests that 'the method employed by the counsellor was far less important than the relationship which developed between the counsellor and client' (pp. 41–2).

I feel that I have put to rest some of my own scepticism and evolved an even stronger belief in both the philosophy and practice of the Person-Centred Approach. Respect for the power of the individual is paramount. I would share Patterson and Watkins' (1985) comment that 'one cannot help be convinced that in the long run the philosophy and theory, and the practice as well, of client-centred therapy will prevail' (p. 424).

Acknowledgement

I would like to thank Ivan Ellingham, deputy manager of counselling at Weald College, for his help and support in preparing this work. Also the medical practice that allowed me the flexibility to develop a person-centred way of working.

References

Ashhurst, P. (1993) Studies of the effectiveness of counselling. In R. Corney, R. Jenkins, (Eds.), *Counselling in General Practice*.London: Routledge.

British Association for Counselling (BAC) (1992) *Code of Ethics and Practice for Counsellors*. London: BAC.

British Association for Counselling (1995) *Counselling and Psychotherapy: Is It For Me?* London: BAC.

Corey, G. (1991) *Perspectives on Assessment in the Person Centered Approach: Case Approaches to Counseling and Psychotherapy.* Monterey, Ca: Brooks Cole.

Dryden, W. and Feltham, C. (1995) *Counselling and Psychotherapy: A Consumer Guide.* London: Sheldon.

Friedli, K., King, M. B., Lloyd, M. and Horder, J. (1997) Randomized controlled assessment of non-directive psychotherapy versus routine general-practitioner care. *The Lancet,* 350 pp. 1662.

Horton, J. (1996) Towards the construction of a model of counselling: some issues. In R. Bayne, I. Horton and J. Bimrose (Eds.), *New Directions in Counselling.* London: Routledge.

Inskipp, F. (1993) Beyond Egan. In W. Dryden (Ed.), *Questions and Answers on Counselling in Action.* London: Sage.

Lewis, M. K., Rogers, C. R. and Shlien, J. M. (1959) Time-limited, client-centred psychotherapy: two cases. In A. Burton, (Ed.), *Case Studies in Counselling and Psychotherapy.* New York: Prentice-Hall.

Mearns, D. and Thorne, B. (1988) *Person Centred Counselling in Action.* London: Sage.

Merry, T. (1996) Client-centred therapy: trends and troubles. In S. Palmer, S. Dainow, and P. Milner, (Eds.), *The BAC Counselling Reader.* London: Sage.

MIND (1998) *Understanding Talking Treatments.* London: MIND.

Patterson, C. H. (1985) *The Therapeutic Relationship: Foundation for an Eclectic Psychotherapy.* New York: Brooks Cole.

Patterson, C. H. and Watkins, C. E. Jnr (1996) *Theories of Psychotherapy.* New York: Harper Collins.

Rogers, C. R. (1951) *Client-Centered Therapy.* London: Constable.

Rogers, C. R. (1961) *On Becoming a Person.* London: Constable.

Rogers, C. R.(1978) *On Personal Power.* London: Constable.

Smith, A. A., Irving, J. and Brown, P. (1989) Counselling in a medical setting. In W. Dryden, (Ed.) *Handbook of Counselling in Britain.* London: Routledge.

Thorne, B. (1992) *Carl Rogers.* London: Sage.

Thorne, B. (1994) Brief companionship. In D. Mearns, (Ed.), *Developing Person Centred Counselling.* London: Sage.

Woolfe, R., Dryden, W. and Charles-Edwards, D. (1989) The nature and range of counselling practice. In W. Dryden, (Ed.), *Handbook of Counselling in Britain.* London: Routledge.

Yalom, I. D. (1989) *Love's Executioner and Other Tales of Psychotherapy.* London: Bloomsbury.

Playing the Probabilities in Psychotherapy

Jerold D. Bozarth

Most therapy sessions are, perhaps, founded upon the question of what might be the most effective treatment for a particular client dysfunction. The recommendations for specific treatments for particular dysfunctions are supposedly based upon research findings, with the research that is considered most viable being the true experimental design which is predicated upon probability theory. Hence, it was my original intention to propose a model for effective psychotherapy which emanates from psychotherapy outcome research. Not surprising to many who know me, this model would be predicated upon Rogers' (1957) integration hypotheses of the necessary and sufficient conditions for therapeutic personality change and would be highly sympathetic to his theory of client-centered therapy (Rogers, 1959). I have, over my career, differed with the party line of psychology and psychotherapy treatment methods which are, in my opinion, paradigmatically different from Rogers' contention. However, my conclusions are more drastic than simply finding research support for my particular frame of reference. The situation is alarming!

Our entire mental health education and treatment system is virtually founded on a sham and the pretence of scientific support for the effectiveness of treatment by techniques and methods and expertise (which I label, the 'specificity myth'). Therapist expertise is foremost in the determination of the 'right' method for the particular dysfunction. Sadder yet is the fact that those who perpetuate and those who are educated in the system continue to believe this contention. To add to the alarm, those of us who think we know better do not speak out. The fundamental fictional foundation of the system is that there are specific treatments for specific disorders. It is primarily on this premiss that training and credentials are based and upon which a particular type of practitioner experience is perpetuated. It is implied that there is scientific method research to support this incredibly cost-ineffective system that is dedicated to the principle of specific treatments for specific disabilities.

A recent special issue of the *American Psychologist* on 'Outcome Assessment of Psychotherapy' illustrates the rigidity of the perceptual belief in the fundamental assumption of treatment by method for types of dysfunction. In ten quasi-scholarly articles and five 'comments' revolving around Seligman's (1995) assertions concerning the usefulness of the Consumer Reports survey on mental health in a

---

First published in *Person-Centred Practice*, Volume 6, Number 1, 1998, and appears in amended form as Chapter 19 in *Person-Centered Therapy: A Revolutionary Paradigm*, Ross-on-Wye: PCCS Books.

previous issue of the *American Psychologist*, only one author referred to the importance of the relationship in therapeutic 'encounters' (and this only a tangential reference). All articles abound with the terminology of 'interventions' for treatment. The clear focus is upon the therapist expertise and method of treatment for the particular dysfunction paradigm (the 'specificity myth').

The factors that have most consistently been related to positive outcome over decades of research; i.e. the client-therapist relationship and the self-resources of the client, are virtually ignored.

Furthermore, research reviews on the relationship in counselling are likewise embedded in the 'specificity myth'. Sexton and Whiston's (1994) reasonably thorough coverage of research on the relationship in counselling is indicative of the bias, even though they seek and encourage a different paradigmatic approach predicated upon a 'social constructivist' view. These authors point out that 'it is only the counseling relationship that has consistently been found to contribute to the success of the therapeutic process (Luborsky et al. 1988; Orlinsky and Howard, 1986)'. Sexton and Whiston (p.7) summarize:

> The research has confirmed what was widely recognized: The success of any therapeutic endeavor depends on the participants establishing an open, trusting, collaborative relationship or alliance (Frank and Gunderson, 1990). In addition, research has shown that failure to form such an alliance is strongly associated with client noncompliance with treatment plans (Eisenthal, Emery, Lazare, and Udin, 1979); premature termination (Saltzman, Luetgert, Roth, Creaser, & Howard, 1976; Tracey, 1977); as well as poor outcome (Alexander and Luborsky, 1986).

However, this review of the literature on research concerning the relationship in psychotherapy undergoes a subtle shift of focus. This is reflected by the above statement that 'failure to form such an alliance is strongly associated with client noncompliance with treatment plans . . . ' The relationship is converted to, 'alliance' and defined by 'client noncompliance' when not formed.

In part, this shift is due to the authors' use of Gelso and Carter's (1985) multidimensional model of the relationship. This model is founded upon psychoanalytic premises resulting in an identification of the relationship as real, as unreal and as a working alliance.

The unreal aspect of the model is based upon the concept of transference. The working alliance is an extrapolation of all therapies, focusing on the agreement of goals and tasks by, and the emotional bond of, the client and therapist, but still associated with the psychoanalytic approach. As such, the entire model is presented from the stance of 'therapist expertise and method to dysfunction treatment' ideas, even when the relationship is the focus of discussion. This basic assumption seems apparent from the authors' periodic references to such terms as 'client compliance', 'interventions', and to the measuring of the alliance as the 'client's collaboration' in therapy. Even when considering the relationship, the fundamental assumption of our treatment system is embedded in the paradigm of the 'specificity myth'.

The following overview of the research on psychotherapy outcome demonstrates the fallacy of what I consider to be the fundamental invalid assumption of our mental health system. It is an assumption that permeates and obfuscates conclusions which miss the critical therapeutic variables that might be considered in a way that can develop more viable treatment. In the latter part of the paper, a model is introduced that might more adequately use the results of outcome research.

Method of inquiry

I examined a number of reviews of psychotherapy outcome research studies and also re-examined my own inquiry into effective psychotherapy over the past three decades. The most prominent conclusions from research reviews are as follows:

1. Effective psychotherapy is primarily predicated upon (a) the relationship between the therapist and the client and (b) the inner and external resources of the client.
2. The type of therapy and technique is largely irrelevant in terms of successful outcome.
3. Training, credentials and experience of therapists are irrelevant to successful therapy.
4. Clients who receive psychotherapy improve more than clients who do not receive psychotherapy.
5. There is little evidence to support the position that there are specific treatments for particular disabilities.
6. The most consistent of the relationship variables related to effectiveness are the conditions of empathy, genuineness and unconditional positive regard.

The integrative statement of Carl R. Rogers

The person who has, in my view, come closest to identifying the critical elements of psychotherapeutic effectiveness is Carl Rogers (1957).

His statement concerning the necessary and sufficient conditions of therapeutic personality change is an integrative statement for psychotherapy and helping relationships that is separate from his statement (Rogers, 1959) concerning the conditions as part of client-centered therapy (Stubbs and Bozarth, 1996). In my view, this is an important point in that Rogers' efforts were mostly directed toward this core of 'necessary and sufficient' attitudes for helping relationships rather than towards the development of client-centered therapy (CCT) as many have assumed. From this perspective, it is speculated by Bozarth (1996) that therapists must achieve their own congruence, including the use of their own 'technique system', in order to maximize their capacity for experiencing empathic understanding and unconditional positive regard for the client.

In short, I assert that techniques and theoretical formulations are for the therapist rather than for particular clients and this, essentially, allows therapists freedom to enter the person-to-person relationship with their clients in the best possible way. Although CCT most likely maximizes the probability of such a relationship if the therapist upholds the principles of the approach, the conclusions of the psychotherapy research suggest, as Rogers proposed, that the conditions can be embedded in other forms of therapy and helping situations. Focus on the relationship and the client's inner and outer resources can occur to some extent in all therapeutic endeavours.

The data base
The major reviews that substantiate my conclusions are briefly summarized as follows.

• *H.H. Strupp, R.E. Fox, and K. Lessler, Patients View their Psychotherapy. Baltimore: Johns Hopkins University Press, 1969.*

This study was an early survey of samples from a psychiatric outpatient clinic wherein patients gave their accounts of their treatments. The 'success' patients in this study were those who had high internal motivation and initiative, and viewed discomfort and determination as crucial to their success. The composite 'patient's' view of the 'good' therapist was 'that of a keenly attentive, interested, benign, and concerned listener, a friend who is warm and natural, is not averse to giving direct advice, who speaks one's language, makes sense and rarely arouses intense anger' (p.117).

In addition, they found that inexperienced therapists did as well as highly experienced therapists from the clients' view: 'There were no appreciable differences in outcome or quality of the therapeutic relationship; length of therapy or frequency of sessions had no measurable bearing on outcome, and differences in therapeutic competence, as judged by supervisors, were also inconclusive' (p. 119).

The authors found that their conclusions were 'strikingly similar to the conclusions . . .' which Berenson and Carkhuff (1967) had drawn from their review of counseling and psychotherapy research. Strupp et al. (1969) paraphrase this review:

1. There is substantial evidence that therapists of very different orientations can be equally effective.
2. There is substantial evidence that therapeutic changes occur in a broad front and that they are independent of the therapist's theoretical position and professional affiliation.
3. There is substantial evidence that the efficacy of psychotherapy is primarily a function of a central core of facilitative conditions. These are three: (a) experiential, (b) didactic, and (c) the role model which the therapist provides. This formulation allows for the possibility that within the context of the core facilitative conditions a variety of techniques may enhance therapeutic effectiveness. These techniques, however, remain to be spelled out.
4. There is substantial evidence that facilitative conditions are not entities in themselves, to be communicated by prescribed techniques, but rather that they are present in all effective human encounters.
5. There is substantial evidence that techniques are rehabilitative when they free the individual to engage more fully in the kinds of life activities in which he would have become involved if the facilitative

conditions had been present originally.

6. There is substantial evidence that all interpersonal encounters may have constructive or deteriorative consequences. To the extent that psychotherapy is effective, it maximizes the constructive consequences of the patient-therapist encounter.

7. There is substantial evidence that effective psychotherapy provides the patient with a human experience which is the inverse of the experiences which gave rise to the difficulties in the first place.

8. There is substantial evidence that in effective psychotherapy the patient eventually incorporates into his own life-style the facilitative conditions offered him in therapy. He is influenced by the significant sources of learning in therapy to become more open, understanding, and respectful of himself and others. Thus, what he is learning is new techniques of effective living (pp. 135–6).

Nearly three decades later, the research reviews of psychotherapy outcome research reflect the major notions observed by Berenson and Carkhuff's (1967) review and the Strupp et al. (1969) study of the importance of the relationship: namely, the importance of the clients' involvement in their own treatment and the minuscule influence of 'interventive' techniques.

- ***J.P. Stubbs, and J. D. Bozarth, The dodo bird revisited: a qualitative study of psychotherapy efficacy research. Applied and Preventive Psychology, 3, (1994), pp. 109–20.***

At the Third International Forum of the Person-Centered Approach in 1987, I (Bozarth, 1993) first reported that the prominent conclusion of the time concerning Rogers' hypothesis of the necessary and sufficient conditions for therapeutic personality change was that the conditions were necessary but not sufficient. One was led by the literature to think that this position was well substantiated by research studies. However, my review did not find a single study that supported this position. Dr Stubbs examined the literature several years later in an unpublished paper and also found the results to be confusing. This led us to the qualitative study of 'The dodo bird revisited'.

This qualitative study of psychotherapy research effectiveness reports that Rogers' hypothesis is the most stable major thread running through the effectiveness of psychotherapy throughout, at least, the last four decades. Of five emergent temporal categories of focus, the abiding relationships to outcome that emerged in some form are those that Rogers (1957) hypothesized in his classic integrative statement as core ingredients for therapeutic personality change (i.e. congruence, unconditional positive regard and empathic understanding). Stubbs and Bozarth also note specifically that the predominant temporal category that is the forerunner to the specificity question, i.e. the category that the conditions are necessary but not sufficient, has virtually no research support. We did not find one direct study that supported this assertion. Conclusions were, at best, extrapolations of flawed logic.

That is, the logic that support for Rogers' hypothesis is weak; hence something more must be needed, and that thing is some form of interventive technique.

The major implications of this study in relation to effective psychotherapy are that (1) the major thread running through the four-plus decades of efficacy research is the relationship of the therapist and client, and that a strong part of those data refers to Rogers' attitudinal conditions of the therapist; and (2) the research foundation for the 'specificity question' has abysmal research support and the precursor of the 'specificity' assumption is the unsupported theme of Rogers' conditions being necessary but *not* sufficient.

• *B.L. Duncan, and D.W. Moynihan, Intentional utilization of the client's frame of reference.* **Psychotherapy, 31, (1994) pp. 294–301.**

Concomitant to the publication of the 'Dodo Bird' qualitative study of psychotherapy research, Duncan and Moynihan summarized reviews of quantitative research studies (e. g. Lambert, et al. 1986; Lambert, 1992) to propose the application of the outcome research to practice. Duncan and Moynihan's argument is actually propounded from a very person-centered perspective. They propose a model predicated on recent conclusions concerning the research on psychotherapy outcome. They point out that the reviews of outcome research (Lambert, 1992; Lambert et al. 1986) suggest that 30 per cent of the outcome variance is accounted for by the common factor of the client-counsellor relationship across therapies; techniques account for 15 per cent of the variance, as does the placebo effect; and 40 per cent of the variance is accounted for by extra-therapeutic change variables (factors unique to the client and his/her environment). Such research findings suggest to them the utility of intentionally utilising the client's frame of reference. Indeed, their point resonates the Rogerian view of empathy:

> Empathy, then, is not an invariant, specific therapist behavior or attitude (e.g. reflection of feeling is inherently empathic), nor is it a means to gain a relationship so that the therapist may promote a particular orientation or personal value, nor a way of teaching clients what a relationship should be. Rather, empathy is therapist attitudes and behaviors that place the client's perceptions and experiences above theoretical content and personal values (Duncan, Solovey and Rusk, 1992); empathy is manifested by therapist attempts to work within the frame of reference of the client. When the therapist acts in a way that demonstrates consistency with the client's frame of reference, then empathy may be perceived, and common factor effects enhanced. Empathy, therefore, is a function of the client's unique perceptions and experience and requires that therapists respond flexibly to clients' needs, rather than from a particular theoretical frame of reference or behavioral set (Duncan and Moynihan 1994 p. 295).

Duncan and Moynihan apparently identify Rogerian empathy with specific behaviours and a particular response-set, rather than from the bedrock of the empathic attitude in the theory. As such, they do not seem to realise that they are actually proposing an operational concept that is representative of Rogers' view of empathy and hence propose their model as one different from all other models.

The Duncan-Moynihan article is important to consider here because it summarises the outcome research in a way that focuses on the critical variables in successful outcome. Moreover, it lays out the basis for a therapy model that is predicated upon scientific method hypothesis testing research. Although their model is very aligned to the model of client-centered therapy in its purist form, the emphasis upon the influence of the extra-therapeutic variables of the client as the greatest contributor to outcome may suggest that a more integral consideration of therapist action and reaction within the empathic context may enhance effectiveness.

• *Mental health: does therapy help?* **Consumer Reports** *(November 1995)*
 pp. 734–9.

This survey questionnaire to readers of the Consumer Reports concerning the effectiveness of psychotherapy again buttresses the findings from other reports, e.g. refuting the assertion 'of the usefulness of specific techniques for specific disorders . . .' As a survey, the study is subject to the usual methodological critiques of the scientific method paradigm, such as lack of random assignment, lack of systematic treatment and other factors threatening internal validity. It is noteworthy, however, that Seligman (1995), who is a major champion of the 'efficacy' study (scientific method, hypothesis paradigm studies), changed his view of the way to study psychotherapy effectiveness. He comments that within this framework, the studies of specific treatment for specific dysfunction (which he terms 'efficacy' studies) do not consider the realities of therapy. He elaborates that the efficacy designs seldom go beyond the internal validity of the studies.

His conclusion is well stated: 'The efficacy study is the wrong method for empirically validating psychotherapy as it is actually done, because it omits too many crucial elements of what is done in the field.' In other words, the nature of the methodological designs and their inherent constraints (e.g. control studies, exclusive and manualized treatments, random assignment, limited treatment times, single diagnoses) ignore many crucial elements of the actual practice of psychotherapy in the field.

The Consumer Reports survey and Seligman's assessment are important in that the conclusions of this report are consistent with conclusions of reviews of studies with more 'rigorous' research designs (as, for example, summarized by the Duncan-Moynihan report and the Stubbs-Bozarth study), and the viability of such surveys are acknowledged even though they fall outside of the 'efficacy study' paradigm.

• *A.C. Bohart and K. Tallman, The active client: Therapy as self-help.*
 Journal of Humanistic Psychology, *36/3, (1996): 7–30*

This review of psychotherapy outcome studies concludes that it is the active client who is ultimately the therapist. What makes psychotherapy work? In this review the answer is: 'the active client'. The authors' interpretations of the research buttress the conclusion that the factors clients see as helpful are not usually technique factors but rather more general processes like providing support. It is further concluded that therapists not only must use the client's frame of reference and rely more on the client, but 'we must truly understand that it is the whole person of the client who generates the processes and solutions that create change' (p. 26).

The therapist provides a safe working place for client dialogue, experiencing and exploration; provides a set of procedures that can be used by clients to create new self-experiences as a way to develop new perspectives and solutions; and provides therapist interactive experience and feedback.

- **W. Silverman, Cookbooks, manuals, and paint-by-numbers: psychotherapy in the 90s. Journal of Humanistic Psychology, 33, (2), (1997) pp. 207–346.**

This article is a reaction to recommendations of the Division 12 Task Force Report on Promotion and Dissemination of Psychological Procedures (October 1993). The author points out that the Task Force cited 18 specific treatment interventions from a total of 33 studies worthy of 'empirically-validated interventions' and actually ignored the conclusions that emerge from several decades of thorough reviews of psychotherapy outcome literature. Silverman's analogy to the Task Force's procedures is worth quoting since their thrust is an acceleration of the fiction of the specificity hypothesis. Silverman states:

> Let us try a group hypnotic induction. Please imagine that you are back in graduate school taking a seminar in Psychotherapy Research. The professor asks you to write a paper about effective psychotherapies. You will share your scholarship with the rest of the students in the class so that they can also become knowledgeable on the subject. After delivering your paper to the professor, you tell her that while you did not do a comprehensive review of the literature, you asked several of your other professors what they believed to be effective therapies and then you documented these impressions. Furthermore, in defining effectiveness you would only consider those studies that manualized the treatment process. Notice the look on her face as you explain this to her.
>
> Your paper cites approximately thirty papers as evidence of effectiveness out of the thousands of papers that have been published in the last twenty-five years. From these thirty papers, you list eighteen treatments that are valid, fifteen of which are forms of behavioral modification or cognitive behavioral therapy. As you hand in your paper to the professor, examine her hand for signs of tension. You also inform the professor that regardless of the grade you may receive, you will be making specific recommendations to the Director of Training about what sorts of therapy Clinical Supervisors are to accept. You will also ask the Academic Dean to make specific changes in the graduate curriculum to accommodate your findings. What

autonomic reactions do you notice displayed by your professor from the generalizations you make? Now I want you to imagine what grade you will receive. Do you find this hypnotic induction too unrealistic? Well, it is time to wake up and face reality (p. 207).

Silverman's analogy is not only a clear statement about the thrust of the particular Task Force, but represents the essence of the undermining of effective mental health care by the myth of specific treatment for particular dysfunction hypotheses.

• *J.D. Bozarth, Psychotherapy outcome research designs. Preliminary Report (1997).*

In 1996 I decided to do another perusal of the research designs of psychotherapy outcome research. It is clear that the profession of psychology holds the 'gold standard' (the 'efficacy' or true design study) of psychotherapy research as the *sine qua non* for the determination of psychotherapeutic efficacy (APA, 1993; Dawes, 1994; Seligman 1995), even though there seems little evidence that such research even exists. Such inquiry is further complicated in that, when (if) it exists, such 'studies are unable to demonstrate either clear-cut efficacy or adequate descriptions of the effective therapist or effective techniques' (Kisch, 1980).

The perusal of the 'efficacy' studies covered a span of two decades from 1970 through 1989. Efficacy in this review, however, is defined as 'the power to produce an effect' (Webster 1991), with 'effect' being 'the power to bring about a result'. Seligman (1995) uses the term 'efficacy' to identify scientific method hypothesis testing studies (i.e. the true experimental study). It is unclear to me that the terms 'efficacy' and 'effectiveness' have been so differentiated to any significant degree in previous writings. The studies searched, thus, had a more general meaning than being only those studies identified as 'true experimental designs'.

My intent was, first to identify the general types of studies of psychotherapy, as being quantitative, qualitative or other reports. Second, the quantitative studies were identified by type of design; i.e. pre-experimental, true experimental, quasi-experimental, correlational-causal and *ex post facto* designs (Leedy, 1993). The 'gold standard' is the true experimental design which has adequate random sampling and a control group. By Seligman's definition, all of the studies would be true experimental designs, but the more general definition used for this review allowed a few more studies to be examined.

The initial computer searches (Galin, Eric and PsycINFO) came up with nearly 1000 articles. However, this was rapidly reduced to 64 articles when non-related titles and content (883), non-research papers (21), papers not having an efficacy issue (23), and exceptionally poor methodology (6) were dropped. There remained 26 quantitative studies, 2 qualitative studies and 33 general reviews of the research studies; 3 additional articles were meta-analysis. It must be noted that this search did not include some of the studies of 'effectiveness' reviewed in previous articles (e.g., Duncan and Moynihan 1994; Stubbs and Bozarth, 1994), but, as noted above, they were also not limited to studies of 'efficacy' as defined by Seligman.

Of the quantitative studies (it is in this ball park that we would find the 'gold standard' studies), 10 were pre-experimental designs, 5 were quasi-experimental, 4 were correlational-causal and only 6 were true experimental designs.

The fact that there were only six studies that met the criterion of the 'gold standard' is, of course, revealing in and of itself. When we examine the studies in slightly greater detail, it is even more revealing. The samples represent varying populations including stutterers, the elderly, Russians, depressed women and individuals in crisis. The treatments are also variable, ranging from unidentified general psychotherapy in two of the studies, to 'supportive psychotherapy', focused intervention, assertiveness training and Rational-Emotive Therapy compared with systematic desensitisation. In short, these true experimental design studies have little common ground regarding the question of efficacy, and there is not a hint of replication.

Although some studies not recorded in the particular computer searches were no doubt missed in this search, this inquiry is consistent with other reviews. There are few true experimental designs and, as summarised previously by Stubbs and Bozarth (1994), 'The research concerning specificity of treatment, dysfunction, therapist variables, and client variables is characterized by fragmentation, few replications and lack of generalizability' (p.116).

The data base conclusion

The conclusion is clear: there is no research foundation for the underlying assumption of our mental health care system; that is, that there are specific treatments for specific dysfunctions. The Specificity Myth is replete. I repeat Stubbs' and my previous comment that the direction of the research continues to prove '"significantly insignificant to help" and often obscures what is most significantly helpful' (Stubbs and Bozarth, 1994 pp. 117).

The most clear research evidence is that effective psychotherapy results from the resources of the client (extra-therapeutic variables) and from the person-to-person relationship of the therapist and client. The specificity and systematizing of these variables remain somewhat murky, although they do include Rogers' hypothesized variables of the attitudinal qualities.

The research on relationship reviewed by Sexton and Whiston (1994) supports the conclusion 'that there are significant individual differences among and within clients over time and that these individual differences account for the majority of the variance in counseling outcome (Martin 1990)' (p. 58). The data increasingly point to 'the active client' and the individuality of the client as the core of successful therapy.

As O'Hara (1995) aptly concludes:

> It isn't the technique, it isn't the therapist, it isn't the level of training,
> it isn't the new wonder drug, it isn't the diagnosis. It is our clients'
> own inborn capacities for self-healing, and it is the meeting...the
> relationship in which two or more sovereign and sacred 'I's' meet as a
> 'we' to engage with significant questions of existence. (pp. 19, 30–1).

It is here that we seek to find a model which can efficiently help clients find their own empowerment. We can, hopefully, find a model to replace the cost-inefficient 'Specificity Myth', the model of expertise, specific treatment for specific dysfunction that drives our mental health treatment system. An efficient model should be based on the 'true' findings of the last four decades of research on psychotherapy effectiveness. At the core, Rogers' seminal contributions are a foundation for effective treatment.

This paper was originally presented at the Association for the Development of the Person-Centred Approach Conference, Las Vegas, 1997.

References

Alexander, L. B. and Luborsky, L. (1986) The Penn helping alliance scales. In L.S. Greenberg and W.M. Pinsoff (Eds.), *The Psychotherapeutic Process*. New York: Guildford.

American Psychological Association (1993) *Task force on promotion and dissemination of psychological procedures: A report by the Division 12 Board.* Washington D. C: APA.

Berenson, B. G. and Carkhuff, R.R. (1967) *Sources of Gain in Counseling and Psychotherapy.* New York: Holt, Rinehart and Winston.

Bohart, A. C. and Tallman, K. (1996) The active client: therapy as self-help. *Journal of Humanistic Psychology*, 36, (3) pp. 7–30.

Bozarth, J. D. (1993) Not necessarily necessary but always sufficient. In D. Brazier (Ed.), *Beyond Carl Rogers.* London: Constable.

Bozarth, J. D. (1996) Client-centered therapy and techniques. In R. Hutterer, G. Pawlowsky, P. F. Schmid and R. Stipsits (Eds.), Client-Centered and Experiential Psychotherapy: A Paradigm in Motion. Frankfurt am Main: Peter Lang, pp. 363–8.

Consumer Reports, (November, 1995.) Mental health: Does therapy help? pp. 734–9.

Dawes, R. M. (1994) *House of Cards: Psychology and Psychotherapy Built upon Myth.* New York: Free Press.

Duncan, B. L. and Moynihan, D. W. (1994) Applying outcome research: intentional utilization of the client's frame of reference. *Psychotherapy*, 31, pp.294–301.

Duncan, B., Solovey, A. and Rusk, G.(1992) *Changing the Rules: A Client-Directed Approach to Therapy.* New York: Guilford.

Eisenthal, S., Emery, R., Lazare, A. and Udin, H. (1979) 'Adherence' and the negotiated approach to patienthood. *Archives of General Psychiatry*, 36, pp. 393–8.

Frank, A. F. and Gunderson, J. G. (1990) The role of the therapeutic alliance in the treatment of schizophrenia. *Archives of General Psychiatry*, 47, pp. 228–36.

Gelso, C. J. and Carter, J. A. (1985) The relationship in counseling and psychotherapy: Components, consequences, and theoretical antecedents. *The Counseling Psychologist*, 13, pp. 155–433.

Kisch, J. (1980) Meaningfulness versus effectiveness: paradoxical implications in the evaluation of psychotherapy. *Psychotherapy: Theory, Research & Practice*, 17, pp. 401–13.

Lambert, M. (1992) Psychotherapy outcome research. In J. C. Norcross and M. R. Goldfried (Eds.), *Handbook of Psychotherapy Integration*. New York: Basic Books, pp. 94–129.

Lambert, M. J., Shapiro, D. A. and Bergin, A. E. (1986) The effectiveness of psychotherapy. In S. L. Garfield and A. E. Bergin (eds.), *Handbook of Psychotherapy and Behavior Change*. New York: John Wiley, pp. 157–212.

Leedy, P. D. (1993) Practical Research: Planning and Design, 5th edn. New York: Macmillan.

Luborsky, L., Crits-Christoph, P., Mintz, J. and Auerbach, A. (1988). *Who Will Benefit from Psychotherapy? Predicting Therapeutic Outcomes*. New York: Basic Books.

Martin, J. (1990) Individuals in client reactions to counseling and psychotherapy: a challenge for research. *Counseling Psychology Quarterly*, 3, pp. 67–83.

O'Hara, M. (1995) Why is this man laughing? *AHP Perspective*, 19, pp. 30–1.

Orlinsky, D. E. and Howard, K. I. (1986) In S. L. Garfield and A. E. Bergin (Eds.), *Handbook of Psychotherapy and Behavior Change*. New York: John Wiley, pp. 311–81.

Rogers, C. R. (1957) The necessary and sufficient conditions of therapeutic personality change. *Journal of Consulting Psychology*, 21, pp. 95–103.

Rogers, C. R. (1959) A theory of therapy, personality, and interpersonal relationships as developed in the client-centered framework. In S. Koch (Ed.), Psychology: A Study of Science: Vol. 3, Formulation of the Person and the Social Context. New York: McGraw Hill, pp. 184–256.

Saltzman, C., Luetgert, M. J., Roth, C.H., Creaser, J. and Howard, L. (1976) Formation of a therapeutic relationship: experiences during the initial phase of psychotherapy's predictors of treatment duration and outcome. *Journal of Consulting and Clinical Psychology*, 44, pp. 546–55.

Seligman, M. E. P. (1995) The effectiveness of psychotherapy: the Consumer Reports Study. *American Psychologist*, 50, pp. 963–4.

Sexton, T. L. and Whiston, S. C. (1994) The status of the counseling relationship: an empirical review, theoretical implications, and research directions. *The Counseling Psychologist*, 22, (1), pp. 6–78.

Silverman, W. H. (1997, Summer) Cookbooks, manuals, and paint-by the-numbers: psychotherapy in the 90's. *Psychotherapy*. 33,(2), pp. 207–14.

Strupp, H. H., Fox, R. E. and Lessler, K. (1969) *Patients View their Psychotherapy*. Baltimore: Johns Hopkins University Press.

Stubbs, J. P. and Bozarth, J. D. (1994) The dodo bird revisited: a qualitative study of psychotherapy efficacy research. *Journal of Applied and Preventive Psychology*, 3, (2), pp. 109–20.

Stubbs, J. P. and Bozarth, J. D. (1996) The integrative statement of Carl Rogers. In R. Hutterer, G. Pawlowsky, P. F. Schmid and R. Stipsits (Eds.) *Client-Centered and Experiential Psychotherapy: A Paradigm in Motion*. New York: Peter Lang, pp. 25–33.

Tracey, T. J. (1977) Impact of intake procedures upon client attrition in a community mental health center. *Journal of Consulting and Clinical Psychologist*, 45, pp. 192–5.

Webster (1991) *Ninth New Collegiate Dictionary*. London: Collins.

A Case-study of Therapeutic Support Using e-mail

Alan Brice

e-mail messages are very cool

Introduction

There is a rapidly developing debate about the possibility of offering counselling by e-mail, both for new relationships and continuing established ones, either in electronic mail consultations (in asynchronous time, where there could be a delay of up to several days between messages) or in on-line consultations (in real time, where each participant waits for a reply). The emergence of a range of Internet therapists offering a wide range of support, from agony-aunt type advice to on-line sessions and group discussions, reveals a growing demand for such services. I work in a busy counselling service in an English university and wonder how a university or college counselling service would react to such a demand. Does this constitute something that is worth doing: is it therapeutic? Does it offer a valuable service to clients?

Many writers have taken on the challenge of considering whether e-mail contact can be considered to be counselling. Lago (1996) drew counsellors' attention to these issues and raised a number of the questions that others have begun to address, notably 'Do the existing theories of psychotherapy continue to apply, or do we need a new theory of e-mail therapy?' Lago went on to suggest that :

Themes of therapeutic competence are likely to include:
- the ability to establish contact
- the ability to establish relationship
- the ability to communicate accurately with minimal loss or distortion
- the ability to demonstrate understanding and frame empathic responses

Particular questions are raised for person-centred counsellors, like myself (although I am sure that similar issues, expressed differently, are raised for counsellors of other disciplines). Rogers (1957) stated the first of his six necessary and sufficient conditions for therapeutic personality change as 'it is necessary that . . . [the] two persons [counsellor and client] are in psychological contact': his sixth condition is that 'the communication to the client of the therapist's empathic understanding

First Published in *Person-Centred Practice,* Volume 7, Number 1, 1999.

and unconditional positive regard is to a minimal degree achieved'. Are these possible through computer-mediated communication?

A valuable starting point may be to consider whether all relationships are partial anyway, and whether such experiences as telephoning, of letter-writing, or counselling cross-culturally or with people with disabilities merely heighten the problems involved in trying to develop helpful relationships with any other person.

Murphy and Mitchell (1998) recognise these concerns and consider issues such as 'can you tell that I care?' and the problems associated with a lack of non-verbal cues. They firmly believe that e-mail contact 'offers an opportunity for us to use our skills to help people who might not otherwise be able or willing to access our services'.

Pete Sanders, in his (unpublished) paper to the British Association for the Person-Centred Approach Annual Conference 1998, 'Is There a Future for Relationship-Based Therapy in Computer-Mediated Communication?' tentatively concluded that 'substantial and complex relationships can be established, developed and maintained remotely'. On the other hand, Robson and Robson (1998), who consider intimacy and self-disclosure, conclude that 'the creation of the relationship that is necessary in client-centred counselling could not be facilitated in its wholeness through computer communication'.

The university and college context

Universities or colleges are used to students being away from the campus: on work experience placements, research visits, international exchanges, foreign language study, medical electives, and on holiday over the long vacation. In these circumstances, continuing to offer counselling support can be problematic. Often these absences from university or college are stressful enough in themselves for a student. Some of the students who are coming for counselling before such an undertaking are often anxious about the impending break in the therapeutic support they are receiving. In the past students have written or telephoned; now it seems more likely that they will e-mail.

I have little experience of an exclusively e-mail counselling relationship. However, I have several times continued to maintain contact via e-mail with a current counselling client of mine who has temporarily moved away from the university. This has been in asynchronous time rather than on-line. It has seemed to me to constitute a vital part of the overall counselling process and of the relationship between the client and myself.

Case-study

I shall write about the e-mail contact I have had with a particular student-counselling-service client, who has given permission for this material to be used. My intention is for those unfamiliar with this way of working to get a practical sense of the possibilities and difficulties involved, to make tangible the abstractions about this way of working.

A female student, who had been coming for counselling for about seven months following several years of living with an eating disorder, was due to go abroad for three months. She expressed some anxiety about this, knowing that she would not establish a new counselling relationship in that time, and concerned that a return to compulsive overeating would be unavoidable.

The first contact I received was a letter giving her e-mail address. She wrote about how difficult it was to settle into the new environment and that she tended to panic in such situations, but so far was not 'using food to numb all the things I can't bear to feel'.

I replied by e-mail, suggesting we make use of e-mail contact on a regular basis. Her e-mail response came three days later, enthusiastic about such contact, and explained that she had to use a cybercafé, so she couldn't check her messages every day. Apart from detailing her accommodation and a recent outing, she continued to offer more personal material. She told me of her irritation with a colleague who was being very negative towards her, saying 'this becomes a real strain at times and I'm sick of being told I'm weird . . . I don't really know how to handle it, and I end up analysing the whole thing trying to make sense of it — trying to work out why I keep getting so angry with her'.

I was reminded that I had been surprised by how alive and fresh words seemed via e-mail, and in describing her contact found myself using speech words (e.g. told, spoke, said) rather than writing words to describe the interaction.

The material she referred to was familiar for her, and when I responded I made a point of acknowledging our work together and trying to connect to her empathically — 'I know that positivity is so important for you, especially when you are struggling'. I also offered a self-disclosure: '. . . for a lot of my life, I knew how to be with people who were negative, and I got good at that. I don't choose it now.' I went on to offer an empathic understanding of the process she was in and to prize her for her qualities, again reflecting the relationship we have had: 'I don't see you as a negative person, just someone who used to be around others who were. You are now learning to be what you would choose to be — open, interested, risk-taking, scared of that too, exploring, changing, thrilled by all those things and unsure that you can do them.'

I recognised that my interventions were longer than they would have been if spoken, and referred to established knowledge within our relationship. It seemed necessary to strive for clarity and to try to reflect the depth of that relationship.

Some of the significant differences between letter-writing and e-mailing include the easy and almost casual manner of dashing off a message without the effort to craft a response, something perhaps about the simplicity of writing into the computer and the instant sending of the message. I was concerned to retain the spontaneity of my initial response on reading her messages and yet to balance that with the valuable thinking-time available. I was worried that my message would sound false or perhaps prove that it is difficult, if not impossible, following the question that Murphy and Mitchell (1998) ask, to show that I care, and to fulfil Rogers' core conditions.

In her response, she said, 'It is great to be able to read your e-mails, it's almost like having a conversation'. She went on to disclose a distressing memory of having an accident when she was younger, which had been prompted by something that she had recently experienced. She reflected on that and wrote 'what I learned was that I can create a safe environment for myself to explore such issues even when I'm far away from familiar surroundings'.

She expressed her fear about the difficulty of written communication: 'There are so many more things I want to say but I find it hard to express them in words — like they lose their feeling or something?' and then went on to conclude that message with 'It's great to hear from you — I feel like I have a witness for all the progress I'm making'.

I replied about the memory that it was 'wonderful, terrible, healing perhaps, saddening definitely, becoming history and also very fresh and cruel with it', and confirmed that I was a willing witness. It seemed important to me that I should try to be more explicit in my written communications than I would be when speaking to a client.

Her response made it clear to me that it is possible to fulfil the core conditions, and not in a dry way either. She wrote that she was moved to tears reading my mail. 'The staff in this cybercafé think I'm a nut because every time I read my e-mails, I end up crying. It's not that I'm sad, it's that your words always move me deeply and the tenderness you convey is tangible.'

In later messages she wrote 'I've decided e-mail messages are very cool because people's personalities come through so strongly . . .' and 'being in regular contact is helping me immensely and the familiarity of your words are a tower of strength'.

All the mailings took place when she was able to get access to a cybercafé, which was the central seven weeks of her time away. She sent nine messages and I sent seven.

Supervision

Supervision of this sort of work takes on quite different qualities compared with supervision of face-to-face client work. The totality of the client-counsellor communication can be present, printed out, in a way that even a video tape of a face-to-face session can't quite capture, as that must miss some of the fine detail of non-verbal behaviour, of the sense of presence, of the deep subceptions between two people. It is worth remembering that the totality of the printed e-mail communication is different from the totality of the contact or of the relationship between client and counsellor.

However, it is an amazing tool for supervision. Nothing is hidden, or hideable! I confess that, initially, I dealt with this in supervision by simply speaking about my e-mail counselling work rather than taking the printed messages. However, I knew that I had plenty to gain by poring over the messages with my supervisor, and quickly broke through my anxiety. Supervision by e-mail, of e-mail work, is a possibility that I have not yet explored, but am tempted by!

Review

On my client's return to Britain, we recommenced routine counselling. We discussed the experience of our computer-mediated contact, both reflecting on how difficult we expected it to be, and how easy in fact it had been to express ourselves openly and for personality, care and understanding to come through, assisted by our established counselling relationship. She said she had been 'sustained' by the contact. She reflected that this was different from receiving letters, because it was more alive, more spontaneous and also more personal in that the messages came direct to her.

She commented that, while reading my messages, it had been easy to imagine me in my office, pottering around, making coffee. I suspect that in a purely e-mail relationship such an accurate image would be unlikely.

Indeed there are plenty of stories emerging of people presenting themselves falsely, dangerously so, in 'chat-rooms' (a form of Internet discussion group). Relationships can develop that come to involve face-to-face encounters. More than one student from this university has set out to meet someone they have related to only over the Internet and have had a disastrous experience, including being raped. This raises many important questions for e-mail-only counselling relationships, including authenticity and congruence, or (for counsellors of different theoretical backgrounds) transference and counter-transference.

The client and I both wondered how long it would take to develop a counselling relationship using e-mail only, and guessed that it might not take as long as either of us had initially suspected. Van Gelder (1996) suggests that people can achieve a higher degree of intimacy through computer-mediated communications than in ordinary life. Many who write would reflect on the potential for greater expression of emotion communicating that way than through talking. My experiences as a member of a number of discussion groups on the Internet is that personalities can come through strongly. If an element of my and my client's personalities have done so in this brief study, then it might suggest that complex relationships such as counselling ones *can* be maintained remotely.

References

Lago, C. (1996) Computer therapeutics: a new challenge. *Counselling*, (4): pp.287–9.

Murphy, L. J. and Mitchell, D. L. (1998) When writing helps to heal: e-mail as therapy. *British Journal of Guidance and Counselling*, 26, (1), pp. 21–32.

Robson, D. and Robson, M. (1998) Intimacy and computer communication. *British Journal of Guidance and Counselling*, 26, (1), pp. 33–41.

Rogers, C.R. (1957) The necessary and sufficient conditions of therapeutic personality change. *Journal of Consulting Psychology*, 21,(2), pp. 95–103.

Van Gelder, M. (1996) The strange case of the electronic lover. In R. Kling (Ed.), *Computerisation and Controversy.* London: Academic Press; cited in Robson and Robson (1998).

Further relevant reading

Bloom, J. W. (1998) The ethical practice of Webcounselling. *British Journal of Guidance and Counselling*, 26, (1), p. 53–9.

Ingram, J. (1996) Cybertherapy: pariah or promise? (on-line). Available: http://cybertowers.com/selfhelp/ppc/viewpoint/cybparpr.html

Lea, M. and Spears, R. (1995) Love at first byte? Building personal relationships over computer networks. In J.T.Wood and S.Duck (Eds.), *Under-studied Relationships: Off the Beaten Track.* Thousand Oaks, Cal.: Sage, pp. 197–233.

Sampson, J.P.Jnr, Kolodinsky, R. and Greeno, B. (1997) Counselling on the information highway: future possibilities and potential problems. *Journal of Counselling and Development,* 75, pp 203–12.

Walther, J.B. (1992) Interpersonal effects in computer-mediated interaction: a relational perspective. *Communication Research,* 19, pp. 52–90.

The Quality of Acceptance

Mary Kilborn

Unconditional positive regard

One of the core conditions presented by Carl Rogers as necessary for personality change to occur involves, in his words, the therapist 'experiencing a warm acceptance of each aspect of the client's experiencing as being a part of that client'. He goes on to explain that 'it involves as much feeling of acceptance for the client's expression of negative, 'bad', painful, fearful, defensive abnormal feelings as for his expression of 'good', positive, mature, confident, social feelings, as much acceptance of ways in which he is inconsistent as of ways in which he is consistent . . . It means a caring for the client as a separate person, with permission to have his own feeling, his own experiences' (Rogers, in Kirschenbaum and Henderson, 1990, p. 225). D. Mearns and B. Thorne offer the following definition:

> Unconditional positive regard is the label given to the fundamental attitude of the person-centred counsellor towards her client. The counsellor who holds this attitude deeply values the humanity of her client and is not deflected in that valuing by any particular client behaviours. The attitude manifests itself in the counsellor's consistent acceptance of and enduring warmth towards the client (1988, p. 59).

Aim of this study

As a person-centred therapist who aims to offer unconditional positive regard, I am aware of the high demands this makes upon me. As Brian Thorne comments, 'Acceptance of this order is not easily accomplished for it requires of therapists a capacity, from deep within themselves, to accept persons as they are and not as they would wish them to be' (Thorne, 1992, p. 38). I see it as my responsibility as a therapist constantly to explore deep within myself, to increase my own self-acceptance to the point where I can fully accept my clients. In addition to my personal and professional development, I decided to undertake a study of this area of my work in order to establish how much my clients felt accepted by me. Further to this, I wanted to find out whether my supervisees felt at the receiving end of unconditional positive regard. I wanted to get a feel for how much the people I work with on a therapeutic or supervisory level actually felt accepted by me.

Preparing the study

When I started planning the study, I came to the conclusion that it would be helpful

First published in *Person-Centred Practice*, Volume 4, Number 1, 1996.

to seek the views of other person-centred therapists on the subject of unconditional positive regard. I wanted to discover how important this core condition was for them and how they felt they were succeeding in offering it. I decided I would attempt this by using an open-ended questionnaire, to leave them free to bring up any issues they wished. I chose mainly therapists known to me, therapists who, like myself, defined themselves as purely person-centred. I received replies from therapists in Scotland and England. I also sought the views of person-centred therapists in France where I have been doing some supervision training. In this case, therapists were openly invited to reply. This study will consider the views of twelve therapists, of whom four practice in France.

My main interest, however, is the response of *my clients*. I wanted to try in some way to get a sense of just how accepted they felt, a sense of the quality of presence I offer in the relationship. I have been involved in another study which sought client views and I know the importance of proceeding with care and delicacy. I wanted to try to avoid any possibility that my approaching a client with a questionnaire would have a detrimental impact on the counselling process. I therefore took care as to which clients I chose. I did this on a purely subjective level. Would being asked to fill in a questionnaire in any way disturb the client? Was our relationship good enough for the client to feel able to refuse? I approached clients who had been in therapy with me for some while, over six months, and whom I felt might benefit from a chance to focus on the acceptance in our relationship. Eleven clients out of twelve completed the questionnaire and their responses will be considered here.

I chose a very open questionnaire, in an attempt to get a fresh response. I considered I could not use the term 'unconditional positive regard', as I thought this might sound rather heavy and abstract, so I used the words 'total acceptance'. In retrospect, I would have preferred to have used the term 'unconditional acceptance', as will become clear when I discuss the client responses.

The last group of responses I sought were those of my *supervisees*. I have a fairly large supervision practice of experienced therapists and therapists in training. Here I was seeking to discover, again through an open questionnaire, whether I was succeeding in offering unconditional positive regard to my supervisees and whether that was beneficial to our work. By its very nature, supervision or consultancy as it is sometimes termed, has an element of the supervisor monitoring the practice of another practitioner. As I am a person-centred supervisor, I expect my supervisee to do a high amount of self-monitoring. Nevertheless, I was interested to know whether being a supervisor and offering unconditional positive regard sat well together.

This study takes a case study approach, offering a snapshot of my work as a person-centred practitioner, incorporating feedback from my own clients and supervisees and the views of other therapists.

The therapist questionnaires and responses

As stated above, twelve therapists responded to a questionnaire consisting of four open questions. The first invited them to consider **the importance of unconditional**

positive regard (Question 1) in their work. All of them saw it as forming one of the central planks. Words and phrases such as c*entral, essential, fundamental, absolutely crucial, supremely, underpins my work,* were used. Some spoke of the need of it to create trust, others mentioned warmth. A number of the therapists linked unconditional positive regard with empathy, stating that these two fed into each other. One therapist likened it to the cement which is needed in large quantities to hold the building together.

Another offered a word of caution. She felt that her unconditional positive regard could be so strong, flow so naturally, that some of her clients have felt unable to bring up the negative side of themselves. She therefore seeks to 'mute' its obvious expression. This links in with a criticism which has been levelled against person-centred therapists, which is that they cannot or do not deal with the negative feelings of the client. This therapist appears well aware of the danger of making everything seem too warm and positive.

In terms of **what ways they feel they succeed in offering unconditional positive regard** (Question 2) to clients, a number of the therapists spoke of it being best when it 'happens effortlessly', 'flows naturally, when it seeps out of me'. Others spoke of attempting to accept themselves and accepting their feelings towards their clients, 'monitoring my self-regard'. One spoke of the struggle to understand the client, another of valuing the humanity of the client, even if the behaviour is experienced as being difficult. Looking beyond to the 'essential being of the client' is mentioned by a therapist whenever she experiences difficulty accepting a client. One therapist spoke of 'the solidity and enduring nature of my commitment' to his clients, which does not preclude criticism and discomfort. He states the view that British counselling culture often substitutes a kind of 'polite withholding' for unconditional positive regard. The responses of some of my clients mentioned later show the importance of this point.

Some therapists spoke of the way they communicate their unconditional positive regard, what they refer to as 'prizing the client'. A number mentioned 'spoken and unspoken communication', 'through my eyes', 'through discreet touch', 'through specific and carefully crafted verbal expression'. It sounds as if unconditional positive regard may flow naturally at times but that the therapists also carefully monitor their attitude and their responses.

One therapist who described her client group as 'a very unaccepted part of the population' explained that her acceptance involved the non-disclosure of illegal actions and also acceptance of the failure to attend. She offers an open-ended appointment slot which clients sometimes keep and sometimes do not. She adds that acceptance does not mean that a no-show is not acknowledged as part of the therapeutic process.

The main point that emerged from the question concerning **occasions when the therapists find it difficult to offer unconditional positive regard** (Question 3), was that this happens when it touches on 'an area which I find difficult to accept within myself', 'my personal blocks', 'issues which I have not resolved in myself', 'directly tapping into my own stuff'. One therapist said she experiences not being able to enter the world of the client when the client awakens her own 'anger, fear, sorrow'. Another explains this happens when he is 'caught up in self-recrimination about my own behaviour, usually outside my therapeutic work'. Another speaks of times she feels empathy for the partner of a client, especially when she senses games are being played. She speaks of getting hooked into analysing the games rather than being with the person.

Specific examples offered were 'a client being abusive, violent or chauvinistic to a partner, a client who talks about undermining/abusing children, exploitation of power', 'someone who expects others to change rather than himself or herself', 'someone who feels the world owes them a living', 'a client who shows hatred for his mother', 'when I am confronted by a rigid, authoritarian personality', 'when I am confronted by a person who has no sense of the sanctity of the human infant, or a woman who has no sense of the unique identity of the human foetus'. Two therapists spoke of their difficulty when clients do not trust them, keep them at a distance, reject their empathy and unconditional positive regard, think that the therapist is after their money and no more! Therapists themselves may find it hard at times not to receive acceptance when they are striving to offer so much themselves.

When asked about **ways in which they can improve the quality of unconditional positive regard** (Question 4), the majority of therapists spoke of continued self-development, with particular attention to self-acceptance, which they see as so strongly linked to their acceptance of their clients. One therapist spoke of increasing self-forgiveness. Heightened self-awareness was also mentioned as helping therapists attend to their own prejudices. A number of the therapists asked spoke of supervision, describing how much he gained when he experienced his supervisor's unconditional positive regard as greater than his own. Finally, self-care and self-nurturing on the part of the therapists was mentioned, for example, walks in the forest, meditation, and prayer. How can therapists offer unconditional positive regard, warmth, love even, to their clients if they cannot offer it to themselves?

Client questionnaires and responses

My main interest in this study was, as I have already stated, my client responses. I hoped to learn from them, and that they would inform and improve my practice. As also stated, I was keen not to put my own wishes and needs before those of my clients. My responsibility is to each one of my clients as an individual and I would consider it professionally irresponsible to involve any one of them in a research project for my own benefit, if that very process were in some way detrimental to them. My hope and aim, therefore, was that in the case of each client, the very taking part in the project would become part of and enhance the therapeutic process.

I chose those clients whom I sensed would benefit from the opportunity to focus on some aspect of their relationship with me. Many of my clients know that I enjoy going to conferences and writing papers, and some welcome the feeling that they are playing a part in that process. Nevertheless, I tried not to make assumptions about their willingness to take part. I asked each one if they would be prepared to take the questionnaire away and look at it. I specifically said they were free not to fill it in. They were asked not to put their name to the responses, if they did not want them personalised. They were offered a stamped addressed envelope to return it to me anonymously if they wished. In the event, the majority gave me back their responses in person and a number wanted to talk about what they had written. Three said they were keen to fill in the questionnaire but found the actual doing of it rather difficult. These took a long time to return them but they continued to declare themselves keen to get it done. I received two by post, not because they wanted to remain anonymous, but because they kept forgetting to bring it to the session. I received eleven returns out of twelve. The twelfth client found herself getting very confused and distressed trying to focus on the questions. She was able to talk about her confusion and distress with me but in retrospect I feel I made an error of judgement in asking her, despite the fact that she had been seeing me over a long period of time.

The client questionnaires consisted of five questions which I tried to keep as open as possible. I asked how they felt about my attempt to offer total acceptance and how far they felt I managed to offer it. I asked if there were occasions when they did not feel accepted and whether there was anything about me or my way of being which got in the way of their feeling accepted, and I finally asked if there was anything in themselves which made it hard for them to feel accepted by me.

The responses to the first question as to **whether clients expected, sought or welcomed my total acceptance** (Question 1) were varied. Some said they had not come to therapy expecting it and that they were learning to experience it as part of the therapeutic process. They then welcomed it, one commenting that it 'does wonders and helps me to accept myself'. Others said, 'basically yes' and that is what they came for. As one client put it: 'Isn't that what we all want from each other? Kids from their parents? Isn't that the meaning of "Do unto others as you would be done to"?' Yet, those clients who had come looking for and expecting acceptance found that at a deeper level it was not that easy to trust. Another client who said she expected it admitted that after two years of therapy she was slowly finding it easier to believe in! (The exclamation mark is hers. A number of clients commented on the need for time so that trust can develop. Three clients question whether such a thing as total acceptance is possible. One of these says she tries not to seek it actively as that would take her away from her own self. (Here, I question whether she is talking more of approval than acceptance. One client took the trouble to point out that, for her, acceptance is me seeing her as she is, whereas approval is me liking what I see. This point was not specifically mentioned in the questionnaire. If clients ever ask for my approval, I usually say something about acceptance of them as people rather than approval or disapproval of their actions.) As one client stated honestly, 'I find the idea of total unquestioning, non-judgemental acceptance difficult and unlikely. I do not expect it, I can't seek it . . . it does not relate easily to my relationship with other people. I welcome it, but I find it difficult to accept in myself.'

One client, who took the trouble to write a long response to my questionnaire and also took the risk of being extremely open and honest, commented that she welcomes the fact that I 'strive for total acceptance' but wishes I would make more use of the dynamic that I don't succeed! (Her exclamation mark.) This is a client who is highly challenging to me as a therapist and to whom I respond defensively from time to time. I do try to look at the dynamic when I am aware of what is happening but I still have a lot to learn with her.

When asked **how far I manage as a therapist to offer total acceptance** (Question 2), the majority claimed that I do offer total acceptance. One felt that after a long period of time, she now felt safe. Another explained how my acceptance in the earlier sessions was **so** important, my acceptance of her 'dark place', her 'not knowing', her 'silence'. She felt deeply touched. A few clients realised they had difficulty distinguishing between my acceptance of them and their acceptance of themselves. A number of clients were more sceptical, especially those who wondered whether total acceptance was possible. One short comment was, 'You consistently present yourself as someone who is offering total acceptance', which is a long way from saying that this client was experiencing total acceptance. Another, in the same vein, stated, 'I have no doubt of your desire and effort to give this . . . to provide this. You feel strongly in your attempt and hope to offer this.'

One client was far harsher, 'I often have the experience that you practice total acceptance to the point of denying me as an individual . . . At times, I experience your total acceptance as a mask behind which you hide. It drives me on occasions to wanting to say or do something to shock you into a normal human reaction. At times, I long for the honesty of experiencing what you really think — what you really accept in me and what you don't or struggle more with. The sessions that work best for me are those when I experience an openness from you that allows me to meet you as an equal — when you drop a bit the facade of practising extending total acceptance towards me.' This sounds as if I have not succeeded in communicating to the client that I accept her humanity. Also that I have in many ways not been present enough. This latter view is reflected by other clients as will be seen in the responses to later questions.

The next question asked about **occasions when clients have not felt fully accepted by me** (Question 3). A few clients could think of no occasions when they had not felt accepted. Others came up with incidents or moments they have found difficult. One client mentioned how I had seemed particularly confident at the beginning of one session, before we started, which had been such a contrast to the 'pathetic place' she felt she was in. I am now trying to be more careful about comments I make before the session starts and also when it is over.

One thing picked up by a number of clients that relates to the last paragraph is how unsure they sometimes feel if I am 'just listening', or 'quiet', or 'not giving anything away'. They are looking for more active acceptance, otherwise they make assumptions about what I am thinking, and that I am judging them. A couple of clients speak of me sometimes not understanding what they are saying, or of 'crossed wires'. However, on the whole it seems preferable that I actively check out. One client says that, after clarification, she feels a 'renewed and strengthened trust' in my acceptance.

One area a client felt I was not accepting of her was spirituality, her way of viewing the world. Such a comment makes me seriously question my level of empathy with this client. My experience is not that I do not accept her spirituality, but I do have to question why she is experiencing me in this way. The client with whom I admitted to acting defensively sometimes, stated that when she stirs something negative in me I can be 'quite harsh and abrupt', and sometimes 'snap' at her. Again, as this is not my view of the way I am as a therapist, it feels as if I have some work to do on myself with regard to when clients do indeed touch a chord in me which makes me react strongly or negatively.

The question which asked about **anything about me or my way of being which may get in the way of clients feeling accepted** (Question 4) revealed nothing new from some clients, who felt they had already answered this in Question 3. One client commented that 'I feel a great warmth, sympathy and interest from you, a balance of seriousness and lightness. Your way of being with me is not intrusive.' One client, who had acknowledged my efforts to be accepting, said he wanted to stress just how important it is for him to feel understood, 'Maybe being understood is being known, and being known by another is to confirm my existence and dispel my terrible internal loneliness'. One other client commented that I am such a different person from her with such a different lifestyle, which makes it hard for her to believe that I can accept her. Another spoke of his background which he assumes to have been very different from mine and which may therefore make acceptance more difficult for me.

Further comments about my way of being related to my face and my looking. One client felt that my face was difficult to read, which sometimes troubled her. Again, an argument for my remaining very active in my acceptance. Two clients said they sometimes did not like to feel me looking at them, one in particular said she felt very exposed. A further client felt very strongly about the fact that I have said that I will try to respond to what she asks for. She felt that I was not accepting of her inability or at least great reluctance to express her needs. 'I feel that if you really accepted me, you'd accept that in me now and not push me time and again into having to ask.' This client and I have often experienced times together when she had felt pushed by me when I feel I have been trying to respond.

The final question asked clients to describe **anything in them that makes it hard for them to feel accepted** (Question 5). A number of clients spoke of their own difficulty in accepting themselves which led to a diffidence in acknowledging my acceptance. One client put it as follows, 'I have a sense of shame about my need, vulnerability, hurt, failures. It's hard for me to accept these bits of me, so hard for me to expect, seek or welcome such acceptance from you.' Some spoke of how hard it is to trust, to believe in my acceptance. One client spoke of a deep-seated sense that, 'I am not worthy of being cared for and that any love or warmth that is extended towards me is purely for the function I fulfil in someone's life'. She also spoke of her fear and panic that I would not really be there if she needed me, as had so often happened in her life before. Another client spoke of the fear that he would not be able to express himself clearly, another spoke of wondering how honest she could be. Finally, one client mentioned his concern that he was being ripped off financially and that he would not get his money's worth, which links in with one of the therapist's earlier comments about some clients believing all you really want is their money.

Supervisee questionnaires and their responses
As stated above, my aim in asking supervisees to answer the questionnaire was to discover to what extent supervisees feel they experience my unconditional positive regard, something I do try to offer them within the confines of the supervisory relationship. The questionnaire was basically the same as that offered to clients.

The responses to the first question as to whether my supervisees **expected, sought or welcomed my total acceptance** (Question 1) was not dissimilar to that of clients. A number spoke of having expected it from the start, others said that they had not really expected it but were growing to appreciate it. One supervisee admitted to being 'a bit confused' that I had asked — 'I suppose I took it for granted and just assumed you did accept me.' Some supervisees alluded to the supervisory nature of the relationship. One explained, 'I would not be able to bring all of my work with clients to the sessions if your acceptance was not there. I need to sense it in order for me to talk about the "less successful" areas of my work.' Two supervisees said that they saw me in a role of authority and this had made it hard at the outset to believe I could offer total acceptance.

In response to **how far I, as supervisor, manage to offer total acceptance** (Question 2), a number felt they had received far more acceptance than they had hoped for. One supervisee said he had been deeply touched by the warmth of my acceptance. A couple said they felt accepted, but not totally, although they did not elaborate on this. Some felt more accepted as time went by. A small number thought that the fact that they were still in training meant that I could not offer total acceptance.

It was in Question 3, **those occasions when you have not felt fully accepted by me** that I learnt most about my supervisees' attitudes towards me. Two commented that I was more accepting when they were 'less sure' about their work than when they felt they were doing well. I suppose I have to say that I can understand that I may give this impression. I do see supervision as a time for teasing out difficulties and not telling your supervisor how well you are doing. However, as the two supervisees commented, where is my total acceptance if I do not want to hear that they feel they are doing well? One further supervisee told me that she had been feeling more self-accepting and then she had felt my response suggested I thought she was getting complacent. This is an area I was not particularly aware of and will be more conscious of it in the future.

One supervisee who is in training to be a pastoral counsellor says she has felt my 'wariness and lack of acceptance of my faith and spiritual issues. This has led me to feel you have not fully accepted me. The distinction between acceptance of my person and acceptance of my faith is difficult for me to make.' I feel this is an area I need to be aware of, inasmuch as a client made a similar comment. Maybe

I need to look more at my own spirituality. However, with this supervisee, I am also concerned to ensure that what she is doing is in fact counselling.

One or two supervisees commented that when I said what I would have done under the circumstances, they felt somewhat criticised. I can understand this. On the whole, as a supervisor, I try not to say what I would have done unless asked. I feel that this can lead to the supervisee feeling undervalued. However, obviously on occasions I break my own rule.

In response to **anything about me or my way of being which gets in the way of the supervisees feeling accepted** (Question 4), most said there was nothing. One supervisee said that I have facilitated rather than blocked his development as a counsellor and I have challenged in a manner which has stimulated his growth. Two supervisees said they wished I was more verbally expressive so that they had a better sense of me. One said I hold back if she asks what I would have done, which is in direct contrast to what other supervisees have said. It could be that I behave differently with different supervisees. I know that I do pace myself and wait until I feel a supervisee is ready to receive what I have to say.

The last question as to **anything in you that makes it hard for you to feel accepted by me** (Question 5) again led to similar responses to the clients'. Most spoke of there being a link between their self-acceptance and their feeling accepted by me. One spoke of having been ridiculed at school and her still struggling with a residual fear of that being repeated. One said she expected conditions of worth, of still looking for approval and of her becoming more aware of the need for self-acceptance and self-valuing.

Conclusion

This study has given me some valuable feedback on the level of unconditional positive regard I offer as perceived by my clients and my supervisees. It has also provided me with some helpful input from other therapists. A lot of what is contained in this paper shows not only the importance of offering unconditional positive regard but also of the client/supervisee receiving it as such, feeling comfortable with it. One client suggested that my questionnaire invited more negative than positive feedback and she wrote some questions herself offering very positive feedback to counterbalance the negative in her questionnaire. Maybe I do to myself what some of my supervisees experience. I feel I can learn far more by challenge than by feeling satisfied with myself. Nevertheless, I remain convinced of the importance of unconditional positive regard within person-centred therapy and continue to examine my own self-acceptance. Unconditional positive regard is indeed a core condition, one necessary for personality change to occur.

References

Kirschenbaum, H. and Henderson, V. (1990) *The Carl Rogers Reader*. London: Constable.

Mearns, D. and Thorne, B. (1988) *Person-Centred Counselling in Action*. London: Sage.

Thorne, B. (1992) *Carl Rogers*. London: Sage.

Too Close for Comfort: Levels of Intimacy in the Counselling Relationship

Mary Kilborn

Intimacy and person-centred theory

Intimacy is a concept which appears in the writings of some person-centred therapists but by no means all. In recent years, a number of British therapists have argued that intimacy in the relationship between therapist and client can be seen as an integral part of the therapeutic process. (See, for example, Mearns and Thorne, 1988.) Carl Rogers, when describing the six conditions which must be present for constructive personality change to occur, speaks of the client and the therapist being 'to some degree in contact' (in Kirschenbaum and Henderson, 1990, p. 221) but he does not at that point explicitly speak of a close or intimate relationship. However, his work clearly leads to the possibility of some form of intimacy between client and therapist. Rogers' early descriptions of empathy mention the therapist entering and moving around freely in the client's world (p.226) and in his later years, he states that, when he is at his best as a group facilitator or a therapist, it seems his inner spirit has reached out and touched the inner spirit of the other (p.137). The concept of intimacy arises naturally out of person-centred theory.

Definition of intimacy

Thorne (1991) states that: 'Intimacy is essentially the relationship which occurs at the centre of our own being . . .' (p.144). Malone and Malone (1987) speak of the 'deepest core of our person' (p.17). When Rogers speaks of his inner spirit touching the inner spirit of another, he feels it happens, 'when I am closest to my inner, intuitive self' (Thorne, 1992, p. 137).

Intimacy, then, involves knowing oneself and being able to be present for another person. This would seem to be an excellent description of the therapist's role.

Aim of this study

In my work as a person-centred practitioner, I am comfortable with the concept of intimacy. I remember intimate moments with clients, relish the flow of energy and warmth between us. Yet, I sometimes wondered what clients would make of the suggestion that intimacy, or at least, intimate moments, are an ingredient of the therapeutic process or relationship. This concern made me want to look further

First Published in *Person-Centred Practice,* Volume 3, Number 1, 1995.

into the question of whether my aims and needs as a therapist were in fact in line with my client's needs.

Preparing the study

My plan was to obtain the views of clients and other therapists. However, very early on in the planning stage, I found the process was going to be a very delicate one, as delicate as the subject itself. Intimacy by its very nature is an intangible phenomenon, one that cannot be captured by hard, scientific data. I decided therefore to prepare very open questionnaires, which would by their content influence respondents as little as possible.

Early on I came to the conclusion that I would only collect data from my own clients, as the subject was so central to the relationship between therapist and client. I wanted to get clients to speak openly about their attitude to intimacy in their relationship to me.

I had planned to approach clients who had not been long working with me but it proved impossible to devise a questionnaire in which I could be sure I was getting the information without impacting negatively on the therapeutic process. I concluded that I would have to question clients who were already in a trusting relationship with me. I chose ten long-term clients on the simple intuitive basis that I felt their participation was likely to be more beneficial than detrimental to the counselling process.

So as to gain an initial and fresh response from people not well versed in person-centred theory, I decided that I would ask people setting out on a course of training to be volunteer counsellors. I gave questionnaires to forty trainee counsellors on their first day of training to gain their initial responses on the concept of intimacy in the counselling relationship.

I then approached person-centred therapists well known to me as, at this stage, I wanted to seek the opinions of those therapists whose orientation was more likely to be similar to my own. I was looking to see if there was a common understanding. Ten colleagues responded to the questionnaires.

The trainee counsellor questionnaires and responses

The purpose of the questionnaire was to get an initial response from the trainees as to the use of the word 'intimacy' to describe the closeness of the relationship between client and counsellor. The responses from three open questions are summarised here.

The vast majority of the trainee counsellors had severe reservations. Nineteen out of the forty felt it was an inappropriate term, having connotations of sexual familiarity and secrecy. They thought it suggested crossing professional boundaries and was more a term to be used of equal, personal relationships, not counselling and therapy. Some suggested it was 'too close', like 'baring your spiritual soul'. Seventeen out of the forty were ambivalent. They too felt uneasy about the word 'intimate' being used for a professional relationship. However, these respondents also felt that the term intimacy captured aspects such as 'trust', 'caring', 'love', 'being able to say absolutely anything', being able to express feelings of pain. One or two pointed out that they were happy with the term but felt that it could be 'misconstrued' by the public at large. Only four of those asked felt wholly positive about the concept of intimacy.

Conclusions to the trainee counsellor questionnaires

It would seem that the use of the term 'intimacy' for the trainee counsellors raised many warning bells. The term which has such positive connotations for many person-centred therapists is not necessarily understood in that light by those unfamiliar with person-centred theory. This would suggest that my reticence to use such a term with clients just entering therapy had some foundation.

The client questionnaires and responses

I took great care with each client involved to explain the exact nature of the research and gave each one the option of refusing to take part. However, all ten agreed to and all ten returned to the next counselling session with a completed questionnaire.

Again, the questions were very open, giving clients the opportunity to respond in any way they liked.

The span of time I had been seeing the clients ranged from six months to three years. Seven women and three men participated, although I decided not to focus in any way on gender. In terms of describing the closeness with me, none of the clients had any reservations with the term intimacy. They came up with a wide range of responses some of which I shall mention here. They spoke of a growing sense of trust, the release of being able to be honest, the cessation of the struggle and moving towards calm and peace, a sense of warmth, acceptance, no fear of judgement, care, openness. The pacing not being pushed or hurried, a sense of steadiness and consistency were aspects alluded to by some. Being able to be completely open and revealing things never spoken of before were also seen as significant, one client spoke of 'nakedness, exposure, nowhere to hide, no defences'. A point made by most of the respondents was the need for a sense of equality in the relationship. One client spoke of our 'respective journeys', another 'being known by you and knowing you'. One commented: 'It is important I experience your vulnerability'; another clearly stated that the closest moment for her was when I shared something of myself, she felt that this sharing had moved our relationship on more than anything else. This client stated she saw it in terms of us having intimate moments together rather than an intimate relationship, which is exactly a conclusion I have been moving towards in the course of this study.

In response to difficulties in themselves which may get in the way of their having a close relationship with me, the counsellor, clients spoke in terms of lack of self-esteem, feelings of unacceptability and unworthiness. Two mentioned the difficulty in believing anyone really wanted to listen to them. A number mentioned fear of intimacy itself and letting other people get close. Some spoke of fear of my judging them, of my seeing them not coping, of breaking down in front of me. One spoke of her fear of being 'different' and 'out of step'. Finally, three mentioned their reticence at being honest with themselves, let alone sharing things with me.

When it came to difficulties in something about me, the counsellor, or something I did, there were a variety of revealing responses. A number mentioned their original difficulty with the fact that they, the clients, were expected to direct the sessions. One stated that at the beginning of the sessions, she felt she had to 'make all the contact'. The same client said she sometimes felt 'abandoned' by me when I did not reach out to her in the way that she would have liked. Some mentioned not always knowing where my comments came from and what to do with them. One said that she occasionally saw comments of mine as stating an opinion and this made her wary of offering a differing one. One wondered whether my calm, unworried manner was really 'complacency', another whether my 'warm concern' was 'put on'. All the comments made me reflect on just how difficult it is to be really there for clients in an open, honest manner which they find beneficial to the therapeutic process. For me, the fact that the clients were able to make these points and in some cases, discuss them with me, suggested that our relationship had a reasonably healthy openness to it.

On the subject of how the relationship between me and the clients had developed, all ten were clear. They felt that we had grown closely together, more intimate. A number commented on how unsure and unsafe they had felt at the beginning. One mentioned finding me 'cold and distant', another was 'frustrated by the lack of judgement'. Whereas one found my voice patronising on the phone, another was immediately attracted to my voice before she saw me. A number of respondents said that the development of their relationship with me was not a smooth process, there were periods of developing closeness, periods of withdrawal. One particular client, who has times when she does not come to therapy, said that she takes a break when she feels we are not so close. Two clients referred to the feelings of intimacy with me as 'scary', a third said it was 'risky', 'different to anything I have ever known'. One of the clients stated that he has not yet understood how to respond to his growing trust in me. He feels that has 'curtailed the feeling of closeness and intimacy made available' to him by me. However, the common element in the growing feelings of closeness is that clients have felt safe to bring out issues, explore feelings, which cause them a huge amount of pain. Without the intimacy, they would have been unable to do this. Although it seems to be a delicate and painful business, intimacy would appear to be at the core of clients getting in touch with their inner pain.

There were no negative comments about filling in the questionnaire while still in therapy. Eight welcomed the chance to take stock and write down their experiences of our relationship. One spoke of being 'allowed and encouraged to open up without fear of castigation'. Two respondents admitted to spending a long time over the questionnaire, in one case, many hours! The client who had made some strong statements about feeling abandoned by me said she had wanted to 'protect me from the hurt' that some of her answers might cause. She insisted on telling me all she had written, so that I did not have to read it on my own.

Conclusions to the client questionnaires

As far as I can tell, the experience had been a beneficial one for all my clients, another dimension in their relationship with me. They all seemed to be quite comfortable with the concept of intimacy within the professional relationship, the fear being that the intimacy sometimes led to the expression and feeling of very powerful and painful emotions.

The therapist questionnaires and responses

It was immediately obvious that for the ten therapists who responded, intimacy was a really important concept for them. They attempted a definition with energy, conviction and warmth. However, they too did not find it that easy. As one therapist wrote, 'It is really hard to define in a concise way, although I "know" when it is there. It surfaces, becomes palpable, in some sessions more than others.' Many wrote that it was a 'two-way thing', 'a sharing of real selves', 'a feeling of being completely "at one"', 'an at-one-ness', 'an experience of connectedness', 'a profound intensity experienced by both therapist and client'. Three were quite clear that it was not a permanent but a momentary state, it existed 'in the present moment'. Two mentioned that often no words were needed. Whereas some spoke of 'depth' of feeling, others spoke of 'transcendence', which may have 'a spiritual quality'. One therapist expressed it in a way which combined our original definition of intimacy with the comments of my clients: 'When the connection between myself and my client is close enough for her/him to *really* feel safe to take the risk of talking about something threatening and *touching* to their *core* being, and when I *know* and *acknowledge* how close to this core self I am being invited to see, then I sense what I would call "intimacy"'.

Not surprisingly, all the therapists alluded to one, two or all three of the core conditions when responding to the question on how intimacy comes about. Some took care to point out that the conditions needed not only to be offered but experienced by the client. Some spoke of patience, pacing and the slow building up of trust. Half the respondents mentioned 'self-disclosure', 'sharing enough of myself', 'transparency as a human being because this allows my client to access my vulnerability', 'risking ourselves', concepts which match the client statements that intimacy implies the therapists sharing their own vulnerability. However, two therapists were at pains to stress that intimate moments in the counselling relationship may well happen but could in no way be aimed at or striven for.

When it came to describing what gets in the way of intimacy, eight of the ten therapists mentioned fear. For themselves, they mentioned fear of letting go, fear of trusting, fear of what will happen next, fear of client dependency. In clients, they experience a fear of being authentic, a fear of being known, a fear of being needy, a fear of incurring disappointment. One respondent spoke of 'out-of-touchness' with self, either on the part of herself or her clients, which impedes intimacy.

Conclusions to therapist questionnaires

It was clear that the ten person-centred therapists felt wholly committed to the concept of intimacy. They all concurred that intimacy had in some way to do with the core of a person, the innermost felt sense. The greatest hindrance to arriving at this felt sense was fear, either on the part of the client or of the therapist, or of both.

Conclusions to the study

This small study has attempted an introduction to the concept of intimacy as viewed by forty trainee counsellors, ten clients in therapy and ten person-centred therapists. It would appear to support the theory that person-centred therapy is based on the relationship between the client and the therapist. It would further suggest that the core conditions of empathy, acceptance and congruence, as offered by the therapist and perceived by the client, provide the environment for a relationship to build up between the therapist and client, a relationship in which moments of intimacy are possible. It would appear also that such intimacy can greatly assist the therapeutic process. Clients entering therapy may have no expectations of or indeed desire for intimacy. They may, as did the trainee counsellors, find the concept unprofessional or threatening. However, over time, they may discover that intimacy is indeed possible within a professional relationship and that this can enhance self-knowledge and the ability to get closer to others, as experienced by the ten clients questioned in this study. The person-centred therapists in the study are offering the conditions for intimacy to occur, they are not aiming for it. When it occurs, it can offer memorable moments to both client and therapist. Or, to give Carl Rogers the last word: 'Our relationship transcends itself and becomes a part of something larger. Profound growth and healing and energy are present.' (In Kirschenbaum and Henderson, 1990, p. 137).

References

Dowrick, S. (1992) *Intimacy and Solitude*. London: The Women's Press.

Kirschenbaum, H. and Henderson, V. (Eds)(1990) *The Carl Rogers Reader*. London: Constable.

Lerner, H. G. (1989). *The Dance of Intimacy*. London: Pandora.

Malone, T. and Malone, P. (1987) *The Art of Intimacy*. London: Simon and Schuster.

Mearns, D. and Thorne, B. (1988) *Person-Centred Counselling in Action*. London: Sage.

Rubin, L. B. (1983) *Intimate Partners*. New York: Harper and Row.

Scarf, M. (1987) *Intimate Strangers*. London: Century.

Slade, H. (1977) *Contemplative Intimacy*. London: Darton, Longman and Todd.

Thorne, B. (1992) *Carl Rogers*. London: Sage.

Thorne, B. (1991) *Person-Centred Counselling: Therapeutic and Spiritual Dimensions*. London: Whurr.

The Personal is Political — and the Political is Personal: A Person-Centred Approach to the Political Sphere

Keith Tudor

This article describes the meeting of two spheres — the therapeutic sphere with its focus on healing the psyche — the internal, intra-psychic world — and the political sphere of the external, social, civic world. In describing this encounter between the psyche and the social, the article develops two directions of movement — the politicisation of the personal and the personalising of the political. This provides a frame for discussions developing a person-centred approach (PCA) to understanding the relation between these two, often separated spheres and, particularly, to understanding the impact of local, national and international events.

The personal *is* political

This early feminist slogan summarised one of the concerns of the Women's Liberation Movement to highlight issues which had previously been seen as personal and private. Relationships between women and men, sexuality, abuse, child care, housework, etc. became the subject of public debate. Later, other movements put issues of race, culture, sexuality and disability on the agenda — issues which affect personal beliefs, attitudes, feelings and behaviour as well as public policies and popular culture. Here the *focus* of enquiry is on the *personal* whilst the *direction* of concern and debate is towards the *political*, for instance by subjecting particular (hitherto) 'personal' conflicts, say between a heterosexual couple, to a political analysis using concepts such as those of patriarchy and class relations. Generally, this has an effect of widening our understanding from the particular to the general: in the above example, to understand a personal conflict as an example of distorted gender relations.

This sphere includes the politics *of* psychology and of therapy. This is based on a belief that therapy as an activity is *itself* political: as a social phenomena it is inevitably political. For those who believe and claim that therapy is — and should not be — 'political', a few comments on the history and organisation of therapy may place this in context. Historically, psychoanalysis became seen as a branch of

First published in *Person-Centred Practice*, Volume 5, Number 2, 1997.

science within medicine and psychiatry. One implication of this is that psychoanalysis in particular and psychotherapy in general has developed an (unhealthy) obsession in psycho*pathology* — the origins of the *illness* of the psyche — rather than an equal concern with what might be referred to as psycho*sanology* — or the *health* of the psyche (see Tudor, 1997). Another implication of this incorporation into the medical/psychiatric establishment was the search for respectability and acceptability in the way in which psychotherapy was/is organised and psychotherapists were/are trained. The struggle against the hegemony of the medical model, of fixed ideas about human nature and change, and of closed, self-generating training institutes (institutions), forms a crucial, if largely ignored, part of our collective psychohistory.

The person-centred tradition has made a particular contribution to the politics of therapy, founded on a politics of the person. In a challenging address to the American Psychological Association (APA), Rogers asked if they (we) dared to develop a *human* science, to be whole people, to be designers rather than repairers — in all spheres of life — and to do away with professionalism: 'as soon as we set up criteria for certification . . . the first and greatest effect is to freeze the profession in a past image. This is an *inevitable* result' (Rogers, 1973/1990a, p. 364). Tn his ideas about education, Rogers (1983) challenges traditional theories of 'top-down' education and training. Rogers' regret at his involvement in establishing a board of examiners within the APA is paralleled by Thorne's (1995) more recent concerns about the vicious circle of accountability and the lack of soul in, effectively, the developing closed shop of British Association for Counselling individual counsellor accreditation. Kearney (1996) offers a critique of counselling based on considerations of (the absence of) class and politics and, in this issue, extends this to the training of counsellors (Kearney, 1997). Rogers applied his ideas to the field of personal politics in his book *Carl Rogers On Personal Power* (Rogers, 1978) whose subtitle is *Inner Strength and Its Revolutionary Impact*. In this he discusses the organismic tendency towards fulfilment as a constructive basis of human motivation and for 'a harmonious politics of interpersonal relationships' (p. 243) — in relation to the helping professions, the family, partnership, education, administration, oppression and intercultural tension. Recent work on and in large groups is an example of the therapeutic application of the PCA in developing a person-centred politics of community and the social world (see Caspary, 1991; Lago, 1994; Wood, in press).

Others, too, have challenged the received theories and practices of the various traditions and schools of psychotherapy ever since Freud first coined the term a hundred years ago. For example, in the early days, those on the radical Left such as Reich and Adler attempted to account for social as well as psychological realities. More recently, the establishment in 1995 of the organisation Psychotherapists and Counsellors for Social Responsibility (PCSR) and its journal *Transformations* is a sign that a significant number of therapists are interested in the social sphere. Two recent books also have contributed to political understanding of the personal sphere: Mowbray (1995) puts the case against psychotherapy registration and House and Totton (1997) argue for pluralism and autonomy in the *activity* (as distinct from the profession) of psychotherapy and counselling.

The political is *personal*

Here the *focus* of enquiry is on the *political* sphere whilst the *direction* of understanding is towards the *personal* and therapeutic, for instance the impact of politics and the political world on 'personal' life. This is the therapy of politics: the healing power of the political (the way civic society is organised, particular policies, etc.) as well as its potential for denying personal experience and distorting the way we understand ourselves. Traditionally, some political systems have impacted more than others on people's personal lives. Generally, socialist governments influenced by Marxist analysis, have tended to emphasise the social by favouring planned economies and societies and developing certain social policies which legislate in the personal sphere such as fertility, abortion, child care and, topically, parental responsibilities. Generally. conservative governments tend to emphasise the individual — epitomised by Margaret Thatcher's famous comment that 'there is no such thing as society' — thus promoting the philosophy of the free market, both economically and socially, and often leaving themselves open to accusations of a lack of caring about issues such as poverty, homelessness, mental illness and distress. In such societies, the emphasis is, respectively, on the community and on the individual.

From the early days of psychoanalysis, therapists have been concerned with and have used their analytic insights to understand the wider, social/political sphere. Freud published his book on *Civilisation and its Discontents* in 1930; at the same time Reich was applying his theories on human character structure to analysing *The Mass Psychology of Fascism* and Jung was writing about the unconscious connections between peoples across cultures and time. In the 1960s a number of humanistic psychiatrists and therapists were actively involved in political movements and struggles, viewing this *in itself* as radical therapeutic practice. More recently, in its organisation of topic groups, PCSR clearly views therapy as concerned with the politics *of* . . . disability, ecology, economics, gender, race and culture, sexual diversity, etc.

The person-centred tradition has made its own contribution to this direction of enquiry, particularly through Rogers' development of the notion of personal rather than institutional power and his emphasis on the emerging person rather than organisations or political parties as the spearhead of 'the quiet revolution'. His work with groups in conflict and in what he referred to as some of the world's 'hottest' areas of tension (Northern Ireland, Central America and South Africa) reflects the development and practical application of the PCA to the political sphere:

> Politically, then, if we are in search of a trustworthy base to operate
> from, our major aim would be to discover and possibly increase the
> number of individuals who are coming closer to being whole persons
> — who are moving toward a knowledge of, and harmony with, their

innermost experience, and who sense, with an equal lack of defensiveness, all the data from the persons and objects in the external environment' (Rogers, 1978, pp.250–1).

This elaborates Aristotle's dictum that 'man [sic] is by nature a political animal': our organismic tendency and the basis of human motivation is towards actualising ourselves *and others*. Here, Rogers is also elaborating the need for harmony both with our inner (intra-psychic) *and* our external (extra-psychic) worlds. Yet, despite Rogers' own work and other notable examples, and despite the depth of its theoretical understanding of the person and her/his environment, the PCA has not developed a widespread understanding (even analysis) of the external environment/ world outside therapy and its impact on people — a gap in application which this article seeks to redress.

Developing a person-centred analysis of the political sphere

Historically, psychoanalysts using psychoanalytic and psychodynamic concepts have been at the forefront of developing analysis of society and social events — most popular psychological commentators and columnists, too, are more or less explicitly influenced by psychoanalysis. Although the person-centred approach has necessary and sufficient concepts with which to understand events in the social sphere as well as their impact on people's lives and internal worlds, it has not been as developed or applied to the political world. To illustrate this, I discuss briefly three recent events in the British political sphere in terms of the PCA: the general election (in terms of person-centred personality theory); the recent referenda on devolved powers to a Scottish parliament and a Welsh assembly (in relation to human development); and the death of Diana, Princess of Wales (with reference to Rogers' six conditions).

Many will view the British general election in May 1997, rather than the founding of the Social Democratic Party sixteen years earlier, as breaking the mold (in both senses!) of British politics. Rather than focusing on the nature of the electoral system, the votes cast, particular political personalities, etc., here I am more concerned to understand what the result represents. In all elections, when it is apparent which party has won, an interesting transition takes place: in this case the political and partial (Labour) party becomes the government; the Leader of the Opposition becomes Prime Minister. The government led by the Prime Minister becomes the government of *all* the people, even those who did not vote for them and, indeed, those who did not vote at all. The defeated party bows to the will of the people — generally with the grace not to tell us that we made a mistake! In May this transition took on a different (political) hue. In 1945 when Labour won a landslide victory the incoming Prime Minister, Clement Atlee, in speaking to party workers and, perhaps reflecting an anger born of years in opposition and years of class oppression, said 'We are the masters now.' Following Labour's victory this year and also speaking to party workers, Tony Blair, deliberately echoing and challenging Atlee's sentiment said 'We are the *servants* now'. In this and Blair's subsequent statements about the third or middle way of politics, in the government's proposals for constitutional reform as well as reform of the voting system and in its invitation to the Liberal Democrats to sit on a Cabinet Committee on such reforms: the government appears to be espousing 'one nation' consensus politics. This may be understood in terms of Rogers' (1951) personality theory in which the total personality comprises two overlapping circles which, in a state of psychological tension, represent experience and self-structure (see Figure 1).

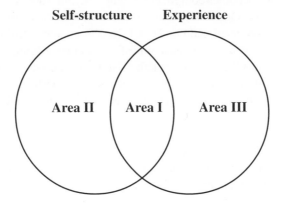

Self-structure   **Experience**

Area II   **Area I**   **Area III**

Figure 1. The total personality (Rogers, 1951).

Experience, 'the immediate [phenomenological] field of sensory and visceral experience' (Rogers, 1951, p. 525), suggests that there are situations, issues and problems in the social world and responses and solutions to these phenomena. The concept of self-structure, 'the configuration of concepts which has been defined as the structure of the self [which] includes the patterned perceptions of the individual's characteristics and relationships' (ibid. p.525) may be applied to an organisational structure such as that of a political party. Person-centred personality theory may thus be applied to the personality of the body politic.

• Area II. Social and other experiences are distorted and values are perceived as experience. Most politicians claim that they have the truth, that all their policies are right, that all the other parties' are wrong — and that the public perceives this to be the case and supports them (if only we knew all the facts). Thus most political issues — the economy, tax and spending policies, education, health, etc. — become polarised *and distorted* as for/against, us/them and good/bad.

• Area III. Experiences are denied to awareness because they are inconsistent with the self(organisational) structure. Some within and outside the Labour party criticised Tony Blair for consulting Margaret Thatcher about his first 'Heads of States' conference. In effect they denied her experience as it is inconsistent with their criticism of her — and inconsistent with much of their organisational structure and culture which has, over the years, been defined by their opposition to her. (One of the problems of the British Labour Party has been that, over the last eighteen years, its identity has been defined only by opposition.)

• Area I. The concept of self (i.e. organisation) and organisation-in-relationship is congruent with our experience. No one and certainly no one political party has the monopoly on the truth. Thus the British government is open to political partnership; the Liberal Democrats state that they will provide a 'constructive opposition', supporting the government on policies on which they agree and maintaining their opposition to policies on which they disagree. Thus, in political life, experience becomes congruent with the structure (organisation) of politics — and vice versa. One example of this is the way the business of the House of Commons is organised and conducted. Recent changes (to Prime Minister's question time and the reorganisation of committee meetings and times) are designed to reflect life in the twentieth — and twenty-first — centuries, thereby making this political life more accessible to those with families (rather than maintaining a structure which reflects the needs of eighteenth century landed gentry).

Such analysis also has its application in therapy. One client, who generally viewed her life as a battle between two oppositional aspects of herself, talked about being surprised at her own excitement at the result of the election. As she discussed this in therapy, she talked about the new government as representing a new politics of consensus (Area I) rather than the old politics of adversarial positions and polarities. Subsequently she drew on this as a potent metaphor for the resolution of her personal conflicts.

The recent referenda on devolving powers to a Scottish parliament and a Welsh assembly which resulted in 'Yes' votes (overwhelming in Scotland and more muted in Wales) is an example of people voting for more devolved local powers and responsibilities. This may be viewed in terms of individual — and, more generally, national — self-development and differentiation as well as devolution. For Rogers (1951), the self is 'the awareness of being, of functioning' (p. 498) and is synonymous with self-awareness and self-experience. Widening this to a 'we' self-concept (Nobles, 1973), a sense of family, collective, tribal and even national identity in an awareness of and desire to be and to function as 'we' is understandable. Developmentally, the self is a differentiated portion of the perceptual field (Rogers, 1951, 1959). Again on a wider level, this provides an understanding of increasing moves on the part of identified and identifiable parts to differentiate from larger wholes, particularly when those 'wholes' are countries, nations, 'blocs' or geographical areas which have been united by conquest (as in the case of Wales by England) or artificially amalgamated by historical expedient or treaty (as in the case of Scotland and England — and, for that matter, six counties of Ireland). From our understanding of development and differentiation, it is perhaps not surprising that, at the same time as the European Community is expanding and certain powers are being centralised, many peoples throughout Europe are expressing their desire for the powers and responsibilities of government to be experienced and expressed more directly and personally.

The death of Diana, Princess of Wales — and, perhaps more significantly, the *impact* of her death — appears to have taken the public, including republicans and commentators, by surprise. As with the other examples, whatever one's own opinions and partiality, Diana's impact on people may be understood, appropriately enough, in person-centred terms. As an integrative model, Rogers' (1957/1990b) six conditions of interpersonal relationships is especially well suited to application to relationships in the wider social/political sphere. Diana clearly made *psychological contact* with people she met — and, arguably, with people she did not meet: 'probably it is sufficient if each makes some "subceived" difference in the experiential field of the other' (p.221). This perhaps accounts for the number of people who were surprised at the strength of their reaction to her death. In her work with the homeless, those with AIDS and leprosy, and with victims of land-mines — 'the constituency of the rejected' as Diana's brother Earl Spencer put it in his funeral address — she had an acute sense of *the vulnerability of others*. In this sense, and especially in recent years, she appeared *congruent*: often communicating her awareness of self and others on a range of personal and social/political issues. She showed compassion and love (*unconditional positive regard*) towards the people she met through her charitable work, despite perhaps not having the same regard for herself — in his address her brother commented that her desire to do good for others had the effect of releasing her from 'deep feelings of unworthiness'. Significantly, the reading at her funeral service, 1 Corinthians 13, ends with the famous phrase about faith, hope and charity — which translates as love. Similarly, Diana appears to have expressed her *empathic understanding* for many people's experience, again perhaps born out of her own vulnerability and difficulties. Finally, people she met said that they had felt her regard and empathy and many thousands, even millions, of others report having felt touched by (having *received*) her love and understanding. Diana's impact may thus be viewed as having fulfilled the necessary and sufficient conditions by which interpersonal relationships are enhanced — even at a distance.

Conclusion

These are but three topical examples of how the PCA may be used and developed as a framework for understanding the wider world and its impact on our personal worlds. Rogers' basis for harmony between innermost experience and the external environment requires us to be at ease with — and in — both the personal and political spheres and to the movement between the two: to develop our congruence with ourselves as individuals-in-political-context. In his ground-breaking work covering issues such as masculinity, nationalism and political material in the clinical setting, Samuels (1993), drawing on analytic (Jungian) psychology, successfully moves in both directions at the same time. This article is a contribution to developing a *person-centred approach* to understanding the political nature of the personal and, particularly, the personal nature of the political.

References

Caspary, W.R. (1991) Carl Rogers — Values, Persons, and Politics: The Dialectic of Individual and Community. *Journal of Humanistic Psychology,* 31, (4), pp. 8–31.

House, R., and Totton, N. (1997) *Implausible Professions. Arguments for Pluralism and Autonomy in Psychotherapy and Counselling.* Ross-on-Wye: PCCS Books.

Kearney, A. (1996) *Counselling, Class and Politics.* Manchester: PCCS Books.

Kearney, A. (1997) Class, Politics and the Training of Counsellors. *Person-Centred Practice,* 5, (2), pp. 11–5.

Lago, C. (1994). The Need for Connectedness and Community: Therapy for a Masturbatory Society. *Counselling,* 5, (2), pp. 120–124.

Mowbray, R. (1995) *The Case Against Psychotherapy Registration.* London: Trans Marginal Press.

Nobles, W.W. (1973) Psychological Research and the Black Self-Concept: A Critical Review. *Journal of Social Issues,* 29, pp. 11–31.

Rogers, C.R. (1951) *Client-Centered Therapy.* London: Constable.

Rogers, C.R. (1959) A Theory of Therapy, Personality, and Interpersonal Relationships as Developed in the Client-Centered Framework, in S. Koch (Ed.), *Psychology: The Study of a Science Vol 3. Formulations of the Person and the Social Context* (pp.184–256). New York: McGraw-Hill.

Rogers, C.R. (1978) *Carl Rogers on Personal Power. Inner Strength and Its Revolutionary Impact.* London: Constable.

Rogers, C.R. (1983) *Freedom to Learn for the 80's.* New York: Macmillan. (Previous edition published 1969.)

Rogers, CR. (1990a) Some New Challenges to the Helping Professions. In H. Kirschenbaum & V.L. Henderson (Eds.), *The Carl Rogers Reader* (pp. 357–375). London: Constable. (Original work published 1973.)

Rogers, C.R. (1990b) The Necessary and Sufficient Conditions of Therapeutic Personality Change. In H. Kirschenbaum & V.L. Henderson (Eds.), *The Carl Rogers Reader* (pp.219–235). London: Constable. (Original work published 1957.)

Samuels, A. (1993) *The Political Psyche.* London: Routledge.

Thorne, B. (1995) The Accountable Therapist: Standards, Experts and Poisoning the Well. *Self* and Society, 23, (4).

Tudor, K. (1997) Mental Health Promotion: The Contribution of Psychotherapy. In M. Money and L. Buckley (Eds.), *Positive Mental Health and Its Promotion* (pp. 21–4) Liverpool: Institute for Health, John Moores University.

Wood, J.K. (in press). *The Person-Centered Approach of Carl Rogers: Toward An Understanding of Its Implications.*

Class, Politics and the Training of Counsellors

Anne Kearney

In my recent book (Kearney, 1996), I argued that counselling is not a politically neutral activity, rather that it is one which is embedded and is inseparable from the political culture of Western capitalist society at this particular stage in its evolution. I claimed that person-centred counselling (and every kind of counselling and psychotherapy for that matter) has lost its 'cutting edge' as a potentially transformative activity in social as well as personal terms.

In seeking acceptance and respectability as a profession on a par with other professions (and thus entitling its members to status and privilege), I believe that counselling is becoming more routinised, less dynamic and less challenging to the norms of society than practitioners like Rogers intended it to be (see Yalom, 1995).

In trying to offend nobody, counselling questions less; in pursuing political neutrality it is in danger of condoning inequality and oppression; in trying to find safe fences to sit on it fails to publicly criticise the oppression of women, of Black people, of disabled people and, most importantly, it fails to acknowledge the enormous inequalities imposed on people by the class system.

In summary, in my book I argued that mainstream counselling is increasingly (if by default) on the side of the powerful at the expense of the dispossessed and that the increasing professionalisation of counselling roots it even more firmly in a middle-class white context. This may limit what it can offer to the majority of people who do not belong to that social grouping.

This has happened with other 'helping' professions which in an earlier political climate such as that of post-war Britain held a set of ideals in education, in health care and in welfare policy which emphasised equality of opportunity regardless of gender, race or class. As the political climate changed so the aspirations of these professions adapted as we can see very clearly with rationing of services in the National Health Service, the inaccessibility of higher education for many people and the inadequacy of welfare benefits for millions of people who are disabled or ill or unemployed.

The legacy of the Thatcher ideology and its political consequences have produced a similar dilution of former ideals in counselling (see Kearney, 1996). Interpretations of Rogerian counselling which emphasise the individual as distinct from 'the individual in her/his social context' have gained precedence over readings

First published in *Person-Centred Practice* Volume 5, Number 2, 1997.

of Rogers' work which charge the counsellor with a social as well as a personal responsibility to clients (see Hutton, 1995). Broader goals, for instance of social change, have with rare exceptions been largely ignored in counselling journals, textbooks and training manuals. Trainees are not expected to be familiar with or knowledgeable about the society in which they and their clients live, and political education is seen to be outside the scope of counselling training. The pressures of the present political climate with its emphasis on market forces and economic accountability, as well as the adoption of so-called 'quality control' measures, have had direct consequences for the ethos and ideology of counselling. In particular, the political climate of the eighties and nineties has inhibited counsellors from examining and recognising some of the social and political assumptions and prejudices of counselling itself. Gender issues and race issues, together with those surrounding disability and sexuality, are slowly becoming recognised elements on training courses. However, the class basis of counselling and the power issues surrounding class remain, for the most part, obscured and ignored.

In this article I want to suggest that the tendency to train counsellors from within a particular ideological framework (which I view as wider than a particular theoretical orientation) which in itself is rarely if ever scrutinised, is a major factor in reinforcing the trend towards a focus in counselling on 'not rocking the boat' politically. An ethos of counselling has developed which, however unintentionally, enhances its status as a profession. The cost of this is to limit its potentially liberating role in opposing social forces which oppress clients. The political is then seen as something external to the client's frame of reference and therefore 'not our business'.

I have suggested earlier that I believe that most current person-centred counsellor training courses are highly selective in terms of which aspects of, for example Rogers' work, they choose to emphasise. Rogers himself saw person-centred counselling as having the potential to challenge and change the political structures as well as the internal structures which inhibit self-awareness and development. He considered that facilitating the client's opposition to those structures was and is a legitimate part of the therapeutic work of counsellors. I would go further and suggest that it is a responsibility of counsellors to be active in opposing those structures.

The shift from this focus to the more limited one which now dominates most training and structures for accreditation is itself a consequence of the present political climate which denies the class-based nature of peoples' experiences. As with all major changes, the political and ideological shifts such as that which took place during the Thatcher years necessitated and resulted in the socialisation of people into a new set of political values and beliefs (see Kavanagh, 1990). No less than any other area of social life, counselling itself and counselling training has been affected by these new values. In subtle and not-so-subtle ways the process of counselling training is itself a process of socialising trainees into a set of beliefs and norms which fail to challenge the social status quo. Further, I suggest, most counselling training does this by default by not equipping or encouraging counsellors to oppose and question their trainers' values or even their own.

Much of this can be seen before counselling training even begins. Training is an expensive business and it *is* a business as it currently operates in most colleges of further and higher education and in the private/independent sector. There is little remission of fees or bursaries for those people who cannot afford to fund themselves and most trainees find that training imposes severe financial strains on themselves and their families. Training as a counsellor, with training fees, supervision and the requirement to have personal therapy, can easily cost £5,000 whilst training as a psychotherapist can cost £15,000. Such training is simply not accessible to most people and this fact inevitably skews the recruitment of trainees in favour of the employed middle-class. Whilst even this population may have to borrow the money to fund themselves, they often have credit available to them as well as a cultural confidence in the concept of borrowing large sums of money. Most working-class people do not share this value and are reluctant to get into debt even if such credit were available to them. Where there is the equivalent of 'assisted places' or bursaries, these tend to emphasise gender and/or race or disability — never social class. This is not to suggest that women, Black or disabled people should not be assisted financially; my point is that the failure to recognise class as a major cause of social disadvantage reveals a lack of awareness and a particular set of values which demonstrate some of the ideological foundation of many counselling courses.

The majority of trainers are from similar backgrounds and this has direct and indirect consequences for the way in which training takes place. Predominantly middle-class trainers, training predominantly middle-class trainees may — and, I believe, does — result in certain attitudes, beliefs and norms being (perhaps unwittingly) imported into training as 'normal' or 'natural' and, as such, not open to discussion. In this way, class-specific, culturally-relative ways of thinking, feeling and doing may not only go unchallenged, but may not even be noticed either by trainers or trainees. A simple example illustrates this. In my own work as a supervisor, I work with trainees and qualified counsellors who have trained on a range of courses in an area in which a great diversity of counselling courses exists. Rarely has any one of my supervisees, in giving a profile of the client they want to discuss, referred to the social class of that client. Even more rarely has a supervisee seen a class difference between herself/himself and the client as involving a set of issues they might wish to explore in their supervision. Class is simply not seen as an issue that might have an impact on the therapeutic relationship. It would seem — and most counselling literature would support this — that in training, trainees are invited to explore various types of oppression which influence their work with clients, but remain unaware of the most influential and all-embracing source of all oppression: that of social class.

The process of training people to be counsellors has various elements, including the acquisition of skills; learning a body of theoretical knowledge; the development of a set of beliefs and attitudes consistent with the purpose of the training and very importantly, the moulding of the trainees' sense of identity. Each of these elements is affected by the great power imbalances between the trainers and trainees in much the same way as the therapeutic process is affected by the power dynamics between the counsellor and client. Whilst the latter are, to a greater or lesser extent, acknowledged in the counselling relationship, the power inherent in the training relationship (e.g. the power of the trainer ultimately to fail the trainee) appears to be discussed less. Yet it is obviously the case that the power entrusted to trainers to judge and assess trainees' work will have a profound effect on the interaction between trainer and trainee. A part of this will be the trainees' tendency to comply with what they see to be valued by trainers, both in terms of attitudes and beliefs. To the extent that trainers take the political status quo as 'given' and therefore not a topic for discussion and possible disagreement, this is likely to invite conformity to that norm by trainees. It would be a brave (if not foolhardy!) trainee who would challenge the unspoken, taken-for-granted ideology of their trainers who have the power to pass or fail them in their assessed work.

Many, if not most, trainees feel de-skilled at various stages in their training, and there seems to be some assumptions that this is inevitably part of the process of undergoing training. I believe it to be inevitable only within a particular paradigm of training, one which de-powers trainees and reduces their sense of identity as skilled, competent adults. Many trainees feel their status reduced to that of child, dependent on adult (trainer) approval. This is particularly difficult for working-class students who may have to cope with the additional de-powering effect of training in a middle-class ethos. The de-skilling effect of much counselling training denies the fact that most trainees are already highly skilled interpersonally and that counselling training requires refinement of those already existing skills, not the damaging of them. This damage can be further increased by what I think of as 'counsellor-speak' — the use of phrases and cliches which have the effect of inhibiting trainees' spontaneity and of undermining their confidence in their ability to communicate meaningfully with their clients. Again, it is likely that it is working-class trainees — and eventually, of course, working-class clients — who are most affected by this. Language is more than simply a means of verbal labelling and description, it is also constitutive of who we become and it is my view that 'counsellor-speak' ('I am aware that you . . .'; 'I sense that . . .', etc.) actually influences trainees to become certain types of people. I am not, of course, arguing that language is the *only* factor which does this, rather that it is the *vehicle* for that 'becoming'.

I am suggesting that counselling training, like all other types of training, has a hidden curriculum, which contains a particular paradigm: one which leads to particular definitions of what is 'real', what is important, what is possible. The paradigm contained in and informing most counselling training is one, I believe, which defines the scope of counselling and does so in terms which denies the political nature of counselling as an activity. This charges counsellors with certain responsibilities and relieves them of others and it absolves counsellors from the need to examine the ideology of counselling itself.

The hidden curriculum, at least partly, justifies the drive to ever-increasing levels of accreditation (see Orbach, 1994; Mowbray, 1995; Thorne, 1995). Increased and increasing professionalisation has been an example of the way in which counselling organisations like the British Association for Counselling (BAC) impose a set of values on practitioners which are difficult to resist and which, if resisted, may pose a threat to their livelihood — most adverts for counsellors now require applicants to be BAC accredited or working towards it. In the same way, trainees have little or no say over the structure and content of their training — some person-centred courses are notable exceptions to this. More worrying, as with the accreditation issue, the hidden agenda remains hidden (probably even from trainers themselves) and it is these absences in training — the failure to examine the ideological nature of counselling — which seem to me to perpetuate particular interpretations of counselling and to give it its current political acquiescence.

It is not my intention to put forward a conspiracy theory of counselling training. My object is to suggest that, in ignoring the political and especially the class nature of counselling ideology, a set of values and beliefs may be internalised by trainees, indeed may be required to be internalised in order to qualify as professional counsellors. To the extent that those beliefs and values preclude the exposure of the non-neutral nature of counselling as an activity, counsellors are in danger of being trained to be part of the process by which disadvantaged clients continue to be disadvantaged. I do not believe that to be the intention or motive either of counsellors or of trainers, but I do believe that it may be one of the unintended consequences of current counsellor training.

References

Hutton, W. (1995) *The State We're In*. London: Jonathan Cape.

Kavanagh, D. (1990) *Thatcherism and British Politics*. London: Clarendon Press.

Kearney, A. (1996) *Counselling, Class and Politics*. Manchester: PCCS Books.

Mowbray, R. (1995) *The Case Against Psychotherapy Registration*. London: Trans Marginal Press.

Orbach, S. (1994) *What's Really Going on Here?* London: Virago, London.

Thorne, B. (1995) The Accountable Therapist. *Self and Society*, 23, (4).

Yalom, I. (1995) Introduction. In Rogers, C.R. *A Way of Being*. Boston: Houghton Mifflin. (Original work published 1980.)

Who is the 'Person' in the Person-Centred Approach?

Judy Moore

Introduction

Over the past three years my thinking about the social context of person-centred counselling has been heavily influenced by questions about the nature of 'reality' and the concept of 'self. These questions, and the influences to which I have opened myself in order to begin to answer them, have led to a recognition that I might well also need to question what I mean by the 'person' — a term that I had hitherto never seen fit to challenge — if I am to address the full complexity of what it means to be alive as a human being and to continue to work within the person-centred approach.

Much work has been done in recent years, particularly in the field of women's studies, to demonstrate that we live in a social reality that is constructed on particular belief systems, passed down from generation to generation and now reinforced by a complexity of media images and propaganda that dictate by what standards we should live and what kind of 'person' (depending upon age, class, gender, ethnic origin and other variables) we should be. Some of this work is discussed by Hawtin and Moore (1998). The distress that impossible standards and aspirations can generate in individuals is ably demonstrated by David Smail in *The Origins of Unhappiness* (1993). While agreeing with much of Smail's argument, I was left unsatisfied by his definition of 'reality' and puzzled by the question of what happens to an individual's actualizing tendency in the variety of social contexts in which we happen to find ourselves. I hope to make a fuller study of these questions in due course, but for the purpose of this article I should like briefly to consider the nature of 'reality' and the 'self' in the light of some of Carl Rogers' own definitions and how these relate to my current understanding of Japanese views of the nature of the person. By considering the concepts of 'reality' and 'self' from the perspective of a culture that is not my own 1 have begun to see how limited were some of my assumptions about the social context in which I work and how limited was my view of the person.

In 1994 I first became interested in Japanese perspectives on the person-centred approach through attending a presentation on the pioneering work of Fujio Tomoda at the 3rd International Conference for Client-Centered and Experiential Therapy at Gmunden, Austria. Tomoda was one of the main introducers of client-centred

First published in *Person-Centred Practice*, Volume 5, Number 2, 1997.

therapy into Japan and has translated much of Rogers' work into Japanese. Subsequently one of the authors of the Gmunden paper, Yoshihiko Morotomi, an associate professor from Chiba University, became a visiting fellow at the Centre for Counselling Studies at the University of East Anglia, where I work, from March to August 1997. 1 have learnt a great deal from his insights and willingness to communicate his perceptions of his culture, enabling me to deepen my understanding of some of the concepts to which he and his colleagues first introduced me.

Reality

David Smail asserts that 'we are in no fundamental doubt about the reality of the world in which we find ourselves' (1993, p. 210). He argues that we need to de-mystify the processes that are at work in our society to give power to the business-oriented 'mediocrity' that dominates us. His view is that all is explicable if we study it with sufficient attention, that we can locate the sources of oppression to the 'distal' forces of the economy and business culture while acknowledging, in terms of individual lives, that 'not only is there a current set of influences bearing down upon the person, but there have also been former sets of influences, so that the person is shaped by a history as well as by present circumstances' (ibid. p. 65). Madness, as *he* sees it, is not a person's 'loss of contact with reality' but rather 'reality's failure to make contact with and to explicate the personal experience of the sufferer' (ibid. p. 90).

Smail is critical of counsellors and therapists because of the emphasis that they place on individual responsibility, ignoring the shaping influence of distal forces and unwittingly colluding with the forces of oppression:

> Over and over again the orthodox theoretical stance favours some
> kind or other of 'internal' pathology. It is as if horticulture had never
> progressed beyond a notion that the growth and health of plant life
> depended on the internal adjustment of each individual specimen
> rather than upon the conditions in which they grow (ibid. p. 90).

Although I could not agree more that we need to take into account the hidden influences that shape our perception of ourselves and our social realities, I found myself at this point finding something lacking in Smail's horticultural analogy and thinking of Rogers' image of potatoes thrusting out shoots in the dark, manifesting an inherent impulse to grow even in less than ideal circumstances. A mechanistic view of reality such as Smail's does not take into account the directional movement of the actualizing tendency, the complex twist at the apparently simple heart of the person-centred approach and one which, I believe, brings us into a different dimension of understanding. While knowing that it is vital that we try to develop our awareness of the sources of oppression in our lives, I want to hold that awareness in balance with an understanding of the primacy of the actualizing tendency, defined by Rogers in *A Way of Being* in the following terms:

> There is one central source of energy in the human organism. This source

is a trustworthy function of the whole system rather than of some portion of it; it is most simply conceptualized as a tendency toward fulfilment, toward actualization, involving not only the maintenance but also the enhancement of the organism (Rogers, 1980, p. 123).

Within Western culture it is difficult to find terms that adequately define this directional force or to acknowledge the existence of a reality that operates at a deeper level than that which can be dissected, even on a psychological level, in terms of conventionally predictable cause-and-effect. The operation of the core conditions on the actualizing tendency takes place on a level that is more to do with a way of 'being' rather than a way of 'doing'.

I find it unsatisfactory to consign the notion of 'being' to vague definitions of 'the spiritual' and I think there is a place within the person-centred approach to explore the notion of different realities — and different layers of experiencing — much more fully than has hitherto been done. In an essay entitled 'Do we need "a" Reality?', written in 1974, Carl Rogers asserts a very different view of the notion of reality from that later propounded by David Smail:

> Can we today afford the luxury of having 'a' reality? I am convinced that this is a luxury we *cannot* afford, a myth we dare not maintain . . . It appears to me that the way of the future must be to base our lives and our education on the assumption that there are as many realities as there are persons, and that our highest priority is to accept that hypothesis and proceed from there. Proceed where? Proceed, each of us, to explore open-mindedly the many, many perceptions of reality that exist. We would, I believe, enrich our own lives in the process. We would also become more able to cope with the reality in which each one of us exists, because we would be aware of many more options (Rogers, 1980, pp. 104–5).

Just four years prior to Rogers' essay, Tomoda, after deeper reflection on the true meaning of the concept, had changed his original Japanese version of Rogers' term 'nondirective' from a very literal translation to 'mui-shizen' which means 'doing nothing and being natural' which is the central concept of Taoism. Hayashi et al., in their 1994 paper on the work of Tomoda, make it clear that 'mui-shizen' is no easy way of being:

> . . . it is extremely difficult to master the way of 'doing nothing'. Tomoda states that no one can directly educate, guide, or counsel others: a counselor can only create an atmosphere or a relationship in which clients can do whatever they want; and once such a relation has been established, the *internal power that is fundamental and makes a human live properly without help from outside will be activated* (Hayashi et al., 1994, pp. 2–3, my emphasis).

The concept of 'mui-shizen' brings a different dimension to Rogers' 'core conditions' of personality change, one which I find extremely exciting and challenging, not only in terms of my own development as a person who wishes to be capable of offering a climate for growth but also to our Western understanding of the person-centred approach.

'Self'

It seems to me that we need to give equal consideration to the notion of the 'self' that happens to be occupying any given 'reality' if we are to move towards a deeper understanding of the person. Rogers points out in the eighth of his nineteen propositions about personality and behaviour that 'there are many puzzling and unanswered questions in regard to the *dawning concept* of the self '(Rogers, 1951, p. 497, my emphasis). Both here and in his 'Theory of Therapy, Personality and Interpersonal Relationships as Developed in the Client-Centered Framework' (1959) Rogers is clear that there are many potential ways of viewing the 'self'. In a long digression in his 'Theory of Therapy' he gives an account of how his own and his colleagues' understanding of what he terms the 'construct' of 'self' had developed to this point. Rogers' main focus in this digression is the development of an understanding of the configurational quality of the self-concept, but he also displays an openness to other ways of viewing the 'self' that prefigures his later openness to other definitions of 'reality':

> At all times. we endeavour to keep in the forefront of our thinking the fact that each definition is no more than an abstraction and that the same phenomena might be abstracted in a different fashion. One of our group is working on a definition of self which would give more emphasis to its process nature. Others have felt that a plural definition, indicating many specific selves in each of various life contexts, would be more fruitful (Rogers, 1959, p. 203).

Tomoda not only translated Rogers' 'Theory of Personality and Behaviour' into Japanese but also published a booklet entitled 'Jiko no Kouzou' (*The Anatomy of Self,* 1969) in which he presented his thinking on Rogers' self-theory. According to his Japanese colleagues, Tomoda is uneasy with the use of the term 'self' within Rogers' work since, from his perspective, working out the meaning of self is an 'everlasting theme' for human beings (Hayashi et al., 1994, p. 4). Tomoda regards the self as being multi-layered (three possible layers which he defined in 1992 are an 'essential' self, a 'narcissistic' or 'conceptual' self and the 'subject' of a relational interaction with another person) and, to avoid any objective definition, instead of 'self' Tomoda uses the expression 'a living organism commonly equated with "I"' throughout his 1969 booklet (Hayashi et al., 1994, p.4).

Yoshihiko Morotomi has further explained how vastly different is the Western from the Japanese concept of the person. In the West the ego (Tomoda's 'narcissistic' or 'conceptual' self) is given much stronger definition and value; in Japan the life of the individual is seen as inextricably interconnected with all living things:

> We, the common Japanese people, feel that the life of human beings
> is a part of the great life of nature itself and that true happiness should
> be realized when we live following the law of nature as a whole
> (Morotomi, 1997, p. 2).

This reflects the 'we' self concept found in many collective cultures which also
carries an awareness of an historical and cultural reference group (see Nobles,
1973). Taking this further Morotomi goes on to explain that in the Zen tradition
'the realisation of one's true self is identical with the realisation of absolute
nothingness, a profound sense of being at one with everything, including the divine'
(1997, p. 4).

It fascinates me that this view of the interconnectedness of all things should
relate so closely to Rogers' hypothesis of the 'formative tendency' in which the
living force of the actualizing tendency becomes part of a much greater living
force:

> I hypothesise that there is a formative directional tendency in the
> universe, which can be traced and observed in stellar space, in
> crystals, in micro-organisms, in more complex organic life and in
> human beings. This is an evolutionary tendency toward greater order,
> greater complexity, greater interrelatedness (Rogers, 1980, p.133).

At the end of the essay in which this definition appears Rogers speculates that this
hypothesis 'could be a base upon which we could begin to build a theory for
humanistic psychology', adding, 'it definitely forms a base for the person-centered
approach' (1980, p.133).

Conclusion

Carl Rogers was clearly open throughout his career to the questioning of concepts
such as 'self' and 'reality' and in his later years to exploring the deeper levels of
interrelatedness implicit in the formative tendency. I have been very heartened by
this openness since the time that I first began to consider questions around the
social construction of reality within the person-centred approach and was brought
up against much deeper and less comprehensible issues than I would ever have
imagined. I feel privileged to have been so challenged in my thinking as 1 have
been by Japanese colleagues. When asked how he would define the 'person' in
the person-centred approach, Yoshihiko Morotomi drew a diagram placing the
'ego' at the top of a vertical line, the 'felt sense' part-way down and the 'true self'
of the Zen tradition at the bottom: he was clear that, for him, the 'person' is at the
bottom, the deepest level.

One of the many questions I am left with is: how do we see the 'person' in our
Western tradition of the person-centred approach? In this article I have given some
early stages in my own thinking but I am aware that mine is an idiosyncratic view,
formed by very particular influences in recent years. My eventual aim is to make
a much fuller study of how an individual's actualizing tendency operates within

different realities, knowing only at this stage that it is openness to different realities that shapes the 'self'— and hence the 'person' — we happen to be at any given time.

References

Note: Unfortunately Tomoda's work has not been translated into English so all references to his work are taken from Hayashi et al. (1994).

Hawtin, S., & Moore, J. (1998). Empowerment or Collusion?: the Social Context of Person-Centred Therapy. In B. Thorne & E. Lambers (Eds.), *The Person-Centred Approach: A European Perspective.* London: Sage.

Hayashi, S., Kuno, T., Morotomi, Y., Osawa, M., Shimizu, M., and Suetake, Y. (1994) A Re-evaluation of Client-Centered Therapy through the work of F. Tomoda and its Cultural Implications in Japan. Unpublished paper, presented at the Third International Conference of Client-Centered and Experiential Therapy, Gmunden, Austria.

Morotomi, Y. (1997) Person-Centered Counselling from a Viewpoint of Japanese Spirituality. Unpublished paper presented at the University of East Anglia, Norwich. [Published in modified form in *Person-Centred Practice,* (1998) Vol 6, No1, pp. 28–32.]

Nobles, W. W. (1973). Psychological Research and the Black Self-Concept: A Critical Review. *Journal of Social Issues, 29,* pp. 11–31.

Rogers, C.R. (1951) *Client Centered Therapy.* London: Constable.

Rogers, C.R. (1980) *A Way of Being.* Boston: Houghton Mifflin.

Rogers, C.R. (1959) A Theory of Therapy, Personality and Interpersonal Relationships, as Developed in the Client-Centered Framework. In S. Koch (Ed.) *Psychology: A Study of a Science. Volume 3. Formulations of the Person and the Social Context* (pp. 184–256). New York: McGraw-Hill.

Smail, D. (1993). *The Origins of Unhappiness.* London: Harper Collins.

The Personal is Political: Re-reading Rogers

Rose Cameron

*I see ... revolution as coming not in some great organised movement, nor in
a guncarrying army with banners, not in manifestos and declarations, but
through the emergence of a new kind of person ... (Rogers, 1978, p. 262).*

'Carl Rogers is not known for his politics', wrote Farson in 1974. This, sadly, still
seems to be the case in 1997. Farson continues by saying that he has come to think
of Rogers, 'as a political figure . . . one of the social revolutionaries of our time'
(1974, p. 197), a view with which 1 am very much in agreement. Not only does
Rogers seem to be largely unrecognised as politically radical, but is often critiqued,
increasingly from within the person-centred world, as politically reactionary. In
response to the view of Rogers as, if not reactionary then, certainly politically naive,
I outline the profound radicalism I see in Rogers' thought. In doing so, I specifically
respond to Jones' (1996) charge of cultural imperialism, Holdstock's (1993) view
of the self-actualising tendency as an ethnocentric and male-centred concept and
Waterhouse's (1992) accusation of victim-blaming liberal individualism.

The actualising tendency

In his paper, (reprinted in this volume, pages 242–249) Matthew Jones (1996)
suggests that viewing the self-actualising tendency as universally applicable implies
a form of cultural and intellectual imperialism. He sketches an image of the person-
centred counsellor as a missionary, clutching a battered copy of *On Becoming a
Person,* 'ready to lead the natives to enlightenment, ready to interpret their
experiences in terms of self actualization' (Jones, 1996, p. 22). My argument with
Jones begins with the word 'interpret'. Person-centred practice is not, and never
has been, about interpretation. Jones calls upon Spinelli (1994) to prove that Rogers
does in fact interpret his client's experience in terms of his own theoretical beliefs.
In order to illustrate this, he isolates one sentence from a half-hour interview
(Rogers, 1986/1990) in which Rogers seems to be 'making an evaluation as to
what is the "real" Jan and what is not' (Jones, 1996, p. 24). What Jones fails to
mention is that Jan, the client, makes this evaluation herself earlier in the session,
long before Rogers does. In fact, Rogers, in his commentary, rebukes himself for
failing to hear and acknowledge it at the time (Rogers, 1986/1990). Although it
happens to be in keeping with a person-centred view of personality structure, the

First published in *Person-Centred Practice*, Volume 5, Number 2, 1997.

idea of the 'real' Jan originates with Jan herself. Rogers' comment is from the client's frame of reference — it is not an interpretation. Interestingly, Jones makes no mention whatsoever of the importance Rogers gives to respecting the client's internal frame of reference as unique and of entering into it as fully as possible. He does, however, make several references to what seem to be post-modernist versions of the same idea. Jones concludes by resolving to restrain himself from 'proactively introducing theoretical concepts into my practice' (Jones, 1996, p. 25). In doing so, he arrives by the most circuitous route at what promises to be something more easily recognisable as person-centred practice.

The imposition of one's own view via interpretation, however subtle, is antithetical to the practice of the person-centred approach (PCA); it is therefore, I believe, very important that we are *aware* of our own beliefs about human nature. When we are *unaware* of what our own beliefs are, or indeed that we have any, we are in danger of regarding them as given, facts, obvious, objectively 'true' or right. Jones acknowledges this, yet seems to argue that person-centred practice is put at risk by a clear awareness of the philosophical position implicit in person-centred theory.

Rogers does indeed regard the actualising tendency as universal. This does not, in my view, imply that he was a proponent of the modernist paradigm and a covert cultural imperialist, and I must confess to finding Jones' line of argument on this point contradictory and confusing in the extreme. It seems to me that Rogers cannot be exclusively defined, as Jones attempts to do, as either a modernist or post-modernist thinker. Rogers constantly emphasises the value and importance of respecting a multiplicity of realities and personal, internal frames of reference — particularly in his paper 'Do we need "a" reality?' (Rogers, 1980), which surely allies him with post-modernist thought. Jones seems to pay no heed to this, concentrating instead on the fact that Rogers believed the self-actualising tendency to be universal. Cultural imperialism is, for Jones, inherent in any universal generalisation. He implies, and Holdstock (1993) explicitly argues, that contemporary person-centred thought ought to drop the belief in the actualising tendency as universal.

The universality of the actualising tendency is, for me, not only the cornerstone of practice, but also of person-centred politics. Rogers' view of the actualising tendency as the *only* psychological drive is one of the unique aspects of person-centred theory and practice. Movement away from defensive destructiveness and towards greater social responsibility is a characteristic of this tendency. The political implication of this position is that we do not *need* to be controlled by an external authority. We, individually and collectively, not only have the right to self-determination and group determination but, given the necessary conditions, can be trusted to use our power responsibly.

Jones draws on Holdstock's 'powerful argument for the revision of the person-centred concept of the organismic self-actualising individual' (Jones, 1996, p. 21). Holdstock also lays the charge of ethnocentricity at Rogers' door, as do Sue and Sue (1990), on the grounds that in his view the self is not 'born out of the social or sharing process' (Holdstock, 1993, p. 241). I disagree strongly with this interpretation. The self-actualising tendency, inherent in all organic life, is the drive to become what one truly is. A seed will not grow without soil, light and water. A baby, as Rogers points out, will not thrive without love. Relationships with other people are as necessary to the development of the organism as they are to the development of the self-concept. We need each other in order to become ourselves.

Another belief underpinning Rogers' view of the self is that the self may be distorted by socialisation. Once growing, a seed can only become what it is — a carnation perhaps. However, I can to some degree, manipulate it into being what I want it to be. I may for instance, give it only inky water, in which case it will produce a purple blossom rather than the red one it would have had otherwise. Similarly, I may be given all sorts of conditions of worth and injunctions which encourage me to display socially constructed characteristics. In this analogy, the purple blossom is equivalent to the self-concept. Carrette (1997) claims that person-centred theory sees the interaction between self and environment as 'unfortunate and unnecessary' (p.8). This is not the case. Misfortune — and maladaptation — arises only if the environment is not loving, affirming and nourishing. Contact with others is something that, as a person, I need. If the contact I have available is accepting and affirming, I will become more fully myself, like the red carnation. If it is conditional, manipulative and oppressive, I will become a distorted version of myself, like the purple carnation.

Rogers, writing against the behaviourist belief that we are only what we have been conditioned to be, emphasises the uniqueness of the individual. He also emphasises the potential for personal power if that uniqueness is respected. The more fully functioning a person is, the less vulnerable they are to a hostile environment. There was, for example, nothing the South African apartheid system could do to make Nelson Mandela lose his integrity and self-respect. Rogers says that the strength and personal power developed by living our uniqueness leads us to be true to oneself in the face of manipulation and oppression. He does *not* say that we have no need of community acceptance and support in the development of that uniqueness. The actualising tendency needs to be nourished by acceptance, warmth, and understanding.

Feminism, autonomy and relatedness

Holdstock (1993) draws on Josselson (1987) to critique Rogers from a female perspective. Whilst I agree that 'women move along the world through relational connections' (Josselson, 1987, p. 169), and 1 value my ability to interconnect with others, I am aware that the feminist struggle is also about extricating ourselves from engulfment in relational identity. It is about no longer being lost in our identities as wife, mother, sister, daughter, but having a sense of ourselves as separate and autonomous — and relational. The hand that rocks the cradle may hold up half the sky (to mix feminist images), but as long as we are seen as the only hand that can rock the cradle we remain tied to biological and social determinism. In concluding his (sic) 'reflections from within the female perspective' (Holdstock, 1993, p. 234).

Holdstock suggests, in a manner which clearly assumes the idea may seem somewhat novel, that: 'we should make heroic the achievement of intimacy and care. Skills in this regard certainly do not detract from functioning effectively in any work situation' (p. 237).

In puzzling as to why Holdstock seems to not regard this attitude as fundamental to the person-centred approach (I almost found myself checking to make sure we were talking about the same Carl Rogers) it occurred to me that, in our gender-influenced, post-modernist co-creation with the text, Holdstock reads an emphasis on autonomy, independence and separateness, whereas I read an emphasis on interconnectedness, relationship and contact.

Power and responsibility

Waterhouse (1992), writing from a feminist perspective, and Sue and Sue (1990) from a transcultural perspective, both accuse the PCA of liberal individualism and of blaming the victim. Both works seem to read the word 'responsibility' as synonymous with 'blame'. Waterhouse, talking of women and children being commonly blamed for rape and sexual abuse, concludes: 'Rogers, and indeed many person-centred counsellors fail to grasp that in the context of unequal power relationships some people have more responsibility than others for a particular life event' (1992, p. 65).

Rogers does not deny the reality of unequal power relationships, nor does he suggest that we are responsible for the actions of others such as rape and abuse. What he does do is suggest that we can reclaim what personal power we do have as a means to challenging authoritarian power. The idea of personal power and of personal responsibility is as fundamental to the theory of feminism and any other form of liberation politics as it is to person-centred theory. The feminist message is that we can challenge what we have been taught and change our lives, both individually and collectively. True, we need affirmation and support from others to do this. Rogers' position is no different — we are unlikely to realise our full potential unless a part of our environment becomes more affirming and supportive. Waterhouse, I have no doubt, would be outraged by Rogers' claim that, 'in its consciousness raising efforts, as well as in its political and legal activities, the Women's Liberation Movement is essentially person-centred' (1978, p. 45). 1 see a great number of shared values between a feminist and a person-centred perspective. Both value interrelatedness, tenderness, intuition, fluidity, subjectivity, connectedness to feelings, and the ability to nurture; qualities which our culture sees as feminine, and values less highly than those it sees as masculine. Being rooted in a similar set of values, the growth of feminist consciousness has striking similarities with the growth of person-centred consciousness. Both began with individuals talking about their personal experience, one to one, then in small groups, then larger groups, and finally by introducing new awareness into institutions like education and health care. Accounts of being in feminist groups bear a striking resemblance to accounts of being in person-centred groups. Both began with a great deal of emphasis on expressing and trusting feelings and on personal empowerment, and on individuals becoming who they were, rather than who they were expected to be.

It is clear that Rogers was well aware of the political implications of his philosophical assumptions, and shared with feminism the desire that all power relationships become transformed: 'what is new and highly threatening to the establishment is that the new politics of relationships presents evidence to show that it works . . . It is the realisation that it is a *viable alternative* to our present ways of seizing and using power that makes it most threatening of all. It is, not only in principle but in cold fact, a quiet revolution' (Rogers, 1978, p. 140).

The PCA is most strongly allied with feminism in that both are concerned with dismantling hierarchical relationships on an individual and a collective level. The power dynamics of hierarchical relationships revolve around status, and 'power *over*' authoritarian power. Feminist theory, like person-centred theory, advocates a way of relating that comes from self-status rather than power that is born out of fear and contempt. Not only does personal change and growth lead to collective change, but personal change, whether this is within an individual or between individuals, is in itself a political act.

References

Carrette, J. (1997) Rogers' nineteen propositions and the therapeutic relationship. *Person-Centred Practice.* 5, (1), pp. 7–13.

Farson, R. (1974) Carl Rogers, Quiet Revolutionary, *Education,* 95, (2), 197.

Holdstock, L. (1993) Can we afford not to revision the person-centred concept of the self? In D.Brazier (Ed.), *Beyond Carl Rogers.* London: Constable.

Jones, M. (1996) Person-Centred Theory and the Post-modern Turn, *Person Centred Practice, 5,* (1), 19–26.

Josselson, R. (1987) *Finding Herself: Pathways to Identity Development in Women.* London: Jossey-Bass.

Rogers, CR. (1978) *Carl Rogers on Personal Power* London: Constable.

Rogers, CR. (1980) *A Way of Being.* Boston: Houghton-Mifflin.

Rogers, C.R. (1990) A Client-Centered/Person-Centered Approach to Therapy. In H. Kirschenbaum and V.L. Henderson (Eds.), *the Carl Rogers Reader* (pp.135–57). London: Constable.

Spinelli, E. (1994) *Demystifying Therapy.* London: Constable.

Sue, D.W. & Sue, D. (1990) *Counselling the Culturally Different.* Toronto: John Wiley.

Waterhouse, R. (1992). Wild Women Don't Get The Blues. *Feminism and Psychology,* 13, (1), 65.

The Person-Centred Counsellor as an Agent of Human Rights

Suzanne Keys

Please listen to me as a person and not as a drunk

This client's words sum up the crux of my understanding of both human rights and person-centred counselling. In this article I consider the relationship between the Universal Declaration of Human Rights (hereafter referred to as UDHR: see United Nations, 1948) and the person-centred approach, the core conditions of the person-centred approach as sufficient response to the UDHR, and the human rights of the counsellor.

Practice context

I work in a drop-in project in London where 60–70 people, mostly those who are homeless or at risk of homelessness, come each day to eat, drink, chat and access a variety of sessional services: an advice worker, a solicitor, a health worker, a chiropodist, an optician, a resettlement worker, a vocational guidance worker, an alcohol support worker, a priest and an art and carpentry worker. Since December 1997 I have set up a counselling service, one day a week, as a pilot project.

As a counsellor I work alongside these other professionals to respond holistically to the social, physical, spiritual, emotional and psychological needs of the service users. I am thankful to work as part of a team where practical welfare issues can be tackled by other professionals. This means I don't feel overwhelmed and powerless when faced by the complexity of the social welfare needs of my clients. The majority of my client group are 40–55-year-old men (hence the use of the masculine when referring to clients in this article) who have insecure accommodation and spend their days drinking in the park. Many have mental health needs and have had contact with psychiatric services in the past.

The project aims to defend the human rights of this marginalised group.

The UDHR and person-centred counselling

The counselling service has an essential role to play because it is addressing some of the most intangible, and therefore most often ignored, elements of the UDHR. The most striking of these are:

• The peoples of the United Nations have in the Charter reaffirmed their faith in

---

First Published in *Person-Centred Practice,* Volume 7, Number 1, 1999.

fundamental human rights, *in the dignity and worth of the human person* and in the equal rights of men and women and have determined to promote social progress and better standards of life in larger freedom (Preamble, UDHR).

• Everyone has the right to a standard of living adequate for the *health and well-being* of himself and his family (Article 25, UDHR).

• Everyone has *duties to community in which alone the free and full development of personality is possible* (Article 29, UDHR).

These key concepts underpin the work that I do with my clients. The Declaration gives an urgency and a political edge to my practice. It is a mandate to facilitate, enable and empower people through valuing, understanding and authentic relationship. The Person-Centred Approach provides me with a theoretical framework from which to respond to these key challenges. At the heart of person-centred theory is respect for the dignity and worth of human beings, belief in a person's potential to become, acknowledgement that the definition of 'health and well-being' goes beyond the physical, and that it is in a facilitative relationship that those who are ostracised from community can begin to grow, develop and reconnect.

Too often the reflex response is to provide the homeless person with a home and the alcoholic person with a detoxification programme. However, as long as a person has not chosen something for themselves, these solutions are short-term. What is therefore essential is a high quality of listening which empowers the client to make his or her own choices. Much alcohol counselling is conditional on abstinence or goal-setting. Person-centred counselling may be thought of as 'not enough'. In my experience it is. It allows for self-determination through an acknowledgment of a person's human rights.

My clients and I work hard at establishing trustworthy relationships which provide the context from which they can grow, develop and make choices. I have no techniques and strategies specific to this client group, but I do work from a very strong theoretical framework. I start from the premiss that I am not an expert on my client's life and what he should do. Each individual has the resources within himself to know what is best for himself. Despite the undeniable impact of social welfare needs on the psychological well-being of some of my clients, I am consistently aware of each individual's actualising tendency:

> . . . the deep motivation that can always be counted on — the vital tendency of the organism to actualize itself, to move toward fulfilment of its potential (Rogers and Sanford, 1980, p. 33).

In the most adverse of circumstances it is astonishing how a human being still struggles to grow and to become and how those who are most dislocated from society can still reach out towards relationship, desiring to belong.

One of my clients lives in a room with no electricity, no gas, no hot water, a hole in the door, no furniture, no cooker, no TV — and yet he wants to live, give up drinking, learn to read and write, achieve some of his potential, strive towards fulfilment.

The core conditions as sufficient response

Working with this client group has reinforced my belief in not only the necessary but also the sufficient nature of Carl Rogers' six conditions for therapeutic growth (Rogers, 1959). I want to briefly pick up on three of these conditions: psychological contact between therapist and client; unconditional positive regard of the therapist for the client; the therapist's empathic understanding of the client.

Psychological contact between therapist and client

I have been struck by how much I have taken this first condition for granted in previous therapeutic relationships. In the Centre, psychological contact with clients has often felt tenuous: very short sessions, very little eye contact, very abrupt endings. Many of my clients are extremely isolated from mainstream society and have few relationships, so making contact in itself is a huge and often frightening step. Although the client may feel powerless in many other areas of his life, it is often I who feel disempowered and deskilled by the abruptness of some encounters. There is a long and fragile process of building up trust. This process in itself is fundamental, therapeutic and empowering. It is much more than just a basis for working together: it is *the* work.

Unconditional positive regard of the therapist for the client

It is of vital importance that the counsellor offers her clients a warm acceptance of who they are as human beings. Of course this is true of all person-centred practice, but I have been acutely aware of the therapeutic value of this attitude in my work at the Centre.

Some of the clients are hard to accept: they have had years of practice of being heavily defended and have deeply entrenched survival mechanisms which keep in place a self-concept which says they are evil, bad, nothing but drunks, completely unlovable. This self-concept is often reinforced by society's response. People who drink on park benches are ignored and abused. No one likes to get too close to someone who is dirty or smells of alcohol or urine.

My consistent offering of unconditional positive regard is, therefore, crucial and I have to be extremely attentive to every aspect of our encounter. This is signalled in a variety of non-verbal and significant ways.

First, it is signalled by the physical environment in which the counselling takes place. This is as welcoming as possible: plants, pictures, comfortable chairs. It may seem obvious, but in this context it is of heightened importance because of the contrast to the client's living arrangements and the potential emotional impact of that contrast. It is also especially difficult to achieve when the only room available is a small laundry with no windows.

Second, it is signalled by the accessibility of the counselling service. The counselling is on-site; the client can gain immediate access to it rather than be referred to yet another agency in a different place. There are already a lot of other places and institutions where service users have to go and make new contacts and introduce themselves again. Here, many have already established relationships with other members of staff before they come for counselling. It also makes the number of appointments easier to remember if a variety of services can be accessed in one place.

Counselling is accessible also because I am pro-active in the drop-in: I don't stay in my room but drop in myself for tea, to say hello to those service users I know (not as clients usually), meet newcomers and talk about counselling, thus demystifying both the counsellor and the counselling process. Unlike other areas of service users' lives, there are no conditions of access to counselling. The service is not specifically to do with, for example, drinking or bereavement or homelessness. There are no forms to fill out or criteria to be fulfilled. The client is free to choose what use he wants to make out of the session.

Third, my intention to be unconditionally accepting of my client is signalled by my consistent presence: I am there every week at the time arranged whether the client comes or not. My acceptance of the client is not conditional on his attendance, however frustrating his failure to turn up may be for me at times. This is particularly important for a client group who are renowned for what is known as their 'chaotic nature' and are often chastised and denied services because they do not attend appointments.

Fourth, it is signalled by my flexibility: my time boundaries are flexible. A session can be anything from 10 to 60 minutes, it is the client's choice. Sometimes it is hard for me to accept the unpredictability, and I wonder about boundaries and mutual respect. However, I realise that some of my clients cannot 'stand' more than ten minutes of a counselling session to begin with. For someone who has had very little acceptance in his life, it seems almost painful to admit even the smallest bit of it into awareness.

Finally, it is signalled by my acceptance of the client's story. Many of the service users are treated with suspicion and mistrust by most people they meet. They are seen as unreliable and therefore untrustworthy, especially if they have been drinking. Their stories are very often not heard and not believed. In a counselling session, their story *is* believed and they can come even if they have been drinking, although most choose themselves not to come if they think the amount of alcohol they've had will impede the relationship. Trusting in the client's ability to know his own limit is of immense importance. Offering such unconditional positive regard is difficult, but I believe my intention to do it is fundamental to the growth of the client.

The therapist's empathic understanding of the client

My empathy is often challenged in working with this client-group. Perhaps I find it hard to enter into a client's world which often seems at first to be so categorically different from my own. I get blinded by material and practical differences.

I also find it difficult to empathise with someone whose self-concept is so far removed from his 'organismic self'. How can I be in the frame of reference of someone whose view of himself is so damaged? Someone who is in such pain he wants to take up a machete and kill the first person who upsets him. Or a 37-year-old man who is contemplating life without drink for the first time since he was eight years old? How can I begin to understand? Tentatively, respectfully and painfully.

Empathy is precisely what is called for: ' I want you to listen to me as a person not a drunk'. As Rogers put it:

> Empathy is in itself a healing agent. It is one of the most potent aspects of therapy, because it releases, it confirms, it brings even the most frightened client into the human race. If a person can be understood, he or she belongs (Rogers and Sanford, 1980).

Belonging is what many of my clients are craving. The counselling relationship, however tenuous, is, I believe, the first step in that process. Once an individual feels heard and genuinely accepted, perhaps for the first time in his life, then he may begin to feel empowered to make choices about his life.

Working within the person-centred framework I am nurturing the profoundest of human rights:

1. the right to be in relationship
2. the right to be respected, accepted and valued
3. the right to be heard and to belong

This is central not only to my theoretical stance on counselling, but also to my own philosophy of life and my spiritual belief system.

These are fundamental human rights, regardless of a person's material status, and these rights merit a response. The question is: as a society, how do we respond? It is not enough that government and charities fund hostels and homelessness projects, because these are addressing only some of the human rights laid out in the UDHR. Person-centred theory offers a response, as do person-centred counsellors whose practice is grounded in their 'faith . . . in the dignity and worth of the human person' (Preamble, UDHR), and whose skills are to facilitate the 'free and full development of personality' (Article 29, UDHR). Too often, however, it is cost-effectivenesss that takes precedence over human rights: step-by-step programmes, medical models and practical solutions fit more easily into funding criteria.

The human rights of the counsellor

In my work as a counsellor I, along with my clients, need to have my rights recognised and respected.

> Everyone has the right to work . . . Everyone who works has the right to just and favourable remuneration (Article 23, UDHR).

I work as an unpaid professional, and this has consequences:

1. on the long-term future of the service I offer,
2. on my status; and
3. on the credibility of the profession I belong to.

First, I offer an invaluable service to clients who cannot afford to pay, in an agency where fund-raising is an annual nail-biting scramble to find the necessary funds just to continue. I provide a much-needed quality service, which I am passionately committed to, but which I may be forced to give up if and when I find paid work. These are the very clients who need consistency and long-term support. These are the very clients whose human rights are most at risk of abuse and yet counselling is provided by a volunteer or not at all.

Second, in a society where value and status are placed on a person through how much she earns, it is very demoralising to be working as an unpaid professional. As a recently trained counselling graduate, however, I am not alone. I, along with many others in the UK, am caught: I need my British Association for Counselling accreditation to gain paid work, and to obtain accreditation I need to have 450 hours of counselling experience. I have no option but to work unpaid to gain the necessary experience to find paid work. How are newly trained counsellors expected to survive financially? They need to earn enough to sustain themselves not only materially but also psychologically for this most arduous of professions.

Third, I expect my professional body:
- to recognise that I not only need training in counselling but also in marketing, outreach work and fund raising;
- to provide me with support and encouragement, particularly at this stage of my counselling career;
- to fight to ensure our status and credibility as a profession. I know of few other professions where trained and skilled professionals are expected to work as volunteers post-qualifying.

Our profession needs to recognise that it can play a key role in society's response to fundamental human rights, but to do this it cannot rely on the unpaid work of professional counsellors.

Postscript

This article has been adapted from a ten-minute paper I gave to a working group at the International Round Table for the Advancement of Counselling at UNESCO in Paris in August 1998. The title of the four-day conference was 'Counselling as a Profession: Status, Organisation and Human Rights'.

Fifty years ago on 10 December 1948, the Universal Declaration of Human Rights was adopted by the General Assembly of the United Nations. At this time of renewed interest in the Declaration and in human rights issues, the person-centred approach and its practitioners have much to offer and be proud of. We can also use the UDHR as a vehicle to underpin what we do in order to aid the general public's understanding of what it is we are about and its relevance for today's communities.

In preparing this paper, the Declaration has come to life as I realise that it is not only by supporting Amnesty International in challenging physical and political injustices that I am engaged in upholding the UDHR, but in fact that I am daily at the forefront of tackling human rights abuses and upholding the spirit of the Declaration through my work as a person-centred counsellor. I find this reassuring, empowering and awe-inspiring.

References

Rogers, C. R. (1959) A theory of therapy, personality and interpersonal relationships, as developed in the client-centered framework. In S. Koch, (Ed) *Psychology: A Study of a Science,* Vol. 3, *Formulations of the Person and the Social Context. Maidenhead, Berks*: McGraw-Hill, pp. 213–15.

Rogers, C. R. and Sanford, R. C. (1980) Client centered psychotherapy. In G. H. Kaplan, B. Sadock and A. Freeman, (Eds.) *Comprehensive Textbook of Psychiatry, 5th edn.,* Williams & Wilkins.

United Nations (1948) Universal Declaration of Human Rights (UDHR). New York: UN.

Towards a Person-Centred Understanding of Consciousness and the Unconscious

Paul Wilkins

The problems surrounding consciousness and mind are often thought to be among the most complex facing philosophy and science (Velmans, 1996, p. 1).

Introduction

The nature of consciousness (and by implication at least, the unconscious) seems to be an issue which has preoccupied thinkers since the time of the classical Greeks. With the advent of the scientific approach and the positivistic paradigm, particularly as it manifested in behavioural psychology, less attention was paid to the phenomenon although it has always had an important role in some psychotherapeutic models of the person. In philosophy and in science, there is currently a resurgence of interest and a variety of models are offered. Broadly speaking, these models fall into biological, psychological and philosophical or metaphysical categories.

Why should any of this matter to person-centred practitioners? Well, to be honest, the short answer is that I don't know that it does because our declared intention is to work with our client's frame of reference whatever that may be and because, in our practice, the relationship takes precedence over theory. However, I suspect that a person-centred understanding of consciousness would (for example) be helpful in:

- the re-evaluation of the self suggested as necessary by Holdstock (1993, 1996)
- an understanding of what Rogers (1986, p.198) called *presence* and which Thorne considers to be synonymous with his concept of *tenderness* (Thorne, 1985)
- and possibly in going some way in resolving the postmodern dilemma raised by Jones (1996)
- allowing us to develop or extend ways of working with dreams, visions, fantasies etc.
- providing a rationale for addressing and using 'other' mind abilities such as intuition, imagination and creativity in the course of growth and healing.

First published in *Person-Centred Practice*, Volume 5, Number 1, 1997.

It is also true that, if we are to be able to offer a person-centred framework which would serve as a paradigm for counselling and psychotherapy as a whole (as proposed by Ellingham 1995, 1996, 1997) then we must offer a conceptual framework for the psychodynamic notion of the unconscious and for (for instance) the states of the unconscious and the collective unconscious described in psychosynthesis (see Whitmore, 1991, pp. 114–5). I believe, too, that an understanding of consciousness would go at least some way to explaining the experiences of both person-centred practitioners and their clients in the course of the therapeutic relationship. Last (but by no means least), I suggest that if the person-centred approach is more than a psychotherapy, if it is a philosophy and a recipe for living, it must offer a belief system which accounts for the nature of people. This must include a position on the phenomenon known as consciousness.

What is consciousness?

Velmans (1996, p. 2) states 'What consciousness is taken to *be* is partly a matter of arbitrary definition'. He goes on to write that, in common usage, consciousness is synonymous with awareness. This is his preferred definition. Rogers (1967, p. 105) writes of awareness as 'man's unique capacity'. He states that a freely and fully functioning awareness is what gives rise to:

> An organism able to achieve, through the remarkable integrative capacity of its central nervous system, a balanced, realistic, self-enhancing, other-enhancing behaviour.

Rogers (1967, p. 105) writes that when this capacity for awareness is added to 'the sensory and visceral experiencing which is characteristic of the whole animal kingdom . . . we have an organism which is beautifully and constructively realistic'. Clearly, Rogers attaches great importance to awareness and in the above statements he offers a constructive view of people which seems to be at odds with a Freudian view of us as driven by a powerful unconscious (the id). In his 'theory of the fully functioning person' (in Kirschenbaum and Henderson, 1990, pp. 250–1), Rogers makes reference to all experiences being available to awareness. If we take Velmans' view that consciousness *is* awareness and accept that the actualising tendency drives people towards becoming fully functioning, does this mean that Rogers saw becoming fully functioning as becoming more conscious? If so, does this mean that there are degrees of consciousness? Can one person be more conscious than another?

For Rogers, was 'awareness' the whole of consciousness? He refers to 'experiencing' which can be sensed and which has meaning but he refers to 'the conscious self' as denying that experiencing (in Kirschenbaum and Henderson, 1990, p. 157). This suggests some quality of being, some way of knowing which is additional to awareness. He also writes of something he calls the 'nonconscious mind' (ibid. pp. 146, 148) and states:

> I know much more than my conscious mind is aware of. I do not form my responses consciously, they simply arise in me, from my nonconscious sensing of the world of the other.

Elsewhere, Rogers (ibid. p. 270) mentions 'avenues of knowing' which are 'unconscious, intuitive and conscious'. This further complicates the picture. Unconscious and intuitive knowledge seem to be different from consciousness. This raises the question of what or who is doing the knowing? Whatever or whoever does, Rogers believes 'is able to sense a pattern long before it can consciously formulate one'. Rogers also signals his agreement with the concept of a number of realities (ibid. pp. 370–3) and uses terms such as 'expanded consciousness' and speculates about 'mystical experience', precognition, telepathic communication and other paranormal phenomena. Not only all this, but he writes of consciousness as something which has 'altered states' (ibid. pp. 137, 148, 150). While he is dismissive of the analysis of dreams as a therapeutic technique (ibid. p. 234), Rogers does see 'work on dreams, on fantasy, on creative thinking' as legitimate (ibid. p. 277).

Another aspect of consciousness discussed by Rogers (ibid. p. 137) is that of 'presence', a facility which of itself is 'releasing and helpful'. He writes:

> At those moments it seems that my inner spirit has reached out and touched the inner spirit of the other. Our relationship transcends itself and becomes a part of something larger. Profound growth and healing and energy are present.

This suggests that some quality of being can be shared and it seems that Rogers is implying that the sharing is more than simply between two people. Can consciousness be shared? Is there a transpersonal dimension to consciousness? Is this what Thorne (1996, p. 113) means when he writes:

> The gift of self-transcendence can only come when there is a recognition between two people or between a group of persons that we are essentially members one of another and need each other for our completion.[?]

From the writings of Rogers alone, a complex picture of consciousness is apparent. Other person-centred practitioner/philosophers intensify this complexity. Silverstone (1994, p. 291) makes reference to right and left hemispheres of the brain as having different functions. The left hemisphere is 'thinking, analytic, judgmental, verbal' while the right hemisphere is 'non-verbal, spatial, spontaneous, intuitive, creative, non-judgmental'. A narrow definition of awareness (and therefore consciousness) indicates that it is a left brain function. This would suggest that the right hemisphere of the brain is unconscious. I don't think that Silverstone believes this to be true. Are there then two different forms of consciousness one for each hemisphere of the brain? Silverstone (ibid. p. 292) also refers to 'the subconscious' in which is material 'denied to the forefront of our awareness' but from which may emerge 'valuable insights leading to growth and self-awareness'. Bohart *et al.* (1996, pp. 199–211) explore and define experiencing:

> A different way of knowing than knowing through conceptual thinking. It is primarily nonverbal, perceptual, holistic and gestalt-like, contextual, bodily and ecological (ibid. p. 199).

This sounds a lot like Silverstone's right brain functions. It is clear that Bohart believes that conceptual knowing (awareness?) comes from experiential knowing which is also the 'initial inspiration for creativity' (ibid. p. 200). He also believes that 'what we want in therapy is an *experiential* shift'. Awareness is not of itself enough to produce therapeutic change. Coulson (1995, p. 8) writes of 'deeper, transcendent, transpersonal realms of consciousness'. Gendlin (1986) believes that dreams may be useful in experiential psychotherapy/focusing. Are we conscious when we dream? Are dreams an altered state of consciousness or a facility of mind in their own right?

Clearly, there are many views of consciousness and abilities of mind within our tradition and I am sure that I haven't touched on them all. I think that other individuals and other traditions can also contribute to a person-centred understanding of consciousness. For example, Anne Baring a psychodynamic psychotherapist speaking at a meeting of the Scientific and Medical Network in 1995 took the view that consciousness was somehow evolving, that as time passes, as a species, we are becoming more aware, more attuned to the Universe. She also said some very interesting things about the importance of myths. I understand Baring to mean that we are in the process of becoming less concerned with individual consciousness and the concept of self as only a thinking entity. As we move away from the Cartesian notion 'I think therefore I am', we become more aware of the greater potentialities of our minds and more appreciative of the self as a mutable entity defined by its relationship to other people, other things. That being conscious is more than thinking is in agreement with the ideas of Silverstone and Bohart, the idea of a transpersonal self (and I am aware that appears to be a contradiction in terms) seems to agree with Holdstock. I wonder, too, whether the idea of consciousness as evolving is in agreement with the actualising tendency? Could the phenomenon of presence be a prescience of this evolved consciousness?

What is the unconscious?
Although, as Spinelli (1994, p. 146) points out, the unconscious has been written about since the eighteenth century, most of us are most familiar with it as a Freudian concept. Jacobs (1988, p. 8) writes that, for Freud, all mental material and mental processes which could not be easily accessed constituted the unconscious. A major aim of the psychodynamic therapies is to make the unconscious conscious. Jacobs also writes:

> Many of the psychodynamic terms can be more fully understood and appreciated if they can be seen as much as metaphors as literal statements. The unconscious is one of those partially metaphorical images which psychodynamic thought makes considerable use of, in its attempt to make sense of experience. Whether or not the unconscious exists as a separate entity is a somewhat fruitless argument. Like many other concepts in psychodynamic theory it is a useful notion to have, in order to possess a type of therapeutic map (ibid. p. 9).

I think that person-centred practitioners might struggle with the concept of an unreasoning, instinctual and at times destructive id but can we agree the unconscious as a useful notion?

That there is some reservoir of experience which is not immediately available to awareness does seem widely accepted. I wrote above of Silverstone's idea of the subconscious and Mearns and Thorne (1988, pp. 47–51) write about *the edge of awareness*. According to Thorne (1992, p. 82), Rogers does not ignore the unconscious and does accept it as a reality. He writes:

> Rogers would assuredly claim that his respect for the unconscious compels him to refrain from adopting any map of this essentially unknowable terrain which might lead him to impose his view or interpretation upon his client.

From a person-centred point of view, I don't think there is any problem with acknowledging the existence of an unconscious dimension to the mind, at least as the metaphor suggested by Jacobs. It seems clear that, under the right conditions, we have an ability to 'recover' (and I suspect create) experiences, ideas, feelings of which we have been unaware. It follows that we must be equally able to 'lose' these from awareness to an unaware part of our mind. A person-centred consideration of the unconscious is given at greater length in Coulson (1995).

A Person-centred understanding and implications for practice

Above, I have raised more questions than I have answered. This is because I believe the issue of consciousness and the unconscious to be far from resolved. With respect to them, I have the impression that we are just about at the stage of getting a measure of our ignorance. However, I think I can tentatively offer some understandings which contribute to theory and which may be relevant to practice.

Firstly, I suggest that we consider consciousness to be much more than cognitive awareness. This seems too a simple notion even if it includes those things of which we can become aware. It seems to me that consciousness comprises a range of mind abilities. These include intuition, creation and imagination, mystical experiences, the experiencing described by Bohart and many more.

The division of the mind into conscious and unconscious parts may sometimes be a useful metaphor for understanding mental processes but it is unnecessary. It seems to me that there is a constant flow between states of consciousness and in and out of the unconscious. Spinelli (1994, p. 147) offers a phenomenological understanding of consciousness as a relational process. By this he means that consciousness (figure) needs something from which to stand out (ground). He understands this to imply that there is an inseparable relationship between conscious awareness and unconscious awareness.

For me, added to my idea that it has many states, this notion that consciousness and the unconscious are in relationship and that this relationship is in process is important. Ellingham (1997, p. 54) has pointed out how this concept fits a person-centred paradigm and argues how Freud's understanding of the unconscious may fit such a paradigm. I think that the psychosynthesis model of conscious, lower unconscious, middle unconscious and higher unconscious can be as easily understood in terms of process. Transpersonal and mystical states also seem to fit this model for they are entered into, result in a perceptual shift and (for most of us at least) are returned from leaving us with just the barest glimmer of the knowledge we had or a watered-down memory of the intensity of the experience. Things move in and out of consciousness, our state of consciousness can and does change.

I think that an acceptance of the idea of altered states of consciousness and the sharing of consciousness may go some way to explaining some of my experiences as a therapist. For example, it seems to me that when I am truly empathic, when I sense the internal frame of reference of my client to the extent of experiencing sensations and feelings which are 'not mine', I must be sensing *their* experience. I am comfortable with the explanation that I have made some perceptual shift (altered my state of consciousness). This isn't the same as presence/tenderness (of which I also have experience) for it lacks the transcendental quality. I'm not sure, either, that empathy is a mutual sharing of consciousness (although I am open to persuasion that the process of empathy is in some way co-created).

I do wonder if some mundane (as opposed to transcendental) sharing of consciousness is possible. Moreno (in Moreno and Moreno, 1975, pp. 6–7) the founder of psychodrama, wrote of a phenomenon he called tele. This, he said, was 'feeling into one another'. Unlike transference, tele is based on the actual beings of two people in relationship. It is different from empathy because it is a mutual understanding. It is said to often play a part in the way a psychodrama protagonist selects an auxiliary. For example, at a large psychodrama conference, a protagonist selected from over two hundred people someone she had not previously met to play the part of her father. The protagonist was not a native English speaker and, when she became stuck, the director invited her to use her own language. This she did and was responded to by her 'father' in that language. It later became apparent that the 'father' was not only fluent in the protagonist's language but had personal experience of a very similar family setting. Is this evidence of some unvoiced but shared perception, of mutual recognition? If so, does it indicate that consciousness can be a shared process? Similar occurrences are frequent in psychodrama. I propose that the consciousness/unconscious process is actually a process between personal, interpersonal and transpersonal mind states (we need the latter to account for presence/tenderness and other mystical phenomena). If this is true, then I think that the 'self' must result from a process and not merely within an individual but from interpersonal and transpersonal processes too. Wood (1996, pp. 176–7) seems to take this view and also writes of the influence of environmental factors on consciousness. Perhaps, then, consciousness results not only from processes within and between people but between a person and their surroundings? Wood states that understanding these environmental effects:

> is especially relevant to studying applications of the person-centred approach because they may have more to do with a participant's experience than the 'facilitative' methods used.

Perhaps an understanding of consciousness is relevant to the core conditions. If consciousness is in some part a shared phenomenon does that help us with acceptance? It seems to me that the more conscious I am, the better chance I have of being congruent. The more of myself and others I allow into my awareness, the more likely I am to be in harmony. Does consciousness, an acceptance of the unconscious and an understanding of both as parts of the same process help with congruence? Again, more questions than answers.

References

Bohart, A. C. & Associates (1996) Experiencing, Knowing and Change. In R. Hutterer, G. Pawlowsky, P. F. Schmid & R. Stipsits (Eds.) *Client-Centered and Experiential Psychotherapy: A Paradigm in Motion.* Frankfurt am Main: Peter Lang.

Coulson, A. (1995) The Person-Centred Approach and the Re-Instatement of the Unconscious. *Person-Centred Practice* 3, (2), p. 7–16.

Ellingham, I. (1995) Quest for a Paradigm: Person-Centred Counselling/ Psychotherapy Versus Psychodynamic Counselling and Psychotherapy. *Counselling* 6, (4), p. 288–90.

Ellingham, I. (1996) Key Strategy for the Development of a Person-Centred Paradigm of Counselling/psychotherapy. *Person-Centred Practice* 4, (2), p. 12–8.

Ellingham, I. (1997) On the Quest for a Person-Centred Paradigm. *Counselling* 8, (1), p. 52–5.

Gendlin, E. T. (1986) *Let Your Body Interpret Your Dreams.* Wilmette, Il.: Chiron.

Holdstock, L. T. (1993) Can We Afford not to Revision the Person-Centred Concept of Self? In D. Brazier (Ed.) *Beyond Carl Rogers.* London: Constable.

Holdstock, L. T. (1996) Discrepancy between the Person-Centred Theories of Self and Therapy. In R. Hutterer, G. Pawlowsky, P. F. Schmid & R. Stipsits (Eds.) *Client-Centered and Experiential Psychotherapy: A Paradigm in Motion.* Frankfurt am Main: Peter Lang.

Jacobs, M. (1988) *Psychodynamic Counselling in Action.* London: Sage.

Jones, M. (1996) Person-Centred Theory and the Post-modern Turn. *Person-Centred Practice* 4, (2), p. 19–26.

Kirschenbaum, H. & Henderson, V. L. (1990) *The Carl Rogers Reader.* London: Constable.

Moreno, J. L. & Moreno, Z. T. (1959) *Psychodrama Volume II: Foundations of Psychodrama.* Beacon, N. Y.: Beacon House.

Rogers, C. R. (1967) *On Becoming a Person.* London: Constable.

Rogers, C. R. (1986) A Client-centered/Person-centered Approach to Therapy. In I. L. Kutash & A. Wolf (Eds.) *Psychotherapist's Casebook.* San Francisco: Jossey-Bass.

Silverstone, L. (1994) Art Therapy the Person-Centred Way: Its Relevance in Counselling. *Counselling* 5, (4), p. 291–3.

Spinelli, E. (1994) *Demystifying Therapy.* London: Constable.

Thorne, B. (1985) *The Quality of Tenderness.* Norwich: Norwich Centre

Publications.

Thorne, B. (1992) *Carl Rogers*. London: Sage.

Thorne, B. (1996) Person-Centred Therapy: The Path to Holiness. In R. Hutterer, G. Pawlowsky, P. F. Schmid & R. Stipsits (Eds.) *Client-Centered and Experiential Psychotherapy: A Paradigm in Motion*. Frankfurt am Main: Peter Lang.

Velmans, M. (1996) Introduction to the Science of Consciousness. In M. Velmans (Ed.) *The Science of Consciousness: Psychological, Neuropsychological and Clinical Reviews*. London: Routledge.

Whitmore, D. (1991) *Psychosynthesis Counselling in Action*. London: Sage.

Wood, J. K. (1996) The Person-Centred Approach: Toward an Understanding of its Implication. In R. Hutterer, G. Pawlowsky, P. F. Schmid & R. Stipsits (Eds.) *Client-Centered and Experiential Psychotherapy: A Paradigm in Motion*. Frankfurt am Main: Peter Lang.

The Person-Centred Approach and the Re-instatement of the Unconscious

Alan Coulson

The segregation and pathologization of the unconscious

Claxton (1994, p.151), asserts that in Western Culture before the sixteenth century the notion of 'conscious' and 'unconscious' as separate realms of mind was more or less non-existent. Moreover, he suggests that there was then a greater tendency for persons to see themselves as more interdependent and less separate than in modern society. Thus when John Donne wrote his famous 'No man is an Island, entire of itself; every man is a piece of the Continent, a part of the main', he would have been understood as expressing not a special state of mind but a mundane reality.

The, now prevalent, view of mind as conscious, self-sufficient, all-embracing, explicit and rational, and the consequent belief that the only and proper home of human identity is in this realm, is attributed by Whyte (1960) to Descartes. In time the adjective 'unconscious' became reified as 'the unconscious' and the idea of a separate, indescribable cellar of the mind took increasing hold. Thereafter Western Culture has more and more enthroned the conscious, the intellect and the rational while relegating the unconscious to the status of habitat of dark and wild forces which, if liberated, may threaten the established order and undermine the supposed clarity of reason. The work of Freud and his successors gave an added impetus to the pathologization of the unconscious. Claxton (1994, p. 224), however, asserts that there is plenty of evidence, both scientific and everyday, that *consciousness* is much more marginal to our psychology 'than its own inflated picture of itself would have us believe'.

The widespread adoption of a diminished, and mainly negative, version of the unconscious also serves to obscure its potential as our connection to the generic Unconscious, the unfathomable source that lies behind all experience. Claxton (1994, p. 163) argues that the fundamental reason why most of us prefer to remain oblivious to our unconscious is that its existence is felt as a threat to our culturally and socially conditioned Self Systems (broadly made up of loose collections of beliefs about who we are and how we should think and behave) which give primacy to consciousness, rationality, clarity and control.

First published in *Person-Centred Practice*, Volume 3, Number 2, 1995.

In contrast, the Person-Centred Approach is founded on the belief that there is a formative force in the universe, present in individual organisms, including human beings, as an actualizing tendency which, if unimpaired, motivates the organism both to maintain itself and to move towards the constructive accomplishment of its potential. This belief in the wisdom of the human organism as a whole reflects a very different and positive view of the unconscious. Rogers believed that we are wiser than our intellects and that our organisms as a whole have a wisdom and purposiveness which goes well beyond our conscious thought. He describes as 'entirely congenial' Whyte's (1974, p. 107) contention that 'at any moment the *unconscious levels are ahead of the conscious* in the task of unifying emotion, thought and action!' He would surely have agreed too with Whyte's suggestion that:

> It may . . . be wrong to think of two *realms* which interact, called the conscious and the unconscious, or even of two contrasting kinds of mental process, conscious and unconscious, each causally self contained until it hands over to the other. There may exist, as I believe, a single realm of mental processes, continuous and mainly unconscious, of which only certain transitory aspects or phases are accessible to immediate conscious attention.

Expansion of awareness in person-centred processes

It is well established that the person centred encounter group or workshop can have a transforming effect on many participants, leading some to a heightened sense of awareness and a much enhanced feeling both of self-worth and of interconnectedness with others. Such groups can provide an avenue into a level of experiencing which can appropriately be described as spiritual, mystical, transcendental (Thorne, 1988, p. 201).

At the PCA forum in the Netherlands (1992, published 1994, reprinted in this volume) I shared my own experience of a person-centred workshop which had served as a catalyst for personal transformation. I conjectured that, by opening us to deeper, transcendent, transpersonal realms of consciousness, such experiences have the potential to, in effect, connect us with what David Bohm (1980) calls an 'implicate order' behind and beyond our own physical reality and our usually ego-bound awareness. Among the effects reported by members of such groups and workshops are a sense of wholeness and unity, sensations of 'belonging' and of 'flow', experiences of perceptual intensity, unusual degrees of physical energy, and spontaneous feelings of elation and joy. These characteristics are akin to those which are part of the 'mystical' experiences found in every culture and religious tradition (Bucke, 1972) and Carl Rogers himself (1980, p. 128) concludes, 'Hard-headed research seems to be confirming the mystic's experience of union with the universal'.

Altered atates of consciousness and loss of self

What appears to give access to these altered states of consciousness is the temporary suspension of elements of individuals' Self Systems (their everyday habits of perceiving and knowing, and their socially conditioned patterns of belief and behaviour). William James (1902) wrote,

> I have on a number of occasions felt that I enjoyed a period of intimate communion with the divine. These meetings came unasked and unexpected, and seemed to consist merely in the temporary obliteration of the conventionalities which usually surround and cover my life . . . What I felt on these occasions was a temporary loss of my own identity.

I want to concentrate in this paper on the occurrence within person-centred contexts of this temporary loss of identity, a kind of 'short-circuiting' of the Self System. From my own experience and that of others I believe that the climate of trust, openness and psychological safety frequently engendered in client-centred therapy or person-centred groups facilitates this process. In so doing it can open the way for some people's awareness spontaneously to move into hitherto inaccessible regions of the unconscious. In these realms, profound connectedness with self (and Self?), others and the cosmos may be experienced; the individual may thereby gain what William James called 'insight into depths of truth unplumbed by the discursive intellect'.

Before proceeding, it may be helpful to refer in some detail to Van Kalmthout's (1991) useful summary of Rogers' ideas about 'the self', he writes:

> . . . he seems never to refer to a static entity or structure within the person, but merely to the *concept* of self, which, at least in a healthy person, is as changing as the organismic process itself. To put it differently, 'becoming myself' seems to mean in Rogers' theory 'becoming the organismic process' . . . This implies in fact that the self is more an impediment to growth and change than a help . . . individual persons have lost their inner strength through their living in the world of 'conditions of worth'. Their life is governed by the 'self' which is entirely a product of the conditions of worth, that is, a product of external forces. (Remember that to Rogers, 'self' means 'self-*concept*'.) Change essentially means: moving from this outer world into the inner world of the organismic life flow. It logically implies the dying of the 'self', permitting the organism to come to life (p. 8).

The Person-Centred Approach and 'unconscious' processes

Carl Rogers' (1980, p. 126) most fundamental belief was that there is a tendency in the Universe and in human beings toward fulfilment and actualisation, and that this involves not only the maintenance but also the enhancement of the organism: the drive to become more fully-functioning. He believed that 'consciousness has a small but very important part to play in this process . . .' (in the draft manuscript of his chapter he is slightly but perhaps significantly more emphatic: 'Consciousness has a very small part to play in all this'). He goes on to suggest that conscious attention 'can be described as a tiny peak of awareness, of symbolising capacity, topping a vast pyramid of nonconscious organismic functioning'.

Though his emphasis on the fundamental importance of organismic whole self experiencing is of very long standing, it was only in the last decade of his life that Rogers' writing and interviews indicate an increasingly explicit acceptance of, and interest in, the involvement in therapeutic and transformational processes of the transcendent, the indescribable, and the spiritual. In one of his last papers (1986, p. 138) he concludes, 'I am compelled to believe that I, like many others, have underestimated the importance of this mystical, spiritual dimension'. Some of the biographically-based reasons for his hesitation in arriving at this position are indicated by Barrineau (1990, pp. 423–4), and Bowen (1991, pp. 11–12), who states, ' his openness to realities which are not direct consequences of sensory or cognitive experiences began in the middle seventies, when he started to work consistently with intensive groups which had community-building as their main purpose (Rogers 1980, pp. 181–206)'. She quotes an NBC television interview (1983) in which Rogers acknowledges the significance of intuition:

> I hear myself saying things that seem totally off the wall, not relevant in the least to what is going on, yet nearly always strike a note in the client that is very valid and very significant . . . In such moments my inner self is in contact with the inner self of the client in a way that my conscious mind wouldn't recognise it. It's a mystical experience (p. 13).

He claimed that his greater willingness to admit that something mystical is happening was because this view fits with the whole new view of more advanced thinkers in physics and chemistry that the cosmos is non-material and that we have to learn to live in this new Universe (Bowen, 1991, p. 13).

Writers and practitioners in the person-centred tradition other than Rogers have drawn attention to the significant involvement of the less tangibly-manifested aspects of ourselves in the process of therapeutic communication and of healing; these are elements which are often commented on as having a capacity to dissolve interpersonal barriers and unite the participants by allowing them to enter a communal state of altered consciousness. The accounts embrace both psychotherapeutic settings (e.g. Rogers, 1986; Bowen, 1982, 1991; Spahn, 1992; Thorne, 1985) and encounter or PCA learning workshops (e.g. Rogers, 1980; Natiello, 1982; O'Hara and Wood, 1983; Coulson, 1994).

Of Carl Rogers' special gift as a psychotherapist, Bowen (1982) writes:

> It appears to me that he enters into an altered state of consciousness in which the dualism between him and the other person disappears. He becomes at one with the client and, in magnet-like fashion, gathers together in one integrative impression the fragmented and disconnected experiences of the client. The feedback of the therapist's integrative impression allows the client to see things in a new light

and to order his or her chaotic experience. That moment of organisation is the essence of the therapeutic process. Following Prigogine's model, each new organisation that is achieved enables the organism to change into a pattern of a higher order of coherence and complexity. This organisation is possible only when the therapist and the client are on the same wavelength and the boundaries between the I-THOU disappear (p. 19).

Rogers emphasises that in theory it is not a technique which is important, but an ability to enter the world of the other person and to experience the spiritual moment when boundaries between the Me and You disappear: 'It is that moment of communication between two Inner Selves, both of them partaking of the Energy of the Universe. It is a highly intuitive moment.'

Similarly, Spahn (1992) notes that in his many observations of Carl Rogers' way of 'being with' a client or a group there was a striking resemblance to what occurs in the interaction between healer and healee (Le Shan, 1974, p. 107) — that they become one entity in a larger context without either of the two losing their individuality. Spahn suggests that the person-centred approach seems particularly conducive to the 'separateness giving way to unity' phenomenon, and quotes Rogers (1980, p. 129):

> I find that when I am closest to my inner, intuitive self, when I am somehow in touch with the unknown in me, when perhaps I am in a slightly altered state of consciousness, then whatever I do seems to be full of healing. Then simply my presence is releasing and helpful to the other . . . it seems that my inner spirit has reached out to the inner spirit of the other. Our relationship transcends itself and becomes part of something larger. Profound growth and healing and energy are present.

Thorne (1985) describes a similar phenomenon arising in therapy when the interpersonal quality he calls *tenderness* is present:

> Inwardly I feel a sense of heightened awareness . . . It seems for a space, however brief, two human beings are fully alive because they have given themselves and each other permission to be fully alive. At such a moment I have no hesitation in saying that my client and I are caught up in a stream of love. Within this stream there comes an effortless or intuitive understanding and what is astonishing is how complex this understanding can be (p. 9).

He indicates the sense of unity and wholeness which suffuses this experience. Bowen (1991) too, in her exploration of the part played by intuition in person-centred psychotherapy, refers to this sensation: 'An intuitive moment is a moment of wholeness. Our perception is clear, with no conflicting emotions.' She sets intuition in the context of deep empathy and endorses Rogers' hypothesis that at moments when sensitive empathy is deep, the intuition takes over in mysterious ways, and the client and therapist are perhaps in a mutual and reciprocal altered state of consciousness. She suggests that at such times the encounter between therapist and client occurs at a deeper level, which transcends the cognitive mind.

> In the intuitive state we know more than our conscious minds are aware of. Responses arise spontaneously from our non-conscious sensing of the other person's world (p. 25).

Phenomena arising from the unconscious and similar to those so far discussed within one-to-one situations also occur in person-centred groups and workshops. Natiello (1982) discusses forms of knowing within the Person-Centred Learning (Group) Experience (PCLE). As well as logical knowing, the form of knowing which is generally associated with science and education, there is clear evidence of a form of knowing which has been variously termed pre-reflective, organismic, absolute, intuitive, or tacit, and which is more associated with religion, mysticism, philosophy and metaphysics . From reports of participants in the PCLE she concludes that the person-centred approach facilitates the latter form of knowing; an unstructured, non-discriminating, holistic, non-rational, direct experience of reality which:

> . . . occurs in a state of receptivity and heightened awareness when the rational mind — the tool with which we filter out certain aspects of experience for reflection, is at rest. It involves the whole person, with the subconscious, unconscious and conscious acting in unity. It brings together the intellect and emotions. It is, therefore, not irrational but suprarational. It is associated with the condition of being fully open to and absorbed in experience; integrated, flowing. Unlike a rational, intellectual concept, it cannot be generated on cue, or built step by step. It comes unsolicited, and thus is often experienced as arriving from outside the knower (p. 4).

Natiello found that in the PCLE, in a climate bathed in empathy and unconditional positive regard, learners began increasingly to trust others and themselves and to enter a state of non-defensiveness in which they were fully open to their experiencing. Deep insights arose not from rational, logical thinking, but rather in a state of unfocused receptivity. According to one participant, 'The moments of profound insight, a discovery, a knowing by my whole self come when I am experiencing a harmony, a flowing together'.

Natiello concludes:

> I believe that the facilitation and honouring of that state of knowing may be the greatest contribution the person-centred approach can bring to learning. For that is the state in which we tap our potential, our connection with the self, the other, the Universe. It is the condition in which we grasp the holistic, interrelated, interdependent nature of reality that is being described by contemporary physicists (p. 10).

As in the situations described earlier, an altered state is entered into as a consequence of participation in the intense person-centred experience. Within a climate of trust and psychological safety, the learners' customary intellectual control is relaxed and their established habits of perceiving and behaving temporarily set aside.

The hold of the habitual Self System is released or diminished leaving the individual in a state of increased receptivity to experience unfiltered by translation or adjustment to fit a preconceived self-structure. In this state, connection with a deeper order of reality, the 'implicate order', may be glimpsed or rather felt. As Van Kalmthout (1991) observes,

> Contact with this reality is not personal in the sense of limited, subjective experience, but rather transpersonal in that a universal, 'objective order' is met by the individual person. This can only be done, however, when all the burden of knowledge, scientific, religious, personal, etc. is left behind, because this order transcends all this limited knowledge (p. 12).

Drawing on experience in and observation of many, mostly large-scale, person-centred workshops, O'Hara and Wood (1983) introduce the concept of *group mind* and explore how it evolves as the workshop process unfolds. They note that many participants become intensely conscious of their inner symbolic world and may at times surrender everyday consciousness completely, entering deeply symbolic dramatic worlds; consciousness is stretched, both individual and group, to a state of great expansion. It may expand to the extent that a feeling of oneness is present, a feeling in which there is a correspondence between individual and group mind, and individual and group consciousness become unified.

> There is true meeting, an I-Thou encounter between group members. In this state of oneness dreams are shared, people may experience perceptions beyond the reach of ordinary senses, healing often occurs, the future is sometimes glimpsed. In short, many of the phenomena referred to as 'psychic' or transpersonal appear (p. 108).

The previously identified pattern of the setting aside of the Self System allowing the emergence of more flowing, spontaneous thought and behaviour is also present here. At the workshop, individuals enter a field with a minimum of institutional structure within which they may be enabled to leave behind the familiar patterns which shape ordinary consciousness. Stereotypic responses can be recognised and revitalised or are set aside in favour of fresher, more spontaneous responses.

O'Hara and Wood suggest that this is, in effect, a process of surrender, surrender to a larger system, a larger configuration. They conclude,

> The capacity to surrender fixed and partisan patterns in favour of more fluid and spontaneous yet 'globally aware' patterns seems to be a critical factor associated with the achievement of more subtle levels of consciousness (p. 113).

The re-instatement of the unconscious

Having discussed the pervasiveness of unconscious mental processes and forces and emphasised their importance, Claxton (1994, p. 226) makes the cogent point that knowing *about* the importance of the unconscious does not of itself enhance one's insight or alter one's world-view. Most of us are adept at maintaining our self-structures and denying to awareness experiences and information which challenge our *status quo*. I have proposed elsewhere (Coulson, 1994) that major changes of perspective or personal transformation usually require a symmetry-breaking process or psychological 'jolt' before we can surrender our crystallised patterns. As Claxton points out, 'intellectual knowledge is the travel brochure, not the holiday'. He continues,

> If scientific observation can 're-mind' consciousness of the dark waters on which it floats, it takes a moment of mystical insight to give one an immediate, awe-ful experience of the fathomless drop over which the conscious mind is suspended. The identification of the person with consciousness is one of the assumptions that sits at the centre of the Self System. When perception is downstream of that assumption, the mind is bound to ignore its dark roots. But if it were possible, even for an instant, to leapfrog *upstream* of this particular dualism, we would then reclaim our biological birthright of mystery — and also of belonging (p. 226).

The foregoing accounts of profound and intense experiences within person-centred contexts partake of many of the qualities of experiences usually defined as mystical. Such experiences, for a time at least, can place individuals outside the trap of their Self Systems and perhaps, in the longer term, lead to their enjoying more fluid and spontaneous ways of relating to and construing their world. Released from the interference and drain on resources the Self System produces, the organism flows. Buried priorities resurface: the value of love, intimacy and belonging are re-membered. When the Self System is switched off, or at least turned down, we feel less separate, we are instead more able to sense our mutuality, our *inter*dependence. The world looks and feels different and the experience is often one suffused with an inviolable sense of *belonging*. Moreover, this sense of belonging may extend beyond the personal and interpersonal domains to the whole of the nature of the cosmos. Claxton (1994, p. 238) describes the core of mystical experience as a welling-up from some ineffable source within and quotes the seventeenth-century German mystic Jakob Boehme:

> In my inward man I saw it well, as in a great deep; for I saw right through as into a chaos where everything lay wrapped, but I could not unfold it. Yet from time to time it opened itself within me like a growing plant.

The language and imagery here is strikingly similar to that employed by Boehme's twentieth-century near-namesake, physicist David Bohm who (1980) postulates two separate orders of reality. The underlying, higher unseen or *implicate order* contains all that is 'non-manifest' and is characterised by undivided wholeness. Derived from it is the secondary or *explicate order*. This is the place of the 'manifest': the seen, heard, and felt reality we are all familiar with. According to Bohm, all things are *unfolded* from the implicate order into sensate reality, and are then *enfolded* back into the implicate.

According to the *perennial* philosophy (Huxley, 1944), human beings are part of a wholeness that constitutes the fabric of the universe, the ground of being. The intrinsic wholeness of a person, however, cannot be considered apart from the totality of which it is a tiny part. Yet, within each one the totality is enfolded. The mystical experience is one way we may attain direct awareness of this relationship.

In a well-known passage, William James (1902) states,

> Our normal waking consciousness, rational consciousness as we call it, is but one special type of consciousness while all about it, parted from it by the filmiest of screens, there lie potential forms of consciousness entirely different. We may go through life without suspecting their existence, but apply the requisite stimulus, and at a touch they are there in their completeness . . .

For many of us, myself included, intense person-centred workshop or therapy experiences have provided the requisite stimulus.

Acknowledgement

My reading of Guy Claxton's *Noises from the Darkroom* gave me the starting point for this account. Though he was not writing specifically about the person-centred approach, I have drawn extensively on his work here.

References

Barrineau, P. (1990) Chicago Revisited: An Interview with Elizabeth Sheerer. *Person-Centred Review,* 5, (4), pp. 416–24.

Bohm, D. (1980) *Wholeness and the Implicate Order*, London: Routledge and Kegan Paul.

Bowen, M. V. (1982) Spirituality and the Person-Centred Approach: interconnectedness in the universe and in psychotherapy, in A. S. Segrera (Ed) *Proceedings of the First International Forum of the PCA,* (Mexico).

Bowen, M. V. (1991) Intuition and the Person-Centred Approach, presented at the *2nd International Conference on Client-Centred and Experiential Psychotherapy*, Stirling, Scotland, 1–6 July.

Bucke, R. M. (1972) *Cosmic Consciousness*, London: Olympia Press.

Claxton, G. (1994). *Noises from the Darkroom: the science and mystery of the mind*, London: Aquarian.

Coulson, A. (1994). Person-Centred Process and Personal Transformation, *Person Centred Practice*, 2, (1), pp. 11–7.

Huxley, A. (1944) *The Perennial Philosophy*, London: Chatto and Windus.

James, W. (1902), *The Varieties of Religious Experience*, London: Collins (1960 reprint).

LeShan, L. (1974) *The Medium, the Mystic and the Physicist*, New York: Random House.

Natiello, P. (1982) The Nature of Knowing in the Person-Centred Approach, in Segrera, A. S. (Ed), *Proceedings of the First International Forum of the PCA* (Mexico).

O'Hara, M. M. and Wood, J.K. (1983) Patterns of Awareness: consciousness and the group mind, *Gestalt Journal*, 6, (2), pp. 103–6.

Rogers, C. R. (1980) *A Way of Being*, Boston: Houghton Mifflin.

Rogers, C. R. (1983) NBC Television interview, quoted in Bowen, M. (1991).

Rogers, C. R. (1986) A Client-Centred/Person-Centred Approach to Therapy, in Kirschenbaum H. and Henderson, V. (Eds), *The Carl Rogers Reader*. (1990) London: Constable, pp. 135–52.

Spahn, D. (1992) Observations on Healing and Person-Centred Therapy, *Person-Centred Journal*, 1,(1), pp. 33–7.

Thorne, B. (1985) *The Quality of Tenderness*. Norwich: Norwich Centre Publications.

Thorne, B. J. (1988) The person-centred approach to large groups, in Aveline, M. and Dryden, W. (Eds), *Group Therapy in Britain*, Milton Keynes: Open University Press.

Thorne, B. J. (1992) *Carl Rogers*, London: Sage.

Van Kalmthout, M. A. (1991), On the Personal and the Universal, presented at the *2nd. International Conference on Client-Centred and Experiential Psychotherapy,* Stirling, Scotland, 1–6 July.

Whyte, L. L. (1960) *The Unconscious Before Freud*, New York: Basic Books.

Whyte, L. L. (1974) *The Universe of Experience*, New York: Harper and Row.

Dreams, the Unconscious and the Person-Centred Approach: Re-visioning Practice

Prue Conradi

> *One must not defend theoretical models but open new paths to knowledge. That is possible only if one remains true to one's own interior truth* (Carotenuto, 1988).

The motivation for this paper

I agreed to write this paper on request, sharing passionately others' concern that the Person-Centred Approach (PCA) must grow or die. I have now worked for almost 20 years as a person-centred psychotherapist and have experienced significant personal and professional changes of perspective within my own practice. During the last 11 years I have had a deep and developing interest in depth psychology, in Jung, in archetypal psychology, in myths and symbols, in the new writing of James Hillman, in psychology and spirituality, and most of all in dream work, which has now become a central and core element in my own practice. Yet, at the same time I am still deeply committed to the PCA. I do not impose my interests in any way on my clients, but sense I have extended or broadened the *range* of my own inner resources which may now be drawn upon by the client who so wishes. However, I have simultaneously grown increasingly perplexed at the singular lack of literature on the subject of dreams within the Person-Centred Approach.

A religious parallel: the two theoretical frameworks

I am curious about the idea of a practitioner steeped in her original therapeutic orientation (myself and the Person-Centred Approach), actually making a journey into the heart of another orientation (Jungian and Archetypal Psychology), but then returning with a greatly enhanced perspective on her original viewpoint. A parallel could exist with respect to inter-faith — a Jew who travels into Buddhism and subsequently returns to Judaism, not having *become* a Buddhist, but now *owning* a greatly enhanced view of the very Judaism that Buddhism has somehow taught her. One could even say that it is hard to be really critical or reflective if one is too *identified* with the object of criticism. In the same way a Frenchman may be able to comment more pertinently about Englishness than can an Englishman.

First Published in *Person-Centred Practice*, Volume 7, Number 1, 1999.

So I am saying that perhaps we have to get outside our tradition and look back inside. Bernie Neville has, it seems to me, done this in a very refreshing way when he explores the PCA through an Archetypal lens and discovers the PCA to be highly *polytheistic*: 'causing practitioners to have to learn to live with much ambiguity and paradox, in contrast to other therapies which exist more in a single way of knowing, where you will be lucky to hear more than one voice' (Neville, 1992).

Neville takes the Greek Gods and has them speak about why each in turn really has the monopoly on the PCA! Neville's views point to an inherent elasticity in the approach itself, and I believe it is this very elasticity that provides fertile ground for embracing the world of dreams which is currently entirely absent within our tradition. My practice clearly already embraces this dimension; yet, to look for a theoretical backdrop, it is necessary to go outside the current framework of person-centred theory. Without embracing a notion of the unconscious, which is currently absent, I cannot see how such practice can be supported within the present tradition.

Shortcomings of the Person-Centred Approach

One does not become enlightened by imagining figures of light, but by making the darkness conscious (Jung, 1951).

I have always felt that the most significant gap in the PCA is the lack of address to the dark side of life, to the unconscious and to the Self. In the person-centred theory day seminars which we have conducted in Norwich for many years now, these are the very themes that we collectively come back to again and again. This seminar is one in which experienced person-centred therapists apply intellectual rigour to the exploration of their own therapeutic *practice*, exploring openly their actual experience and then holding this up against the theory itself. Are these identified issues mentioned above actual gaps, or shortcomings in a theory that takes too positive a view of human nature? Do these problem areas point to a *deficient* theory of human nature, an inadequate phenomenology? Is the Person-Centred Approach actually significantly different from its historical antecedent client-centred therapy? Is the PCA in fact no more or less than an actual 'approach' as John K. Wood (1994) has posited, simply an *attitude to the person*?

Where can the debate about these contentious questions be conducted? Is there hidden within the current theoretical body a kind of notion of 'sacred cows'? Is there a danger from the 'purist camp', that, through their reluctance or refusal to explore what I would call *the living edge* of the PCA out of fear of a diluted 'eclecticism', the approach will become a kind of dead dogma? Carl Rogers would, I am sure, have *most* deplored this.

I hope that writing about my own practice and interest may enable me to come out of the closet, so to speak, and that this very speaking out loud just *might* have serious theoretical implications for the PCA itself, or at the very least that these thoughts might serve personally as a prelude for further writing on this subject, something I would very much like to do.

A process approach

When I was two-thirds of the way through the few days that I had set aside for the writing of this paper, I began to stumble upon *why* it had been so perplexingly difficult even to begin. In a moment of stuckness and desperation earlier in the week, I telephoned a friend and colleague who asked an extremely helpful question: 'What exactly are you trying to do? Are you writing a comparative study between Jungian Psychology and the PCA, in which case you need to write about the distinctive *differences*, and then compare them; or are you wanting to put across some kind of a *synthesis?*'

I was certainly not wishing to write comparatively, or to create a synthesis of the two psychotherapeutic traditions. My wish was rather more to articulate the personal integration or synthesis I am already living, and breathing, a synthesis of my own which now informs my life and work. At the level of both personal experience and professional practice this synthesis has already occurred for me. However, I realised that I had simply yet to articulate it. The only way I could begin, was to speak *out* of and *at the edge* of my own experience, as opposed to trying to stay within too tight a theoretical framework. I could worry about the theoretical implications later and give myself permission not to have to define too carefully or, exactly, the terms I would use for the time being. So what you read here is a kind of *discursive* paper. After all, Rogers was himself highly suspicious of theories, wishing to liberate himself from the constraints of previous theories and to trust the empirical validity of his own experience.

Historical perplexity

I can and do appreciate how Carl Rogers' own ideas developed out of, or against, the historical background of the psychoanalytic tradition. He deplored, it seems, interpretative approaches and the behavioural tradition. It seems he reacted against the idea of the therapist considered as expert. Instead, he focused on his profound belief that, if certain qualities (the core conditions) could be manifested in the person of the therapist, a facilitative environment would be created and the client could then be fully trusted to discover her own resources and way forward. I have always been deeply moved by Carl Rogers' focus on, first, the primacy of the therapeutic relationship and, second, his returning to, or endowing total trust in, the client, placing the internal locus of evaluation in the *client*, not in the therapist. This is indeed a highly demanding way to work, as those who practise will know, and is often quite oversimplified and misunderstood by therapists from other orientations, who have it seems to me, appropriated the term 'person-centred' with little or no real understanding of the rigour or strict discipline which the PCA exacts.

However, I have been most baffled by *why*, in articulating the values I have just described, Rogers has apparently thrown the baby out with the bathwater. In his desire to honour the above principles it seems he has stopped short of, or mistakenly excluded, the significance of the notion of the 'unconscious' and any real work with dreams. I have sometimes wondered whether he stopped short of these notions out of a fear that such an exploration would indeed be irreconcilable with his deep humanistic values and profound respect for the inner wisdom of the client. Whether this is an assumption that he made, or one that has somehow now become implicit within the PCA, I do take exception to such a view. Rogers himself was seen towards the end of his life to be increasingly open to the exploration of new territory. If he were alive today, I suspect he would thoroughly embrace these questions. I sense the problem that now exists may concern *who* may be deemed eligible to continue with the PCA's evolution. I do not believe there is any contradiction between honouring and respecting the client's own wisdom which Rogers so espoused, while also looking to the client's dream life for further clues and amplification with respect to current personal issues.

I see no contradiction in retaining the core theory of the approach, of trusting and empowering the individual but extending the approach to take better account of the unconscious, symbolic, and metaphorical worlds. It is simply not good enough to say that these realms fall outside of the approach. If a client wishes to explore these areas, as indeed I did and still do, then a therapist has a duty to meet this challenge of accompanying her in this deeper exploration, or else fail in this task of deeper exploration sought by some individuals. It is a well-known maxim that one can go only as far as one's therapist has gone. We are talking here about the necessity for the therapist to discover something of her own psychic inner territory, to learn something of the language of dreams and how they may be fully heard and received, if she is to have the ability and confidence to subsequently travel this terrain with her clients.

My own journey
After nine years of working as a person-centred therapist, I experienced a crisis in my own development, knowing that I wished to explore issues of deep concern which included my own powerful dream-life. However, I was simply unable to find any therapist within the person-centred world who I felt could accompany me into this territory. I felt I had hit the blind-walledness of *self-actualisation*, in terms of one's journey being perceived as a process of exclusively greater and greater *consciousness*, when I knew at some level that I needed to go in the opposite direction and to become more acquainted with, and in tune with, my unconscious life.

I therefore sought and found a Jungian. Subsequently my own experience as a client then preceded a reconceptualisation of myself as a therapist. This work in and with my own inner world had and, I believe, has, its effect within my own practice by extending and broadening my capacity to respond to others in two major ways. First, an enhanced personal flexibility slowly developed with respect to my potential responses to my clients; and second, I discovered a leaning towards greater expressed congruence in my work with clients. This flexibility and enhanced trust in myself, I hope and believe loosened any potential straitjacket which may have been developing as a safe, comfortable or habitualised way of working after many years of continued practice. I sense this is a very great danger for psychotherapists after many years in the profession. However, I then quite naturally discovered the necessity for more differentiation with respect to the ego and the Self.

The Ego and the Self: two languages

So we come to the ego and the Self. It is evident that, within the two theoretical frameworks and the theories of personality, there are differing views of the Self. (Figures 1 and 2, below, further describe the two frameworks.) In person-centred theory we speak of the self-concept, the organismic self, the formative and the actualising tendency. We also have conditions of worth, and the locus of evaluation. In Jungian theory we have personae, ego, complexes, shadow, the archetypal dimension, anima, animus, the Self and the process of individuation. But most significantly, there is much greater distinction between ego consciousness and the unconscious, as expressed by Daryl Sharp:

> It is clear now that we are twofold beings; we have a conscious side which we more or less know, and an unconscious side of which we know little but which is no secret to others. Think of how often we make all sorts of mistakes without being aware of them in the least, while others suffer them all the more painfully. The recognition of the existence of an unconscious side of ourselves is of revolutionary importance (Sharp, 1996).

The Ego–Self axis

I suggest that much psychological thought has fallen into the trap of trying to make itself far too much into a science. In so doing, too much emphasis is placed on the rational or explicable world. 'Knowing' somehow takes a primary role in the psyche over and above the unknown, mystery and the very essence of soul which cannot live and thrive in such an arid ambiance. Where the ego has supremacy over the Self, psychological thought becomes reductive in a terrible way, and as such goes against soul, which always has a way of its own. Soul cannot breathe in the ambience

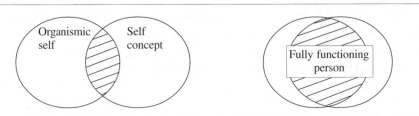

Figure 1: The Person-Centred Approach — the division and relationship between the *self-concept* and the *organismic self.*

• On the left is a person dependent on an external locus of evaluation, who may be a person who wins approval but at the expense of authenticity and without much self-esteem. The shaded area refers to an area of less discrepancy, but possibly great tension is experienced here due to the conflict between the inner and outer realities. The sense of self-worth is likely to be dependent upon conditionality and the winning of approval. This is a conditional/con-tractual world-view.

•A fully functioning person, shown on the right, is one who (a) is open to experience; (b) lives in the present; (c) is able to accept responsibility for own behaviour; (d) has a high degree of autonomy; and (e) is creative.   *Source: My own.*

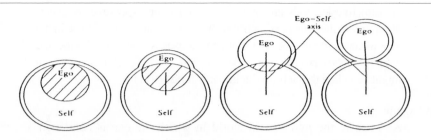

Figure 2: The Ego–Self axis.
At first the ego exists only in potential as a component of the Self. Over time, the ego gradually differentiates itself from the Self and emerges as a force to be reckoned with. The line connecting them represents the ego–Self axis, the vital link that establishes the integrity of the personality.

The first two sets of circles describe a relatively undifferentiated person who is living out of the collective. The second two demonstrate greater differentiation and autonomy, a person able to oppose the collective. The shaded areas represent the relative degree of ego/Self identity. The ego can develop or become self-actualised but, without the ego-self axis risks being cut off from growth. Growth has taken place, but it may then be *the ego that has grown* out of relation to the ground of the Self. *Source: Stevens (1995).*

of the supremacy of ego consciousness. The ego has to become relativised, and to then develop greater powers of discernment and differentiation, if there is to be any hope of living in the service of the Self. Both the instinctual and the archetypal levels are discovered within the psyche and have to be trusted as potential guiding principles, which consciousness disallows at its peril.

The modern world's collective disrespect and violation of nature seems to me a natural and terrible consequence of the individual's overemphasis on rationality, with a corresponding disrespect, inability, or unwillingness to honour the deeper psychic levels within. I say this now because it strikes me as highly important to see this deeper work not as an endless introspective or solipsistic journey without reference to the world, but precisely the opposite, a way in which one may craft a firmer inner foundation from which to live more authentically. As Carl Jung has said:

> The psychological rule says that when an inner situation is not made conscious, it happens outside as fate . . . that is to say when an individual does not become conscious of his inner contradictions, the world must perforce act out the conflict, and be torn into opposite halves (Jung, 1951).

The actual material and focus for this work, I suggest, comes through a dedication to dream-work and to the honouring of the imaginal and the world of imagination. I believe there then follows a kind of re-orientation of consciousness and unconsciousness which Jung speaks about very eloquently:

> If the unconscious can be recognised as co-determining along with the conscious, if we can live in such a way that conscious and unconscious,

or instinctive demands, are given recognition as far as possible, the centre of gravity of the total personality shifts its position. It ceases to be in the ego, which is merely the centre of consciousness, and instead is located in a hypothetical point between the conscious and the unconscious, which might be called the Self (Wilhelm and Jung, 1931).

and again:

> As I see it, the *psyche* is a world in which the ego is contained. Perhaps there are also fishes who believe that they contain the sea. We must rid ourselves of this habitual illusion of ours *if we wish to consider metaphysical statements from the standpoint of psychology* (Wilhelm and Jung, ibid).

It has been my experience that, by carefully attending to the inner world of dreams and the inner psychic life, *a metaphorical bridge* is crafted between the unconscious and conscious worlds, across which material may arise and flow creating a dynamic centre within the personality in precisely the way addressed in the above quotations.

The unconscious is of course extremely difficult to speak about because its very nature is unconscious, but perhaps it can be best imagined symbolically, like the blood in our veins which sustains existence *without our realising it*; or like those who live near a water mill and simply don't hear or notice it; or like a cork bobbing in the sea; or like an iceberg which rises above the water, 95 per cent of which is hidden.

A few years ago I was to offer a workshop on dreams for the first time. On the morning of the workshop I woke with the following dream: *I am with a small*

Figure 3: The context of the larger Self.

To follow dreams is like establishing a connection between the ego and the centre of the personality. The ego–Self axis occurs when the Self is taken to refer to the whole or total personality, one that embraces the centre and the unconscious. Dreams provide the link between the smaller reality of the ego and the larger reality of the whole person or Self. The ego is the smaller circle; the Self is the larger circle and the dot in the centre represents both the personality and the all-embracing totality. The ego is contained within the Self, so the smaller is contained within the larger. This is true even if we are unaware of the larger personality of the Self. But for the ego to gain maximum benefit of a relationship with the Self, there must be an ego–Self axis. Dreams are one way in which the ego–Self axis is created.

Source: Sanford (1978).

group of people, standing in front of them, and in my hands I have a fish. I seem to be squeezing the fish from one end, as one used to turn down toothpaste tubes! I seem quite surprised and bewildered, and out of the mouth of the fish comes some mauve liquid. The other people seem quite delighted and applaud. I remain somewhat bemused.

This dream seemed highly significant both then and now. At a personal level I felt it was offering me much encouragement and affirmation about the day ahead. Collectively, it contains a wonderful way of evoking the sense that dreams will yield their meaning through *work*, that the dream is the starting point, but that we need to meditate and mull on the dream's imagery, to 'work' with dreams, in order that they may yield their meaning.

Prejudice and dreams

I believe there are many misconceptions about analytical work, and about working with dreams, which stem more from ignorance and prejudice than anything else. I sense that the Jungian or psychoanalytic schools mistakenly imagine that the humanistic and person-centred therapist works only at surface issues and not at depth issues. Prejudice from the humanistic and person-centred schools may mistakenly believe that all Jungian therapists invite and work with the transference as the primary and basic working material and that the therapy is reified and out of touch.

Historically, dreams tended to be understood to be the monopoly of psychoanalysis. More significantly, the words dream 'interpretation', or dream 'analysis', quite mistakenly, give the impression that the only way to work with dreams is for the therapist to be considered superior and more knowledgeable, i.e., that the client will somehow necessarily become putty in their hands. One could hardly move further away from the core values or philosophy of the PCA. I wonder whether it is these prejudices that may account for the neglect of this subject more than anything else. There are many ways of embracing dream-work which are entirely consistent with endowing trust in the client, following the client and respecting the material, without falling into any of the traps mentioned above. Furthermore, it seems to me that the PCA offers an unprecedented and truly wonderful *methodology of relationship* which I have not found adequately addressed in Jungian or analytical writings. Conversely, Jungian psychology could enable the PCA to open out and extend significantly the phenomenological world being explored. In this way there is a great deal that the two approaches could offer to one another, both already taking subjective experience as their starting point and focus.

It may be important to add that, in my own practice, there are clients with whom dreams do not feature. I recall a recent woman who had sought me out because she desperately wished to delve into her accompanying dream diaries, only to discover in our sessions that the focus of our work was moving in quite another direction, towards an early childhood experience which had incapacitated her in her later life. Her need, it transpired, was precisely to bring this material to consciousness; her dreams were only a pointer in this direction.

Dreams can, if properly honoured and received, offer to the dreamer great sources of new understanding and re-orientation, within herself, within her relationships to other people and within her relationship to the world. However, a primary orientation point in turning with openness in this direction is a belief in what I would call the 'creative unconscious', as opposed to Freud's notion of the 'regressive unconscious' which we have so often mistakenly been led to believe is the ultimate dark truth about the unconscious. It occurs to me in writing this now how peculiar and ironical it is that exponents of the PCA may be suffering from actual fears about the 'regressive unconscious' when its very own philosophy supports Rogers' positivistic belief in the ultimate goodness or benevolence of the human being. This is indeed a highly ironical contradiction.

It is my experience that the world of dreams operates like the taking of photographs from underneath; offering always a new perspective, one that has not yet been entertained, some nuance not previously considered. However, when the attitude to the dream is correctly open and respectful, and when one is ready to enter into the dream, to befriend the dream and dwell within its world and its imagery, as opposed to too quickly literalising, or appropriating the dream's message, then a great deal of inner guidance becomes available and we are on our way to a newly re-visioned psychology which opens not only inwards, but also more fully outwards to the world. How ? Let me relate a dream of a 75-year-old woman who has given me permission to share this with you.

Dream of a balloon and a bull

The dream was composed of two images, rather than a sequence of events: *First I saw two ascetic young men — very pure and bloodless, effete even — who had just come down from a trip in a hot-air balloon. They looked rather sombre and were agreeing that it had not really been all that marvellous 'up there'. The second image was of a small elegant and sleek black bull, beautifully made and shiny, and her stance was the perfect embodiment of exquisite RAGE. Her head was lowered menacingly and she was ready to butt anyone and everyone. At the same time she was pissing from the back quarters with all the energy of her being!*

The dreamer's interpretation
'These are the two extremes of my nature — the spiritual on one hand, and the physical/emotional/instinctual. The spiritual ascetic side seemed to be dry, lifeless and disappointed. 'It wasn't too marvellous up there.' The bull on the other hand was expressing itself — *her*self — to the full and enjoying every moment of it: *she* personified the complete freedom of the instinctual life and getting rid of, or expressing, heartfelt emotions with a sense of rightness, and was so elegant with it! An animus dream, but with the bull, rather a feminised version. The energy, life and spirit came from the instinctual part of me — the ascetic animus side appeared effete and lifeless. I've overdone the spiritual/ascetic things and not given enough attention to instinctual/natural things, which hold my energy within too, but are trapped.'

Some months later the dreamer reported: 'The message of this bull dream has released years of suppressed energy and resulted in a feeling of physical and psychic substantiality which I had never before experienced'.

Her comments show so well how the dreamer's attitude to the world may be changed if and when the message of the dream has been properly absorbed, and not at the level of idea, but at the level of lived experience.

The personal/universal and the collective unconscious

I believe there are in these two psychological frameworks very marked areas of similarity in their phenomenological approaches, centring in their profound respect and trust in the person, but that their two psychological perspectives differ essentially by beginning at opposite ends of the same continuum. At the risk of gross oversimplification, I suggest that, where Rogers' approach is to begin with the *personal* and to focus on relationship and intimacy, Carl Jung's starting point is a study of the nature and function of the psyche which we could call the collective or the *universal*. (In Jungian psychology this is often termed the objective psyche.) Two experiences of mine come to mind which somehow reflect these two different orientation points, and I feel both somehow demonstrate the notion *that what is most deeply personal is also most deeply universal*.

During a group that I facilitated some years ago in Northern Ireland, a frail, battered and brave woman, who had suffered terribly in her marriage to an alcoholic, wept in her personal angst as she contemplated the appalling blind 'meaninglessness' of her suffering. While of course her experience was a deeply personal one, somehow her speaking about it in the way she did led to a profound universal truth which then came to life within the group. The remaining participants also simultaneously experienced something of the truth that *suffering without meaning* was indeed — or could be — a kind of living hell. It was experienced by everyone in the group that there can be no glory or virtue in suffering *per se*. This was an example for me of a deeply private and personal experience, which once disclosed was experienced as demonstrating a universal truth.

Many years later, I attended a residential conference focusing on dream-work. Here, in a small group setting, a client's dream was shared, without any biographical data being given with respect to the individual life of the dreamer. After one hour of sitting with and exploring the dream, to the certain astonishment of both others and myself, it became possible to guess with accuracy the quite specific and individual life-circumstances and probable dilemmas of the actual dreamer. This was for me clearly an unquestionable experience of what may be called, in Jungian terminology, the 'objective' psyche. I include these two stories, simply to demonstrate the validity and value of both different points of orientation.

Self-actualisation and individuation

I believe the PCA needs a much greater exposition with respect to what is meant by the Self. I believe the term 'self-actualisation', so central a concept to the body of the PCA, needs to be further explored with respect to what exactly is meant by the 'Self'. Does this word 'self-actualisation' carry the same inference as Jung's term 'individuation?' While there is currently such unclarity here, the PCA lends itself, along with other humanistic or psychological approaches, to the challenge of narcissism, *re-enforced*, I suspect, by the way in which everyday speech so frequently alludes to words such as, self-assertion, self-confidence, self-esteem, self-management. It is hardly surprising that the attack of narcissism is now such a common one. *There are clear limitations to an ego-based psychology; without inclusion of the archetypal dimension, the 'work' remains in the domain of ego consciousness and the personal I.*

The Person-Centred Approach and relationship

Perhaps the PCA's greatest strength can be said to lie in its emphasis on *relationship* with the other. However, could it be that herein also lies its weakness? Otherness. Who is the other? I suspect that in therapeutic terms the other is usually the therapist, whereas I suggest that otherness can encompass very much more than this. When the ego is felt to be relativised in the multiplicity of vantage points which begin to open up when one attends to dreams, then the crack or opening or 'aha' moment that may be perceived, offers a moment of pure embrace in what I would call the *Anima Mundi* or the soul of the world.

The need to redeem the world of imagination

It seems to me that a psychology that excludes the world of imagination is guilty of being reductive, in contrast to the possibilities that open up for self-knowledge when the magnitude of the human condition and the journey of the soul are fully embraced. Without this vision we will indeed be poverty-struck, lacking the courage required *to broaden our perspective*. In the modern world, where the psychotherapist may now often be consulted in place of the clergyman, the therapist has a duty and obligation to familiarise herself with the heights and depths of the soul's journey and to consider *how and where the psychological dimension may become, or has become, the spiritual*, if she is to have any hope of responding to the client who wishes to go beyond the dimension of the 'personal' or 'ego' problem and who wishes to restore a religious attitude to life. I recall being profoundly struck on hearing years ago 'Where there is no vision the people perish', and equally struck more recently on considering a colleague propose that 'Little or no real change occurs, except first in the world of the imagination'.

A challenge to the PCA: purism *or* development, or purism *and* development?

I am now able to acknowledge my own very mixed feelings and my initial fearfulness and defensiveness about this articulation in the face of many person-centred purists. Although I respect their position and would *not wish* the PCA to be weakened by a too-permissive inclusiveness, I do not relish being mistakenly condemned as a dissident or heretic! But this is a risk I take. I am ultimately much more concerned with where the truth seems to be taking me than with what would be a more cowardly fear about issues of 'belonging'.

However, there is of course an entirely other position apart from the purist one, which is represented by those therapists who are willing to bring their practice into the open for exploration and to look at what they are actually doing as opposed to what they profess they are doing. I believe the PCA now houses in its national and international communities voices from both camps.

I hope this paper may contribute to and enliven the debate with respect to the need as I see it to extend person-centred theory. I believe, in so doing, one risks the criticism either that one has strayed hopelessly from the core of the approach, or, and this I believe is highly important, one might have exposed actual blind spots in the approach itself, which could challenge theorists to develop and extend the theory further. In other words, by articulating our practice we might see that we have not strayed from the core tenets, but are indeed touching *in our practice*, the very ground upon which new and extended theory now needs to develop.

It seems to me that all theory that is to remain alive must also remain dynamic if it is not to crystallise, calcify and lead to the creation of a kind of stasis or 'dogma', something that Carl Rogers himself would have most deplored. I suspect that the current state of the PCA is now at this boundary or knife edge. Those who are therefore willing to risk opening their current practice to scrutiny may either prove to be making a significant contribution to the development of new theory, or discover they have been 'outed' as heretics or eclectics. However, I suggest that this latter accusation may be a means of 'pathologising' by those who do not wish to challenge or extend the core theory. So be it!

Carl Rogers' dream

In 1979, Carl Rogers attended an international workshop for 90 participants in Princeton, New Jersey. He relates this in his book *A Way of Being,* in the context of the later part of his life, in which he is seen to be most open to the intuitive dimension and mystical experiences. He describes this workshop as being one of the most difficult workshops he had ever experienced, with a consistent lack of communication and the expression of high degrees of anger and unresolved frustration.

A few weeks ago I was in conversation with a colleague, who had been present at this event, when he quite suddenly recalled a dream of Carl Rogers' which had been shared in the context of that community. Carl had reported his dream as one in which '*I had a number of barrels of crude black oil to take to Carl Jung's place of retreat, his tower at Bollingen*'.

In the context of the very difficult and disturbing experience of a workshop that was not proceeding in an apparently 'growthful' way, and where powerful negative feelings were being expressed, this dream does seem to me very fascinating indeed. I would surmise that perhaps it points towards an aspect of wisdom which Carl Rogers obviously perceived as being embodied in Carl Jung's person or work, which clearly seems to concern the unconscious and the dream as a way of accessing it. I wonder what Carl Rogers would have said if he had been given the chance of amplifying the images — the oil, the crude blackness of it, the barrels and the place he was to take these barrels? It seems fascinating that the oil is crude and black, not refined oil, which would be quite different. In this same chapter in *A Way of Being*, Rogers subsequently makes a number of stunning comments:

> I have stated that we are wiser than our intellects, that our organisms as a whole have a wisdom and a purposiveness which goes well beyond our conscious thought. I think that men and women, individually and collectively, are inwardly and organismically rejecting the view of one single culture — approved reality. I believe they are moving inevitably towards the acceptance of millions of separate, challenging, exciting, informative, individual perceptions of reality. I regard it as possible that this view — like the sudden and separate discovery of the principles of quantum mechanics by scientists in different countries — may begin to come into effective existence in many parts of the world at once. If so we will be living in a totally different universe, different from any in history (Rogers, 1980).

Conclusion

I believe that at a theoretical level the PCA needs to challenge and re-examine its concept of self, to consider the ego–Self axis, and to give more credence to dreams and the unconscious. Further, I would argue for a place for the unconscious within the PCA. This would subsequently have significant implications by way of practice, in challenging and extending the therapist's empathic capacity to include the whole world of dreams. In other words I suggest that dream-work can be entertained and embraced only in practice, with a much more differentiated analysis at the level of theory, of what we do actually mean by both the Self and the Unconscious.

I would like to end with two poetic thoughts from Anthony Stevens, who has written a wonderful book on dreams called *Private Myths,* and finally with a short passage from Jung's own autobiography.

> To work on dreams is not a petty form of self-indulgence, but a spiritual ritual of cultural and ecological significance: the more conscious we become as individuals, the more hope there is for our tiny portion of the universe. Dreams may be the last frontier of human psychology. We must also heed Liam Hudson's warning that dreams are our 'last wilderness', to be protected with the same fervour as the rainforests, the ozone layer, and the whale. As the only natural oasis of spiritual vitality left to us, dreams are among our most precious possessions, and we must stand up to those who would diminish the value that we place on them. Whilst scientists will further elucidate the neurological basis of consciousness, what will continue to matter to us and to our planet, is what we do with the consciousness that we have . . . To work with dreams is to understand that we are moved by energies that we do not control. This is a religious understanding. Such energies are experienced as 'divine', because they come from the biological ground of all being: we do not create them, they create us, personal will is sacrificed to the will of the

collective as constellated in its myth; the ego becomes to the Self as the moved to the mover (Stevens, 1995).

Jung recalls playing between the ages of seven and nine in his garden. There was an old wall in his garden built of large blocks of stone, the interstices of which made interesting caves, with other children helping him. He writes:

> In front of this wall was a slope in which was embedded a stone that jutted out — my stone. Often when I was alone I sat down on this stone, and then began an imaginary game that went something like this. I am sitting on top of this stone and it is underneath. But the stone also could say 'I' and think: 'I am lying here on this slope and he is sitting on top of me!' The question then arose 'Am I the one who is sitting on the stone, or am I the stone upon which he is sitting? This question always perplexed me, and I would stand up wondering who was what now. The answer remained totally unclear. But there was no doubt whatsoever that this stone stood in some secret relationship to me. I could sit on it for hours, fascinated by the puzzle it set me (Jung, 1983).

References

Carotenuto, A. (1988) *The Difficult Art: A Critical Discourse on Psychotherapy.* Wilmette, Ill.: Chiron Publications.

Conradi, P. (1996) The PCA to supervision. In M. Jacobs, *In Search of Supervision.* Buckingham: Open University Press.

Jennings, J. L. (1996) The dream is the dream is the dream: A person-centred approach to dream analysis. *The Person-Centred Review.* 1(3).

Jung, C. (1928) *The Relations between the Ego and the Unconscious*. London: Routledge.

Jung, C. (1951) Aion. In *Collected Works Vol. 9.* London: Routledge.

Jung, C. (1983) *Memories, Dreams, Reflections.* Glasgow: Harper Collins.

Kamenetz, R. (1994) *The Jew in the Lotus.* San Francisco: Harper Collins.

Neville, B. (1992) *Jung and the Postmodern Condition.* Paper, presented at the PCA International Forum, Tershelling, Holland.

Rogers, C. (1980) *A Way of Being.* Boston: Houghton Mifflin.

Sanford, J. (1978) *Dreams and Healing.* New York: Paulist Press.

Sharpe, D. (1996) *Living Jung.* Toronto: Inner City Books.

Stevens, A. (1995) *Private Myths.* London: Penguin.

Wilhelm, R. and Jung, C. G. (1931) *The Secret of the Golden Flower.* London: Routledge & Kegan Paul.

Wood. J. (1994) The Person-Centred Approach: Toward an Understanding of it's Implication. In *Client-Centred and Experiential Psychotherapy: A Paradigm in Motion,* collected papers from the 1994 international conference in Vienna. Germany: Peter Lang.

Can Psychodrama be 'Person-Centred'?

Paul Wilkins

In his editorial to the Summer 1994 edition of Person-Centred Practice, [reprinted in this volume, pp. 2–5] Tony Merry explores some of the issues surrounding traditional and non-traditional (heretical?) views of what does and does not constitute being person-centred. It is something which exercises my mind from time to time because not only do I practice as a Counsellor/Psychotherapist (when not even the purest of the pure would be able to fault my approach) but also as a psychodramatist. In an earlier paper (Wilkins, 1993), I wondered if being person-centred was a matter of philosophy and attitude rather than of details of practice. I decided that when I function as a psychodramatist, though person-centred philosophy informs my practice, I probably was not person-centred, per se. I am now re-examining my view.

Merry (1994) writes that the position of those who argue that the core conditions are not sufficient and yet call themselves person-centred is untenable. With this I am in complete agreement. However, I do think that there might be many ways of holding these attitudes within a therapeutic relationship and I am increasingly of the opinion that psychodrama provides a vehicle within which the core conditions may be demonstrated. There are fewer conflicts between the basic philosophy of the PCA and psychodrama than may be imagined and many of its 'techniques' may not conflict with person-centred practice (though it is of course possible to practice psychodrama in ways so far removed from the PCA that I find them distressing!).

Rogers (1986) states that the PCA depends upon the actualizing tendency. Moreno (1985) viewed each person as inherently spontaneous and creative. While I think that Rogers and Moreno had very different ideas about the practice of psychotherapy, I do think that (in essence) they agreed about the drive for growth. If the PCA is ultimately dependent upon the actualizing tendency and that tendency underlies psychodrama perhaps the philosophical gulf between them is not so great? With this notion in mind, I set out to examine my psychodrama practice and the attitudes I hold to my clients when I act as a psychodramatist.

For me, the roots of the PCA lie in phenomenology. Spinelli (1989) states that the aim of phenomenological psychotherapy is 'to offer means for individuals to examine, confront, clarify and reassess their understanding of life, the problems encountered throughout their life and the limits imposed upon the possibilities inherent in being-in-the-world'. Within my one-to-one practice, I set out to achieve

First published in *Person-Centred Practice*, Volume 2, Number 2, 1994.

this aim by entering into the subjective experiencing of my client, attempting to understand it 'as if' it were my own while at the same time offering unconditional positive regard and being fully and congruently present. What is vital is that I enter acceptantly into my client's world, that I am fully present and available to my client (within the context of our therapeutic relationship) and that I am truly myself. For me, this is no different in psychodrama.

As the facilitator of a psychodrama group, my invitation is essentially 'show us how it is for you'. If this invitation is accepted, then the protagonist has an extremely powerful way to communicate her experiential reality. The classic psychodrama offers an ideal way to explore and convey the *Eigenwelt* while the *Mitwelt* (Binswanger, 1968) is the province of sociodrama. I see no inherent tensions between the psychodramatic form and a phenomenological approach to therapy (including the PCA).

When I facilitate a psychodrama, my intention is to enter as fully as I may into the scene the protagonist chooses to explore. In order to do this I must be engaged with her in the empathic process and deeply accepting of her essence. This is no different an intention from that I hold in my one-to-one practice. When I work with an individual I tend to sit a 'comfortable' distance from her, 'diagonally opposite' and to be attentive to what she says, how she is and to my inward sensing of her experience (which may be as 'feelings' or even bodily sensations) — I also hold an awareness of my *personal* reactions and my flow of experience. I may respond to my client from any or all of these experiences. As a psychodramatist, I may vary my physical distance from my protagonist. Sometimes I may actually be in physical contact, at others more distant. Just as when I work with an individual, my intention is to develop an empathic sense of my protagonist and (when it is appropriate) to communicate my empathy. Close physical proximity often makes it easier for me to share my protagonist's experience 'as if' it were my own. This is particularly helpful in the initial stages of a psychodrama for it is only as she feels understood and accepted that the protagonist will wish to proceed to 'tell her story', to share her reality. I am attentive too to the process between me and my protagonist and just as I would 'use' this in one-to-one therapy so I will use it in psychodrama. This will mean that I do my best to remain congruent and (quite probably) to be what Lietaer (1993) calls transparent. My *intention* then is to enter into a relationship with my protagonist and (through the demonstration of the core conditions) to facilitate therapeutic change.

Rogers (1961) states that the effort of the therapist to be accepting, empathic and congruent is appreciated and felt as beneficial by the client. Brazier (1993) writes of the importance of the therapists's altruism in the therapeutic endeavour. Perhaps, then, the PCA is characterised by the effort and intention to be deeply respectful of another's personal experience, to strive to understand it, to believe in their actualizing tendency and to work with them towards actualization? All this is true of how I practice psychodrama.

But psychodrama is 'directive' — this is explicit in the classical psychodrama term for the therapist, *director*. Also it is structured. By some at least, both these are seen as antipathetic to the spirit of the PCA. And perhaps there is a tension.

However, I think that to claim the PCA is not directive and that it is unstructured is unrealistic. The abandonment of the label 'non-directive counselling' long ago indicates an acceptance of the directive element in PCA and structure is visible in the fixed roles we play (therapist and client), in the boundaries in which we operate and even in our adherence to the core conditions. Psychodrama cannot be dismissed as 'not person-centred' simply because it is structured and directed. Perhaps then it is a matter of degree or the client's/protagonist's choice and power within the offered framework that separates PCA from other approaches? Within the person-centred one-to-one encounter, the client has the power to control the content of the session (except, of course, that how the therapist responds profoundly affects just what material and experiences the client brings to the session!). This can be the same in psychodrama, for while some psychodramatists may 'instruct' their protagonists, this is not demanded by the philosophy or the form.

The role of the psychodramatist may be seen to be much more that of the 'expert' than the person-centred practitioner. The psychodramatist has a repertoire of techniques; the person-centred therapist has but herself in relation to her client. This may be true (though I wonder if the PCA is any more 'technique-free' than it is non-directive?) but *if* these techniques are made available to the protagonist in the spirit of the PCA and in the belief in her actualising tendency, is there really any conflict? When a protagonist is exploring and/or demonstrating a scene from her reality and asks a question of a person in an auxiliary role, I may ask her to 'reverse roles'. This is a clear direction and may conflict with the PCA *but* if the protagonist knows that this is likely to happen and that she can say no, is the conflict as great as might be imagined? Is there a conflict at all?

I think that though there *can* be (especially if the protagonist has an external locus of control), there isn't *necessarily* a conflict. What matters here is the sensitivity of the therapist, her intention to seek a better understanding of the protagonist and her ability to 'let go' of any notion that she knows what is best. No more and no less than I expect of myself when I practice counselling. My rationale for working with and accepting the directive element in psychodrama then, is that, to some degree at least, there is always a directive element in psychotherapy — what matters is how this is addressed, that, if the structures and techniques are understood and consented to by those in the client role *and they are free to make as much or as little use of them as **they** find appropriate* and I hold to the core conditions, then this is in essence no different from entering into a one-to-one relationship.

If all I say is accepted and not dismissed as sophistry then the unanswered question is 'why bother?'. If it is possible to be person-centred in the context of psychodrama what does its form offer that it is not available from individual therapy or the encounter group (which may be a more appropriate comparison)? For me, the power and effectiveness of psychodrama lies in two directions. The first of these is that, because it involves an element of action and an attention to the *whole* self, it may offer to the protagonist, the therapist and the group a much deeper understanding of the protagonist's reality and her processes than is easily available through a 'talking' approach. Liesl Silverstone (1994) states that by 'talking about' a client may stay in her 'left brain' and not connect with her 'right brain' (where her intuitive, creative and non-verbal facilities lie). She says that the repressed material in the right brain is needed for integration. In other words, it is needed for self-actualization. She argues that art therapy allows access to this material. So may psychodrama, for it functions at cognitive, emotional, spiritual and physical levels and specifically seeks to use the spontaneity and creativity of the right brain. Secondly, psychodrama is a *group* approach to therapy and so the protagonist is not only in relationship with the therapist but *with every other member of the group* . In a group setting, the protagonist has not only the benefit of receiving the core conditions (and often not only from the therapist but also from other members of the group) but also the benefits of *encounter*. Rogers (1970) wrote at length about the capacity of the therapeutic group ('an awesome thing') and had a deep belief in the wisdom of groups indicating that they are greater than the sum of their parts. My experience echoes and supports this and I regard the encounter element as contributing greatly to the psychodrama group. It is not only from the conscious mind of the protagonist that material emerges to fill the psychodramatic space but also from the process of encounter. Sometimes the 'action' may be entirely contained within the group process and it is not uncommon for my psychodrama sessions never to proceed to a structured scene (or more properly, series of scenes). On the one hand this may raise again the question of why bother with psychodrama if encounter offers as much, but on the other I think it supports my contention that as a person-centred psychodramatist I offer my skills but do not impose them.

I indicate above that part of the power of the psychodramatic form lies in the possibility that the protagonist will experience the empathy, acceptance and congruence not only of the therapist but also of members of the group. This occurs in a variety of ways. Firstly, members of the group who are asked to perform as auxiliaries in a scene enter into (or attempt to enter into) the subjective world of the protagonist in a very real way. In effect, they become elements of it and play a part in making it accessible to others. Moreno (1953) wrote of a 'unit of feeling transmitted from one individual towards another' which he called 'tele'. Though tele doesn't seem to be clearly and unambiguously defined, one of the definitions offered is 'the insight into, appreciation of, and feeling for the actual make-up of another person' (Moreno and Moreno, 1959). Tele is said to be the process through which auxiliaries are chosen and though we don't have a precise equivalent in the PCA, it seems to me to combine elements of the core conditions. I think that often, a protagonist's experience of choosing and utilising an auxiliary is about offering and receiving at least empathy and acceptance. In this way, the protagonist meets some of her need for unconditional positive regard and to be deeply understood. As in one-to-one therapy, even the attempt and intention to 'get it right' is appreciated and facilitative.

The psychodramatic technique of doubling offers a similar opportunity for the protagonist to receive the acceptance and empathy of others. The aim of the 'hit and run' double is to voice a thought, feeling or idea that the protagonist is struggling to voice for herself or that is just below her 'edge of awareness' (Mearns and Thorne,

1988). To do this with accuracy, the double must be linked in an empathic process with the protagonist. The 'permanent double' is charged with being with the protagonist throughout the action and to enter into her (the protagonist's) experience 'as if' it were her own. This too is about being empathic but also accepting.

The last part of any psychodrama session is called 'sharing', in which members of the group are invited to share any personal experiences of which they have been reminded by the content and process of the session (I always end a group with an invitation to share whether or not there has been 'action' and a protagonist). Through the process of sharing, the protagonist has more opportunities to experience the empathy and acceptance of the group but, equally importantly, group members have the opportunity to express themselves authentically and, as they tell their stories, to experience the empathy and acceptance of others.

It is my contention, then, that not only may psychodrama be done in a person-centred way but that it offers a valuable addition to more classic forms of person-centred therapy. It is not better than individual therapy or encounter, still less does it replace them. Rather it is different and offers an extension to the PCA. Person-centred psychodrama (and I feel increasingly comfortable with the term) has at its core the actualizing tendency and a deeply held belief in the power of the core conditions. It is a way of offering these which is unique and powerful and which (while it may not suit all clients or all therapists) allows effective therapy and perhaps to those for whom more orthodox ways are less comprehensible.

References

Binswanger, L. (1968) *Being-in-the-World.* New York: Harper Torchbooks.

Brazier, D. (1993) The Necessary Condition is Love: going beyond self in the person-centred approach. In Brazier, D. (Ed) *Beyond Carl Rogers.* London: Constable.

Lietaer, G. (1993) Authenticity, Congruence and Transparency. In Brazier, D. *Beyond Carl Rogers.* London: Constable.

Mearns, D. & Thorne, B. (1988) *Person-Centred Counselling in Action.* London: Sage.

Merry, T. (1994) Editorial. *Person-Centred Practice.* 2, (1), pp. 1–4.

Moreno, J. L. (1953) *Who Shall Survive?* Beacon : Beacon House.

Moreno, J. L. (1985) *Psychodrama Vol. I: 4th Ed.* Ambler: Beacon House.

Moreno, J. L. & Moreno, Z. T. (1959) *Psychodrama Vol. II: Foundations of Psychotherapy.* Beacon: Beacon House.

Rogers, C. R. (1961) *On Becoming a Person.* London: Constable.

Rogers, C. R. (1970) *Encounter Groups.* Harmondsworth: Penguin.

Rogers, C.R. (1986) A Client-centered/Person-centered Approach to Therapy. In I.L.Kutash and A.Wolf (Eds) *A Psychotherapists casebook.* San Francisco: Jossey-Bass.

Rogers, C. R. (1990) A Client-centered/Person-centered Approach to Therapy. In Kirschenbaum, H. & Henderson, V. L. *The Carl Rogers Reader.* London: Constable.

Silverstone, L. (1994) Person Centred Art Therapy. *Person Centred Practice.* 2, (1), pp. 18–23.

Spinelli, E. (1989) *The Interpreted World.* London: Sage.

Wilkins, P. (1993) Person-Centred or Person, Centred? *Counselling*

Person-Centred Process and Personal Transformation

Alan Coulson

My first participation in an intensive person centred workshop was experienced as a catalyst for personal transformation. Numerous subsequent workshop experiences and the reports of other participants have fed my wish to understand better the nature of the transformation process involved. By 'transformation' I mean a change in which the person's whole life is significantly altered. This may entail extensive changes in the person's external life, but, perhaps more importantly, the transformation is felt as a major shift at the subjective level. In my case I would describe the outcome as a 'redefinition of self'. Such far reaching changes are most often induced by 'jolts' to the system. More often than not, these jolts are life crises which, by creating internal conflicts or upheavals in the person's environment, act as catalysts for changes of perspective, the reordering of priorities and values, and other profound shifts, especially in relationships.

It is this jolting process and the consequent destructuring of established habits, values and ways of perceiving ourselves which provide the point of departure for this paper. Carl Rogers (1959), in a comprehensive, but rarely quoted chapter, describes the process of breakdown and disintegration which frequently precedes a person's shifting towards a situation of greater congruence between their *self* and their *experience*. Additionally, I have found recent work by Gemmill and Smith (1985, 1991) helpful in that their analysis of the process of organisational transformation also seems to fit the kind of personal transformation I am referring to. They employ the theory of dissipative structures, developed in the physical sciences (Prigogine, 1980; Jantsch, 1981); this describes: 'a transition that happens when the internal or external conditions of a system are turbulent enough to push it out of the limited parameters where it was able to maintain equilibrium. Where these conditions occur, the system may either dissipate amidst disorder or attain a more complex and appropriate alignment, a new ordering far from its initial equilibrium'.

Personal experience and observation suggest that transitions most often occur as a consequence of life crises such as illness, divorce, bereavement or redundancy. The intensive person-centred workshop provides a situation within which individuals are encouraged to disclose more facets of themselves than is usually possible in daily life, and within a context of psychological safety, to receive

First published in *Person-Centred Practice,* Volume 2, Number 1, 1994.

extensive and open feedback. My proposal here is that this process enables us to loosen or break down our habitual patterns of behaving and relating and facilitates experimentation with forms which are more spontaneous and more congruent with our inner sense of identity.

Prior to attendance at my first workshop I experienced, though not very consciously, a lack of alignment between my daily social and working life and my essential 'inner self'. However, cultural norms, my upbringing, and the continuous pressure of social and professional expectations had built up within me what Rogers terms *conditions of worth*, ways of selectively perceiving my experience and behaviour according to the judgement of others as to their worthiness or otherwise of positive regard. This established, internalised frame of reference was increasingly at odds with my own felt sense of things so a state of what Rogers (1959) calls *incongruence* between *self* and *experience* had arisen. However, the only very partial awareness I had of this condition, combined with my own deeply ingrained habits and fears, helped to maintain the lack of alignment or congruence and prevented change. The workshop experience provided a 'jolt' which revealed more clearly that a significant degree of incongruence existed between my *self* and my *experience*. It also brought the realisation that many other people saw me rather differently from the image of myself which I had established and internalised over the years. The defence system which had kept my *self-structure* in place functioned less successfully, and indeed was no longer really applicable. Feelings of confusion and disorder ensued. It was as if the kaleidoscope which is me had become somehow 'stuck' and this experience gave it a shake resulting in the pieces inside moving into unfamiliar and often disconcerting arrangements. Nevertheless, at the same time there were also released feelings of greater personal freedom, increased energy and an expanded sense of self. As I became more able to digest what was happening to me and grew more aware of the process of 'becoming' that I was experiencing, the kaleidoscope pieces eventually settled into a more comfortable and pleasing configuration. Moreover, I had a sense subsequently that henceforth they would never quite be so stuck again and the image would continue to evolve. Gemmill and Smith (1985) cite Prigogine's contention that the dissipative self-organising process is the driving force behind the evolution of systems:

> the system that successfully becomes a dissipative structure must also be open to change, must be able to break down old system functions and generate new ones, and must possess certain stabilities that will assist in the reformulation process.

By not having to return to an equilibrium, the dissipative structure is able to maintain a greater sensitivity and responsiveness to its environment.

Four stages may be identified in a transformation of this kind:

First, **Disequilibrium**. In my case this was as described above, a vague sense of being out of alignment, incongruent with myself. However, social and psychological factors had served to keep the *status quo* more or less intact. Rogers (1959) suggests that it is by denying to awareness experiences which run contrary to their *conditions of worth* that individuals normally maintain their selective, distorted perceptions. Similarly, Bertine (1958) argues that the instability of an individual varies *directly* with the extent of area occupied by unconscious content and *inversely* with the scope of consciousness.

Second, **Symmetry Breaking**. The temporary removal of the social and environmental forces which dampened change enabled my thinking and behaviour to undergo an 'unfreezing'. I underwent the process described by O'Hara and Wood (1983): 'By leaving behind familiar patterns which structure ordinary consciousness and entering a field with minimum institutional structure, familiar ego boundaries can be expanded. Each person is challenged and supported to behave more spontaneously than usual, individual expression is liberated.' Experiencing the core conditions of empathy, positive regard and genuineness within the workshop encouraged risk taking and disclosure on my part and also exposed me to the inner worlds of other participants. I found myself confronting a profusion of internal conflicts and inconsistencies, and being thrust towards disorder which upended much of my existing *self-structure*. I believe that it was this upending, this destructuring of established crystallised patterns which made possible the emergence of new and more viable norms by which I could define myself. As Joanna Macy (1984) has observed, 'Going to pieces or falling apart is not such a bad thing. What "disintegrates" in periods of rapid transformation is not the self, but its defences and ideas. Our "going to pieces", however uncomfortable a process, can open us up to new perceptions, new responses.' Moreover, the experience of chaos and disorder may be a significant source of energy for moving the individual towards transformation. Without sufficient disturbance to the existing *self-structure,* the necessary 'escape velocity' to carry the individual beyond the 'gravitational pull' of established patterns of thought and behaviour may not be achieved. Alternatively, the symmetry-breaking process may be interpreted as one of surrender of the person's usual restricted ways of viewing issues, a surrender of our crystallised patterns in favour of a larger perspective and more fluid and spontaneous ways of relating to and construing our world (O'Hara and Wood, 1983).

Third, **Experimentation**. Within the person-centred workshop I experienced freedom to be more *'as I am'*. Since within the workshop there were no particular expectations of me, I had no role or purpose other than to explore and to discover myself in the company of others engaged in the same endeavour. The most valuable outcome was having a better grasp of what *being me* actually means or could mean. An important facilitating element in the person-centred workshop is that the person is largely relieved of the need to function in accordance with utilitarian values and goals. It is through 'play' or spontaneous experimentation which is not under the dominant control of goals or predetermined outcomes that true self-exploration and self-design can emerge (Weick, 1977). A dissipative structure in nature, while remaining open to the turbulence it faces, looks to itself for structure; it must be 'self-referencing' or 'self-creating' (Smith and Gemmill, 1991). Similarly, Rogers (1959) proposes that in the course of becoming more 'fully functioning', persons move away from a situation in which their *self-experiences* are in the main externally discriminated by reference to the evaluations of significant others, and towards one in which their internal *organismic valuing process* is more and more the basis of behaviour regulation.

Fourth, **Reformulation**. I felt that as a consequence of the workshop my awareness was heightened and my sensitivity increased. This process brought me into greater resonance with other participants. O'Hara and Wood (1983) have described very well the self-transcendent state in which individual consciousness surrenders or merges into the group and the boundary between 'I', 'You' and 'We' becomes increasingly permeable and indistinct. At the same time I enjoyed a state of integrative, expanding consciousness which enabled me to achieve a greater resonance and integration with my own inner world, a region within which there were, to an unaccustomed degree, feelings of spaciousness and harmony. Also, more than at any time in my adult life I felt in tune with and part of some entity greater than myself. It was as though not only did I know myself better, but I really *belonged*. Spontaneously and intuitively, I had arrived at a state of consciousness in which my 'kaleidoscope' bits and pieces could organise themselves into a more meaningful and comfortable version of me which felt at once more *authentic* and more connected to everyone and everything else.

A workshop participant quoted by Carl Rogers (1986) eloquently expresses feelings very much like my own at that time:

> I felt the power of the 'life force' that infuses each of us — whatever it is. I felt its presence without the usual barricades of 'me-ness' or 'you-ness' — it was like a meditative experience when I feel myself as a centre of consciousness. And yet with that extraordinary sense of oneness, the separateness of each person present has never been more clearly preserved.

The experiences which form the basis of this account occurred fifteen years ago. Subsequent workshop experiences and other personal growth work have reinforced my conviction that the intensive person-centred group experience not only has the potential for releasing or strengthening our self-actualising tendency and for precipitating personal transformation, but may be seen in a broader context. If the dissipative structure paradigm is applied to the psychology of the person it follows that when the structures of our lives are broken down during the transformation process, deeper structures remain as an ordering mechanism from which the individual's new, more organic reality may arise. Thus the subjective, personal experience of evolving and discovering our deepest centre, and, in the process, opening to deeper, transpersonal realms of consciousness, may be related to David Bohm's (1980) theory which postulates the existence of an implicate order that is a deep structure behind physical reality, one that is not localised in a particular system. Moreover, this implicate order, like the person, is dynamic: it evolves over time. The intensive group experience or other in-depth personal growth work which puts us in touch with deeper, transcendent, transpersonal realms in effect connects us with an 'implicate order' behind and beyond our own physical reality and ego-bound consciousness.

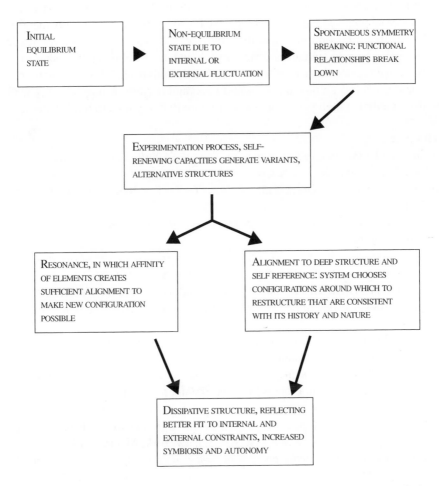

Fig. 1. Dissipative structure paradigm — key process elements in the general change model. Source: Smith and Gemmill (1991).

In one of his last papers, Rogers (1986) acknowledges that profoundly life-changing group experiences partake of the mystical and involve the transcendent, the indefinable and the spiritual. He goes on to make a link with the work of some physicists such as Capra (1982) who, 'As they push their theories further, picture a "reality" which has no solidity, which is no more than oscillations of energy, they too begin to talk in terms of the transcendent, the indescribable, the unexpected — the sort of phenomena that we have observed in the person centred approach'.

It may not, therefore, be too fanciful to consider that what Carl Rogers called our *formative tendency,* our drive to become more *fully functioning,* may be part of a more universal, even cosmic unfolding.

Postscript

Later this year, I retire from thirty-five years of institutional employment, a situation which will destructure much of the existing pattern of my life and remove many of the external points of reference which have for so long contributed to my identity. As I enter this transition my natural (defensive) inclination is to seek reference points and reassuring guidance outside myself and to try deliberately to shape my future. However, my real need is to go more deeply within, allowing the emergence of structures and meanings in their own tempo and rhythm. A poster on my wall reminds me that 'When you trust yourself you will know how to live' (Goethe).

References

Bertine, E. (1958) *Human Relationships — in the family, in friendship, in work.* New York: David Mckay & Co.

Bohm, D. (1980) *Wholeness and the Implicate Order.* London: Routledge & Kegan Paul.

Capra, F. (1982) *The Turning Point: Science, Society and the Rising Culture.* New York: Bantam Books.

Gemmill, G. and Smith, C. (1985) *A dissipative structure model of organisation transformation.* Human Relations, Vol. 38. No. 8, pp. 751–66.

Jantsch, E. (1981) *The Evolutionary Vision.* Boulder, Colorado: Westview Press.

Macy, J. (1984) *Despair and Personal Power in the Nuclear Age.* New Society Publishers.

O'Hara, MM. and Wood, J.K. (1983) *Patterns of awareness: consciousness and the group mind.* The Gestalt Journal, Vol.6, No. 2, pp. 103–6.

Prigogine, 1. (1980) *From Being to Becoming — Time and Complexity in the Physical Sciences.* San Francisco: W.H. Freeman & Sons.

Rogers, C.R. (1959) *A theory of therapy, personality and interpersonal relationships as developed in the client-centered framework,* in Koch, S. (Ed), *Psychology: A Study of a Science,* Vol. 3. New York: Mcgraw Hill.

Rogers, C.R. (1986) *A client-centered/person-centered approach to therapy.* In Kutash, I. and Wolf, A. (Eds), *Psychotherapist's casebook.* Jossey-Bass.

Smith, C. and Gemmill, G. (1991) *Change in the small group: a dissipative structure perspective.* Human Relations, Vol.44, No.7.

Weick, K.E. (1977) Organisational Design: Organisations as self-designing systems. *Organisational Dynamics,* Vol. 6.

Person-Centred Theory and the Postmodern Turn

Matthew Jones

Introduction

One of the things I experience intensely as a sociologist training to be a person-centred counsellor, is the very different ways that these two traditions think about what they do. Frequently I find myself feeling caught between two opposing ways of theorizing and interpreting. In my work as a sociologist, I have been influenced by postmodern critiques of knowledge and this paper is an attempt to understand person-centred theory in the light of some of these critiques.

I feel quite uneasy and unsettled by Carl Rogers' claim to have discovered an essential truth about human beings. I am not, of course, the first person to query his 'optimistic' view of human nature. But I will not be suggesting, as some other critics have, that he has somehow got it 'wrong' and that someone else (often Freud or Skinner) has got it 'right'. Rather I will be arguing that such attempts to legislate what is true for everyone, everywhere, are fundamentally misconceived endeavours. I shall use postmodern critiques of knowledge to argue that what we know, and how we go about trying to know anything, is shaped by the times, places and cultures in which we live. Towards the end of the essay I discuss the implications of these debates for the development of my own person-centred practice. But before I make that attempt, I want to locate Carl Rogers' work within the debates about modernity and postmodernity.

Rogers as modernist

Modernist social theory is based on a belief that demonstrably valid knowledge can be produced about a world which exists independently of the knower. This valid knowledge, it is suggested, can be used as the basis of generalizations, sometimes about whole societies. The modernist project can be characterized as a belief in a knowable world and, with it, a knowable self (Neimeyer, 1995). It's not hard to see Rogers as a modernist. Like many other modernist writers, he is deeply critical of the idea of there being one unifying objective reality. Rogers (1980) writes that the only reality 'I can possibly know is the world as *I* perceive and experience it at this moment' (p. 102). As I shall later argue, it is precisely this concept of reality as experienced which postmodernists have challenged. Rogers' theory is allied to the principles of modernist thought. Person-centred

First published in *Person-CentredPractice* Volume 4, Number 2, 1996.

theory asserts that it has discovered generalizable truths about our psychological make-up. For Rogers, at the core of every one us exists a tendency towards self-actualization.

> By this I mean the directional trend which is evident in *all* organic and human life — the urge to expand, extend, develop, mature — the tendency to express and activate all the capacities of the organism or the self (Rogers, 1961, p. 351, *my italics*).

> It is clear that the actualizing tendency is selective and directional, a constructive tendency, if you will. The substratum of *all* human motivation is the organismic tendency toward fulfillment (Rogers, 1977, p. 242, *my italics*).

Rogers' fully functioning person is an individual in touch with their real self, a person who is self-actualizing. This is true for *all* humans beings, *all* over the planet. In fact, as the above quotations illustrate, Rogers argues that all organic life is characterized by this tendency.

What is postmodernism?
Postmodernism stands in direct opposition to the kind of universal claims that Rogers makes for his theories. The postmodernist project turns nearly every aspect of this modern program on its head. Postmodernity undermines our confidence in a knowable universe, and it fundamentally questions the idea of an essentialized self — 'an individual ego who is the locus of choice, action and rational self-appraisal' (Neimeyer, 1995, p. 13).

Postmodern thinking has been famously characterized by an attitude of incredulity towards all encompassing explanations (Lyotard, 1984).What gives us the right, the postmodernist asks, to see the individual as a unified and coherent being? And how can we ever tell if our theoretical concepts genuinely 'grasp' or accurately 'reflect' this 'individual'? The postmodernist suggests that we can never really know this. Our ability to know reality is always mediated by language and our conceptual frameworks. Therefore we can never have direct awareness of a reality independent of ourselves (McNamee and Gergen, 1992). Barbara Held (1995) offers this example:

> The therapist cannot know the nature of the client and his struggles as they really exist, no matter what the therapist observes in the therapy sessions. Rather, the [postmodern] doctrine insists that the therapist's theories, language, constructions, or narratives about the client always determine just what the therapist observes, and so preclude any direct (ie. theoretically unmediated), undistorted, or even any indirect (ie. theoretically mediated), undistorted knowledge of the client's *true* condition (Held, 1995, p. 7, *my italics*).

So just as the Freudian psychoanalyst will inevitably observe 'intrapsychic conflicts' in their patients no matter what the patient actually says or does, so the person-centred counsellor cannot help but see clients in terms of their 'self-concept' and their 'internalization of conditions of worth'. From a postmodern perspective, the actualizing tendency is not a given, it does not exist *a priori* in clients, but rather is created in the therapeutic dialogue between the counsellor and client. It is for this reason that postmodernists have argued that reality is not so much discovered, as it is actively constructed. One of the uses of this critique is that it allows us to understand how so many different theoreticians (Freud, Skinner, Rogers, etc.) are able to hold completely contradictory views of human nature and of psychotherapy and argue that they, and they alone, are 'right'. That their knowledge is 'true' and the other theories are 'false'.

One of the key points of the postmodern critique of knowledge is that we can never have direct access to reality; rather our experience is always filtered through interpretative schemes. However, it would appear that some experiences are easier to 'filter' than others. One of the problems with grand theories is that they have a tendency to encounter exceptions to their laws. Person-centred theory appears to be no exception. Rogers, himself, writes of the actualizing tendency that:

> I can count on it being present . . . There is, however, one rare exception which has stuck in my mind. I saw a television show of African wild dogs. There was one female who was jealous of another. When the second female was absent from her den, the first would go into the den, remove one of the cubs, and kill it. This went on day after day until the litter was totally destroyed. I can still remember my shock at the that, because it is so uncharacteristic of animals (Rogers, in Kirschenbaum and Henderson, 1990b, p. 253).

Rogers is shocked by this behaviour which doesn't fit into his all-encompassing theory, into what Lyotard would call his 'meta-narrative' — which must by its very nature be able to explain everything. 'I will admit', Rogers writes, 'that there is much that I don't understand about some evil behaviours' (Rogers, in Kirschenbaum and Henderson, 1990b, p. 254). It is to his credit that Rogers is prepared to write of this shocking experience, but I am left wondering of the implications for his theories. Does this mean that the actualizing tendency might not be universally true? And if so . . .

Can we afford not to revise the person-centred concept of the self-actualizing individual?

Zygmunt Bauman (1988) has argued that the main flaw with Western modernist theories (of which, I have argued, person-centred theory is one) is precisely this 'pretension to universality'. For Bauman, this is their hubris, their arrogance. Behind all attempts to 'legislate' what is eternally true, universal and rational, lies an ideological attempt to promote the norms of our own type of society. In other words, while theorists have striven after disembodied truth and rationality, it is the culture and society of Western science and philosophy which is being defended, not timeless mental values (McLennon, 1992).

Len Holdstock (1990, 1993), writing from within the person-centred tradition, makes a powerful argument for the revision of the person-centred concept of the organismic self-actualizing individual. He questions Rogers' conception of the self-contained organismic self, arguing that it is not universal but relative to the West, particularly America. He points to African writers who have argued that the 'self-contained individual' is fundamentally incompatible with conceptions of the self shared by black South Africans. Holdstock writes: 'African culture . . . emphasizes a view of the person that is inextricably interrelated with the larger society, not only of other people, but also of deceased ancestors, animals and plants and even inanimate objects' (1990, p.114). Here the essence of being is 'participation' in which human beings are always interlocked with one another — 'I am, because we are. We are, because I am'. From this perspective, the idea of an individual with firmly drawn self/other boundaries is argued to be entirely illusionary. Holdstock writes: 'It ought to be clear how differently from Africa, the person-centred approach conceptualizes the individual' (p.115).

The logic of viewing the self-actualizing individual as universally applicable — as a truth — seems to me inevitably to imply some form of cultural and intellectual imperialism. An absurd but troubling image of the person-centred counsellor as missionary enters my mind. I can see us enthusiastically disembarking onto the 'dark continent', dressed in sweaty fatigues, our battered copies of *On Becoming a Person* gripped tightly in one hand, brushing away tsetse flies with the other. We're ready to lead the natives to enlightenment, ready to interpret their experiences in terms of self-actualization, ready to differentiate between their conditional and real selves.

One alternative to intellectual colonialism is to ignore other indigenous psychologies altogether and pretend that they do not exist. Petruska Clarkson (1995) relates an incident where a white European Kleinian analyst was trying to build a rapport with a psychologist of African origin. The Kleinian analyst was suggesting that there was a great deal of similarity between Kleinian constructs and the African belief that the spirits of our ancesters are around us. The African psychologist dismissed this as an attempt to turn his real experience of his ancestors' spirits merely into an internal psychodynamic concept. Failing to incorporate the other into his therapeutic discourse, the Kleinian had little choice but retreat, disappearing from the room when a ceremony was held to honour the ancestors present in the room. In order to maintain the integrity of a psychotherapeutic metanarrative, its very nature requires it either to dominate all others, establishing a regime of truth, or else quietly ignore other 'truths' and leave by the nearest available exit, heading no doubt for more sympathetic audiences. But for the Kleinian analyst to stay and encounter his theory's cultural relativity would involve an intellectual demotion from a position where he was *the* legislator of truth, to a much more humble role as *an* interpreter of different cultural traditions and the linkages between them.

Turton (1986) reports that attempts to introduce person-centred ideas into South Africa have not been successful. The failure of a lay black counselling programme in Soweto being attributed to participants experiencing it as irrelevant and inappropriate to meet the needs of the people requiring its services. Holdstock argues for the recognition, acceptance and respect for the spiritually-ensembled individualism of South African culture. Further, and more radically, he calls for what he describes as a paradigm shift where the West reorientates itself in terms of African conceptions of the self. While I firmly believe that engaging with the postmodern critique I have outlined here is a step towards the recognition and respect of other cultural conceptions of self-hood, I'm less certain of the possibility of our transforming our own cultural concepts at will. Western conceptions of the individual may be socially constructed but that does not mean that they are not encountered *as if* they are real, and are not real in their consequences.

Psychotherapeutic knowledge is socially constructed in specific historical and cultural contexts rather than discovered in one and applicable to all. Truth is no longer a discovery, but a political contest for domination. Petruska Clarkson (1995) writes:

> To me it seems not so much a matter of 'Do not impose your values'
> because obviously we will, but rather 'Be aware of what values you
> are indeed imposing and become conscious of this importation of
> the world of ethics and aesthetics which is inevitable when engaged
> in a healing encounter with any other human being' (p.174).

Bereft of its claim to truth, our theoretical knowledge cannot be separated from our values, rather it is understood as a reflection of them.

The end of theory?
Ought I — could I — abandon theory? Attempt to work without the support of any explanatory therapeutic discourses? Some social constructionists are attempting just this. This practice is sometimes described as 'not knowing' (Anderson and Goolishian, 1992). Here therapists attempt to engage with their clients without the aid of any prior explanatory frameworks. Rather each client's experience is explicitly responded to as their own unique perspective. Lynn Hoffman (1992) writes:

> Knowledge being socially arrived at, changes and renews itself in each
> moment of interaction. There are no prior meanings hiding in stories
> or texts. *A therapist with this view will expect a new and hopefully
> more useful narrative to surface during the conversation,* but will see
> this narrative as spontaneous rather than planned. The conversation,
> not the therapist, is the author (Hoffman, 1992, p.18, *my italics*).

I find myself facing a series of deeply frustrating questions in response to reading descriptions of postmodernist therapy: Why can the therapist expect a new narrative to surface? What does the writer mean by 'surface'? Surface from where? Surely, if one believes that 'there are no meanings hiding in stories', then there is no non-conscious mind, no real self or no unconscious from which more useful narratives may emerge?

My hunch is that it is impossible to engage with and listen to clients from a theory-less or 'blank slate' standpoint. For myself, I fear that I would just end up suppressing and hiding my generalizations and interpretations, but they would nevertheless be present. Ernesto Spinelli (1994) concurs. 'It would', he writes, 'be the height of naiveté to imagine that this could possibly be achieved' (p.135). He goes on to suggest a strategy which makes greater sense to me, he writes:

> Rather, the point . . . is simply that therapists should treat their theories and assumptions critically, remaining open to their falsifiability, to the uncertainty of the 'truths' they might contain, and to the alternative possibilities with which their encounters with their clients may provide them (p.135).

Implications for practice

How can I remain open to the uncertainty of the truths contained within person-centred theory? How can I remain open to alternative possibilities which my clients may bring with them? I suspect that I can only attempt to do this by being cautious, by being very cautious indeed. What would a person-centred practice informed by this postmodern critique involve? Gergen and Kaye (1992) suggest that developing a practice which permits this uncertainty involves:

> . . . creating a climate where clients have the experience of being heard, of having both their point of view and feelings understood, of feeling themselves confirmed and accepted. It involves an endeavour to understand the client's point of view, to convey an understanding of how it makes sense to the person given the premises from which the viewpoint arises. At the same time this does not imply an acceptance or confirmation of the client's premises. It implies rather a form of *interested inquiry* which opens the premise for exploration (p.182, *original emphasis*).

I'm astonished at the debt Gergen and Kaye's postmodern 'interested inquiry' owes to Rogers' core conditions of empathy, congruence and unconditional positive regard. When I first read the above paragraph my immediate reaction was to wonder whether embracing a postmodern approach would actually involve *doing* anything different from operating within a person-centred one? Is it really only a case of how we approach and hold theoretical knowledge? The idea is seductive (after all, it gets me out of this predicament). But of course our theoretical beliefs and loyalties directly influence and shape our work, our practice, our lives.

Ernesto Spinelli (1994) has illustrated how Rogers' theoretical beliefs in the self-actualizing organism directly influences and shapes his counselling practice. Spinelli points to a demonstration interview Rogers gave with a woman called Jan. During their half-hour together, Jan talked of her feelings of loneliness. At one point Carl Rogers responded:

> Carl: Simply that one of your best friends is the you that you hide inside, the fearful little girl, the naughty little girl, the real you that doesn't come out very much in the open.[1]

In offering what Rogers later describes as an intuitive response, Spinelli suggests that Rogers is also reading his theory into her comments. This involves Rogers making an evaluation as to what is the 'real' Jan and what is not. This is not to say that Rogers himself doesn't experience his comment as intuitive, but it is simultaneously a theoretical interpretation: the 'real self' he conjures in the image of 'frightened little Jan' is a central component of his theory of personality (Rogers, 1951). Jan comes to experience herself in terms of person-centred theory. Together, in the therapeutic relationship, they construct reality between them.

Being cautious for me involves restraining from proactively introducing theoretical concepts into my practice. For I suspect that doing such a thing may prevent me from being open to 'the alternative possibilities' which my clients may bring with them. This does not mean abandoning person-centred theory, but rather it is a practical way for me to remain uncertain to its 'truth'.

Ending

In this paper I have located Rogers' conception of psychotherapy within a critique of the modernist project. In the light of this postmodern critique I have offered an alternative description of person-centred practice — as a therapeutic relationship involving the co-construction of reality from *both* the client's account of their experiences and the therapist's theoretical framework. This is a way for me to engage with the uneasy feelings I have concerning Rogers' belief that he has discovered a universal truth about human beings. For as I have argued in relation to South Africa, the claiming of such truths also denies and silences other voices.

I've also learnt in writing this paper that I'm not willing to abandon person-centred theory for the more recent postmodern therapeutic movement. My hunch is that postmodern knowledges are best used as critiques of our existing bodies of knowledge — as ways of critically engaging with our theories. For if I embrace a postmodern perspective, as those constructivist therapists have, am I not in danger of turning what is a valuable critique of meta-narratives into just another 'all-encompassing explanation'?

I'm reassured when Irvin Yalom (1989) writes that 'the capacity to tolerate uncertainty is a prerequisite for the profession' (p.13), for I remain profoundly uncertain. It seems at least I am not alone in this, Yalom writes that for the practitioner, certainty is 'rarely the case: instead . . . therapists frequently wobble, improvise, and grope for direction' (p.13).

Wobbling it is then.

References

Anderson, H. and Goolishian, H. (1992) The Client is the Expert: a Not-Knowing Approach to Therapy. In McNamee, S. and Gergen, K. (Eds). *Therapy as Social Construction*. London: Sage.

Bauman, Z. (1988) *Legislators and Interpreters*. Cambridge: Polity.

---

1. Reported fully by Rogers, in Kirschenbaum and Henderson, 1990a, pp.138–152.

Clarkson, P. (1995) *The Therapeutic Relationship*. London: Whurr.

Gergen, K. and Kaye, J. (1992) Beyond Narrative in the Negotiation of Therapeutic Meaning. In McNamee, S. and Gergen, K. (Eds.) *Therapy as Social Construction*. London: Sage.

Hoffman, L. (1992) A Reflexive Stance for Family Therapy. In McNamee, S. and Gergen, K. (Eds.) *Therapy as Social Construction*. London: Sage.

Holdstock, L. (1990) Can Client-Centred Therapy Transcend its Monocultural Roots? In *Client-Centred and Experiential Psychotherapy in the Nineties*. Leuven: Leuven University Press.

Holdstock, L. (1993) Can We Afford not to Revision the Person-Centred Concept of Self? In Brazier, D. (Ed.) *Beyond Carl Rogers*. London: Constable.

Held, B. (1995) *Back to Reality: A Critique of Postmodern Theory in Psychotherapy*. New York: Norton.

Kirschenbaum, H. and Henderson, V.L. (1990a) *The Carl Rogers Reader*. London: Constable.

Kirschenbaum, H. and Henderson, V.L. (1990b) *Carl Rogers: Dialogues*. London: Constable.

McLennan, G. (1992) The Enlightenment Project Revisited. In Hall, S. and McGrew, T. (Eds.) *Modernity and Its Futures*. Oxford: Oxford University Press.

McNamee, S. and Gergen, K. (Eds.) (1992) *Therapy as Social Construction*. London: Sage.

Lyotard, J.F. (1984) *The Postmodern Condition: A Report on Knowledge*. Manchester: Manchester University Press.

Neimeyer, R. (1995) An Invitation to Constructivist Psychotherapies. In Neimeyer, R. and Mahoney, M. (Eds.) *Contructivism in Psychotherapy*. Washington: Amercian Psychological Association.

Rogers, C.R. (1951) *Client-Centered Therapy*. London: Constable.

Rogers, C.R. (1961) *On Becoming a Person: A Therapist's View of Psychotherapy*. Boston: Houghton Mifflin.

Rogers, C.R. (1977) *Carl Rogers on Personal Power*. New York: Delacorte.

Rogers, C.R. (1980) *A Way of Being*. Boston: Houghton Mifflin.

Spinelli, E. (1994) *Demystifying Therapy*. London: Constable.

Turton, R. (1986) Bourgeois counseling and working-class clients: Some problems and political implications. *Psychology in Society*. pp. 95–100.

Yalom, I. (1989) *Love's Executioner and Other Tales of Psychotherapy*. London: Penguin.

I would like to thank Phil Anderson and Maggie Ridgewell who offered constructive comments on an earlier draft.

Contributors

Jerold Bozarth is Professor Emeritus of the University of Georgia, where his tenure included Chair of the Department of Counseling, Director of the Rehabilitation Counseling Program and Director of the Person-Centered Studies Project. He has been involved with the PCA for many years, authoring several journal papers, chapters in books and his major retrospective, *Person-Centered Therapy: A Revolutionary Paradigm*.

David Brazier is a psychotherapist and trainer with a deep commitment to Zen Buddhism. He edited the volume *Beyond Carl Rogers* and is author of a number of books including *Zen Therapy* and *The Feeling Buddha*.

Alan Brice. I worked with homeless people, drug users, young offenders and in psychiatric settings before coming to the University of Newcastle-upon-Tyne — helpful experiences, perhaps, for counselling students! I am from Kent originally, and have lived my adult life up North, and I am now enjoying the shifts towards multiculturalism taking place here.

Barbara Temaner Brodley started practising Client-Centered Counseling in 1955, employing the approach in many different settings over the years including seven years at the psychotherapy research center founded at the University of Chicago by Carl Rogers. She has maintained a practice with individuals, couples and families for 32 years as well as teaching Client-Centered Therapy to graduate students at the Illinois School of Professional Psychology and at the Chicago Counseling and Psychotherapy Center.

Rose Cameron. I stumbled upon the PCA when I wasn't looking for it, and like so many other people, found myself landing on territory I had always known. That I could actually make a living by being with people in a genuine, respectful and empathic way was one of the best pieces of news I'd ever had. I became self-employed seven years ago and still revel in being institution-free.

Prue Conradi is a psychotherapist and supervisor in private practice with 20 years' experience. She also works at the Norwich Centre where she is a Founder Member and was Director until September 1998. Whilst centrally committed to the PCA, she is also deeply concerned with the work of Carl Jung and is interested in bridge-building between the PCA and depth psychology. She has a strongly developed interest in the relationship between psychology and spirituality and with myths, dreams and symbols.

Alan Coulson was a schoolteacher for twenty years then, until retirement, a senior lecturer in management. His commitment to the Person-Centred Approach was established through workshops in the 1970s. Currently he facilitates a psychology study programme for retired people. In addition to articles on person-centred groups, his publications include pieces on cinema and management.

Ivan Ellingham. Introduced to Client-Centred Therapy by Prof C.H.Patterson when completing a diploma in counselling at the University of Aston, I subsequently studied further with him, gaining a PhD in Counselling Psychology at the University of Illinois. Now, as a psychologist working in the National Health Service, I have a particular interest in the development of person-centred practice and theory in relation to so-called mental 'illness'.

Irene Fairhurst is co-founder and past President of BAPCA.Through her work with young people as a youth and community worker, she became aware of the Person-Centred Approach as a way of being. She also co-founded the Institute for Person-Centred Learning and edited the book *Women Writing in the Person-Centred Approach*.

Mike Farrell runs the Barons Court Project, a centre for people vulnerable through mental illness, homelessness and substance abuse in West London.

Sheila Haugh is a UKCP Registered Psychotherapist and BAC Accredited Counsellor working in the UK and on the continent. Involved in the Person-Centred Approach since 1983, she has a private practice in counselling/psychotherapy, supervision and training. She is currently editing a book on empathy.

Jan Hawkins is a person-centred therapist in private practice who runs workshops for survivors and their allies and a diploma course for all in the helping professions who counsel survivors. She is also Director of The Foundation for the Developing Person.

Pam Janecka established a career in nursing and health visiting after graduating in 1984. She developed a special interest in the healing relationship, communication and empowerment. Most resently, she commenced counselling training at the Metanoia Institute, finding the Person-Centred Approach a framework to support and develop these interests. A mother of two young children, her other interests include gardening, yoga, walking and reading.

Matt Jones is in advanced training in the Person-Centred Approach at Metanoia and has worked as a counsellor for several voluntary organisations. He lives in Manchester and is a television scriptwriter.

Anne Kearney is a counsellor, trainer and supervisor working in primary care practice as well as independently. She is a founder member of the Manchester Counselling Collective and has a particular interest in issues of anti-discriminatory practice. She was born in Dublin and has four grown-up children.

Suzanne Keys was born in Haiti, grew up in Belfast and Bath and lived and worked in Italy, France and the Ivory Coast before training at the University of East Anglia as a person-centred therapist. She currently works (now paid!) in London as a day-centred for those who are homeless or at risk of homelessness, at a women's centre and in private practice.

Mary Kilborn has a private counselling and supervision practice. She works as a person-centred trainer at the University of Strathclyde, Glasgow and also in Dijon in France. She is co-founder of a counselling supervision training in Paris. She feels that feedback from clients plays a vital part in person-centred research.

Dave Mearns is Professor of Counselling at the University of Strathclyde, Glasgow. He has specialised in the person-centred approach to therapy since 1972/3 when he was Visiting Fellow to the Centre for Studies of the Person in La Jolla. He has published widely on Person-Centred Therapy and training and currently his work is focussed upon the revision of Carl Rogers' theory of self. When not working he can be found on the golf course.

Tony Merry teaches counselling and psychology at the University of East London. He is Editor of *Person-Centred Practice* and is a founder member of BAPCA. He has written many articles, chapters and books on the Person-Centred Approach and related subjects.

Judy Moore was trained in the Person-Centred Approach by Person-Centred Therapy Britain. She is currently Director of Counselling at the University of East Anglia and a lecturer in the Centre for Counselling Studies at UEA. She has recently become a Buddhist in the Soto Zen tradition.

Liz Nicholls. I am a self-employed counsellor and supervisor. I work both privately and for several agencies in the South Manchester area. I am particularly interested in expressive ways of working to enrich the dialogue in my working relationships and to develop my artistic interests.

John Pratt is a person-centred counsellor and supervisor who has trained and worked with a variety of helpers-as-counsellors. He has authored two books and published in counselling, nursing, physiotherapy and educational journals including research papers on teacher stress and the meaning of touch in care settings. He is the author of two books; *The Caring Touch* and *Counselling Skills for Professional Helpers.*

Garry Prouty, the originator of Pre-Therapy, is the Author of *Theoretical Evolutions in Person-Centered/ Experiential Therapy: Applications to Schizophrenic and Retarded Psychoses*. In addition he has co-authored *Prä-Therapie* and published numerous articles on Pre-Therapy. He is a Fellow of the Chicago Counseling, Psychotherapy and Research Center. Currently he continues to write, lecture and train students internationally.

Ruth Reid is a qualified nurse, health visitor and counsellor working in both nursing and counselling at a London general medical practice within the National Health Service. She also works privately as a counsellor.

Keith Tudor has a background in social work and community politics and is an experienced therapist, supervisor and trainer. He is a widely published author in the field of therapy and mental health and is the series editor of *Advancing Theory in Therapy*.

Paul Wilkins. As well as being a person-centred practitioner, I am an academic working for the Centre for Human Communication, Manchester Metropolitan University. I have written papers and chapters dealing with aspects of the Person-Centred Approach, and books on professional and personal development, and Psychodrama. When not working I like to walk, work on my allotment and enjoy the good things in life.